A
Book
of
Catholic
Anecdotes

A Book of Catholic Anecdotes

John Deedy

Illustrations by Bernadette Leach

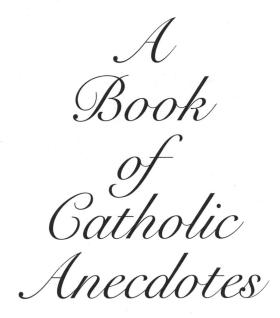

ThomasMore®
A Division of
RCL · Resources for Christian Living™
Allen, Texas

Grateful acknowledgment is extended to the following for permission:

The Tablet, London, for excerpts from Peter Hebblethwaite's article, "Why I Love the Church," September 2, 1992.

Excerpts from *Blessings in Disguise* by Alec Guinness, Copyright 1985 by Alec Guinness, Alfred A. Knopf Inc.

Excerpts from *C* by Maurice Baring, A.P. Watt Ltd., on behalf of the trustees of the Maurice Baring Will Trust.

Send all inquiries to:

Thomas More®
A division of RCL • Resources for Christian Living™
200 East Bethany Drive
Allen, Texas 75002–3804

Toll Free   800–264–0368
Fax   800–688–8356

Printed in the United States of America

ISBN 0–88347–309–7

1 2 3 4 5   01 00 99 98 97

For the Manships, Kings, Kennys, Harpers,
Murphys, Tierneys, Burgoynes, Ahearns, Hageneses
and other civilizers of Cape Ann.

❧ Foreword ❧

In *Playland*, novelist John Gregory Dunne speaks of anecdotes as being "nothing more but factoids of questionable provenance." It is a surprising dismissal from a writer who indulges in anecdotes much of the time. Whether fluff of scholar-ship or ephemera of history, the anecdote very much belongs to language and history. In his introduction to *The Little, Brown Book of Anecdotes*, Clifton Fadiman displays greater respect for the genre. Good anecdotes are entertaining, shedding some sheen, some "decoration," to use Fadiman's word, on history and biography. Certainly, enjoyment was an operative element in conceiving and assem-bling this book.

The "fun factor" in no way diminishes the informational aspects of this book of Catholic anecdotes. Not every line of the book is sworn testimony belonging to notarized statement or documented history. It is the nature of anecdotes to contain embellishments of a particular life story or event. In the old journalistic tradition that names make news, the anecdotes here pivot on persons—who, if not famous, are readily identifiable figures of Catholic history.

Some of the anecdotes are from familiar sources, such as the old 1913 Gilmary *Catholic Encyclopedia* and *Butler's Lives of the Saints*. Some are from cur-rent publications; others are from the memory banks of friends and associates of long standing. Many of the anecdotes here are seeing print for the first time. Some are inspirational, some informative, some mischievous. Others are whim-sical, and still others, irreverent.

It should be acknowledged—and it's an acknowledgment Fadiman also had to make—that, regrettably, there is a gender deficiency in these pages. The number of entries involving women is far fewer than it should be. Catholic history has been overwhelmingly dominated by the male species, and one hopes that if and when a similar compilation is done off in the future, the story will be different.

A number of people have been of special help in compiling this book:

Rev. Paul F. Bailey and Cornelius M. Buckley were invaluable fonts of ideas and information. Herbert A. Kenny, whose head is a veritable storehouse of anecdotes, lent me some of his Catholic ones. George E. Ryan was especially helpful on matters and persons Irish. James O'Toole, Catholic historian, and Bob Burns, retired editor though columnist yet for *U.S. Catholic*, provided assistance. John Wilkins and Sue Chisholm at *The Tablet* of London answered questions relating to British personalities. Maurice Adelman Jr., a friend of forty years, student of the Catholic scene and like myself an inveterate noter of Catholic idiosyncrasies, provided several items for the book. John Sprague of Thomas More encouraged the project from the start and steered anecdotes my way. Also providing help were Sara Miller, Rev. John Jay Hughes, John Horgan, the late Dara McCormack, and the staffs of the Sawyer Free Library in Gloucester, Mass., and the public library in Rockport, Mass.

One word more: Most of the anecdotes, including those culled from print sources, have been rewritten for purposes of this book. In all cases, though, there has been no tampering with quotations.

—*John Deedy*

𝒜

ABBOTT, Walter M. (1923–). Jesuit priest and native of Boston, Abbott was director of the John LaFarge Institute and associate editor of *America*, the Jesuit weekly. He was a *peritus* (expert) at Vatican Council II and was general editor of *The Documents of Vatican II*, the authoritative book of translations and commentaries on the council documents. He was subsequently administrator of Arrupe House, a Jesuit novitiate in Boston.

At Vatican Council I, as Pope Pius IX *(q.v.)* was promulgating the new dogma of infallibility, a huge thunderclap from a summer storm sent fright and awe through the aula of St. Peter's. Vatican II had a kindred moment as the controversial religious-freedom issue was being debated and a Spanish cardinal was addressing the assembly. Abbott was seated high up in an empty tribune observing the proceedings with his friend Father John Courtney Murray *(q.v.)*, a principal architect of the religious-freedom proposal.

Abbott's feet were propped on a solid oak bench, about twelve- or fourteen-feet long, which he was unconsciously rocking. Suddenly the bench tipped forward and crashed to the floor against a big drum. It was as if "a cannon went off in the middle of St. Peter's Basilica," said Abbott. "It was horrendous. Everyone looked around. Is anybody on the floor? Has somebody been shot? After what seemed five whole minutes, but was probably only ten seconds, there was a feeling: well, nobody's dead, nobody's on the floor, and so everything resumed."

The Spanish cardinal went on with his speech. Eyes had turned toward their tribune, but Abbott and Murray stared innocently ahead as if "nothing happened here."

*A*CTON, Lord [John Emerich Edward Dalberg] (1834–1902). English historian and one of the most learned men of his time, Lord Acton in 1859 succeeded John Henry Newman *(q.v.)* as editor of the Catholic monthly, *The Rambler,* which he later merged with the *Home and Foreign Review.* He folded the *Review* in 1864 after a declaration by Pope Pius IX that the opinion of Catholic writers was subject to the authority of Rome.

In 1870, Acton strongly opposed the idea of the dogma of papal infallibility and traveled to Rome to lobby against its ratification. Although disappointed by events, he did not join the Old Catholic separation led by his friend and mentor Johann von Dollinger, regarding "communion with Rome as dearer than life." However, he never reconciled to the notion of papal infallibility and, in 1887, wrote to Bishop Mandell Creighton the letter with his famous maxim: "Power tends to corrupt and absolute power corrupts absolutely."

*A*LBERTI, Leon Battista (1404–1472). A canon at Florence and later abbot of San Sovino in Pisa, Alberti was a brilliant architect and is credited with completing the Pitti Palace in Florence. He built several other churches, including that of St. Francis at Rimini.

> ✎ Alberti was the classical, many-sided Renaissance man. A great scholar and athlete (with feet bound together he could leap over a man's head), Alberti mastered arts and trades, wrote books, and was so quick of tongue that associates collected his serious and witty sayings. He entered totally into life around him and delighted in nature. The sight of noble trees or waving corn fields could bring tears to his eyes, and a beautiful landscape could cure him of illness. Alberti was said to have the gift of prophesy and be able to read into the countenances and hearts of people. Possessed of an iron will, his credo became a motto (albeit sexist) for the ages: "Men can do all things if they will."

ANDREW, Agnellus, O.F.M. (1908–). A British Franciscan, Agnellus Andrew for many years was the British Broadcasting Corporation's consultant on Catholic affairs.

> ✎ Hugh Burnett, a BBC television producer, needed specialized assistance of a religious kind in preparing two satirical programs, one on heaven, the other on hell. He wrote to Father Agnellus asking how he could obtain the official Catholic view on heaven and hell. Burnett received back a one-word memorandum: "Die."

*A*NGELICA, Mother [Rita Rizzo] (1923–). Born in Canton, Ohio, Rita Rizzo entered a cloistered Franciscan order in Cleveland in 1944 as Mother Angelica of the Annunciation. A founding member of the monastery of Our Lady of the Angels in Irondale, Alabama, in 1962, she achieved fame first as a teacher of the Bible and as a publisher. She subsequently branched into television and developed the Eternal Word Television Network (EWTN), a twenty-four-hour-a-day cable religious channel, with programming available in some twenty languages worldwide.

> A fiery traditionalist, Mother Angelica targeted liberal and progressive Catholics, who she believed were watering down the Church's teachings. Over time, she built a devoted following among millions with a message of unqualified loyalty to the pope and the Church's teaching authority. Supporters contributed millions annually to her work, still hers remained a chancy operation financially. Asked to explain the financing of EWTN, she said: "Being broke, we need help. Needing help, we turn to God. Being constantly broke, we are constantly turning to God."

> Known as a risk taker "who would walk off metaphysical cliffs" trusting that God would see her safely down, Mother Angelica explained her propensities for trust and risk taking to a Long Island newspaper reporter, Bob Keeler: "There are times when, unless we are willing to do what seems humanly ridiculous, God will not do the miraculous."

*A*NTHONY of Padua (1195–1231). Born in Lisbon, Portugal, with the name Fernando de Bulhom, he joined the Canons Regular of St. Augustine at age sixteen, but left at thirty to become a Franciscan, taking the name Anthony. A man of learning and great eloquence, he became famous throughout Italy as a confessor, convert-maker, and preacher. He was often forced to preach outdoors, as no cathedral or basilica could accommodate the throngs who flocked to hear him. He was only thirty-six when he died. Within a year, he was canonized, his reputation enhanced as a worker of miracles.

Devotees think of Anthony as sweet and meek, but he had a tongue that could blister, particularly as he preached on favorite themes of his: greed and luxurious living, among both lay people and the clergy. Anthony spared no one, not even the mitered. Invited once to preach at a synod at Bourges in central France, he stunned his audience by launching into a denunciation of the presiding prelate, Archbishop Simon de Sully, the very person who had invited him. *Tibi loquor cornute,* he began: "As for you there, with the miter on your head . . ."

In 1992, the jawbone of St. Anthony was stolen from the basilica at Padua, where it was enshrined and considered a source of miracles. Authorities recovered the relic two months later as it was about to begin a sea voyage to a Colombian drug runner. Why, people asked, would a crime figure want St. Anthony's jawbone?

An Australian journalist based in Italy offered a rationale: St. Anthony has a special place in many a mafioso's heart as a man of honor. A mafioso legend has it that while preaching once in Italy, Anthony heard that his father, a member of the Portuguese nobility, had been convicted of homicide back in Lisbon. Rushing off to Lisbon, Anthony resuscitated the victim, who then acknowledged that Anthony's father had not been the attacker. So who was the perpetrator, the police wanted to know; could Anthony please help them? But the future-saint replied: "I am interested only in proving my father's innocence. It is your job to find the assassin."

AQUINAS, Thomas (1225–1274). An Italian Dominican, Thomas Aquinas is arguably the greatest scholar of church history. His great achievement was the systemization of Catholic belief through the arrangement in orderly fashion of revelation and reason, theology and philosophy. His master works were *Summa Contra Gentiles,* a defense of Catholic Christian doctrine, and *Summa Theologiae,* an exhaustive exposition of Catholic theology.

- Thomas Aquinas was a huge man physically, weighing over three hundred pounds and needing a hole cut into his desk to accommodate his stomach. One day brother monks decided to have some sport with Aquinas, and one of them excitedly pointed out the window, exclaiming, "Come quick, look at the cow flying." Aquinas jumped from his desk and sprinted across the room—to see nothing, of course. The monks had their laugh, but Aquinas had his historic rejoinder: "I thought it more likely that a cow should fly than that a monk would lie."

- As a student in Paris under Albertus Magnus (who was later canonized), Aquinas's great bulk was equated by fellow students with oafishness and dullness, and they referred to him as "the dumb ox." When Albertus Magnus learned of the ridicule, he admonished them. "The roaring of that ox," he said, "will be like the bellow of a bull and one day will fill the whole world."

✍ Aquinas was a modest man and on his deathbed is said to have offered a despairing verdict on his life's work: *Videtur mihi sicut palea,* which in paraphrase is rendered, "It looks to me like a pile of stuff usually found on the floor of stables."

*A*UGUSTINE (354–430). Born in northern Africa, son of St. Monica and Patricius, a pagan Roman official, Augustine passed through licentiousness and Manichaeism en route to becoming the dominant molder of thought of Christian Europe. His *City of God* and *Confessions* still rank among the greatest of Christian documents. He died as bishop of Hippo and is proclaimed as a Doctor of the Church.

✍ As a young man, Augustine lived fifteen years with a mistress, by whom he had a son, Adeodatus. The joys of a sexual relationship long led him to resist a commitment to Christianity (he was thirty-three years old before being baptized) and celibacy. With respect to the latter, he would pray to the Lord, *Da mihi castitatem et continentiam, sed noli modo*—"Give me chastity and continence, but not yet."

✍ Augustine's conversion resulted from a mystical experience he had while sitting with his friend Alypius in a garden in Milan. He fell to the ground, weeping uncontrollably. Suddenly he heard a child's voice in a house nearby chanting *Tolle, lege; tolle, lege*—"Pick up and read, pick up and read!" Augustine leaped to his feet and rushed to snatch up his New Testament. It opened at the words of St. Paul to the Romans: "Not in riots and drunken parties, nor in eroticism and indecencies, not in strife and rivalry, but put on the Lord Jesus Christ and make no provision for the flesh and its lusts."

The long struggle was over. "I neither wished nor needed to read further," Augustine recalled. "At once, with the last words of this sentence, it was as if a light of relief from all anxiety flooded my heart. All the shadows of doubt were dispelled."

❦ Monica, Augustine's mother, was said to be the instrument of his conversion, through her charity, forbearance, and prayers. Augustine recorded in the *Confessions* her rhapsodic satisfaction over his conversion:

> Son, for mine own part I have delight in nothing in this life. What I should do here any longer, and to what end I am here I know not, now that my hopes in this world are spent. There was one thing for which I sometimes desired to be a little while reprieved in this life; namely, that I might see thee become a Christian Catholic before I died. This hath the Lord done for me, and more also, for that I now see thee having contemned all earthly happiness, to be made His servant; what then do I here any longer?"

(Five days later, Monica became gravely ill with "marsh fever," and on the ninth day she died.)

❦ Once committed to Christianity, Augustine gave definition to the faith through more than two hundred works, some three hundred letters, and nearly four hundred sermons. He possessed a felicitousness of expression that inspires to this day. Especially memorable is his prayerful cry to the Lord: *Sero Te amavi, pulchritudo tam antiqua et tam nova, sero Te amavi*—"Late have I loved Thee, beauty so ancient and so new, late have I loved Thee."

In his 1970 book *Catholic Nonsense,* Philip Nobile contends that "a straight nonsensical line runs crookedly from Augustine through Aquinas and right up to Bishop Sheen in our own day." By way of proof that "nowhere or at any time has any Catholic theologian openly taught that nonsense is incompatible with faith or morals," Nobile offers the following:

ON "BATHING"

If anyone, deserving a bath, has washed alone naked, let him do penance with a special fast. But if anyone, while washing lawfully in the presence of his brethren, has done this standing, unless through the need for cleansing dirt more fully, let him be convicted with twenty-four strokes.

Penitential of St. Columbanus, c. 600

ℬ

ℬARING, Maurice (1874–1945). Novelist, poet, and playwright, Baring was born in London and educated at Eton, Cambridge, and Oxford. He entered diplomatic service in 1898, although minus a university degree, and served in several European posts before resigning in 1904 to become a foreign correspondent. He served with distinction in the Royal Flying Corps in World War I, after which he became a full-time novelist, publishing a dozen books of fiction.

   Baring converted to Catholicism in 1909 and is often grouped with G. K. Chesterton *(q.v.)* and Hilaire Belloc *(q.v.)* in a triumvirate credited with the Catholic literary revival in Britain in the early twentieth century. (Some contend, on the other hand, that the association may be due more to a famous James Gunn portrait of the three together than anything else.) Baring was never the public apologist for the faith that the other two were, although in his autobiographical novel C, he alludes to the mind-set that induced his becoming a Catholic:

> "Are you a Catholic?" asked Bede. "No," said C . . ., "I'm nothing—" "Of course not, if you're not a Catholic," said Bede. "There is either that or nothing. There is no third course." "And one can't very well *become* a Catholic," said C. "Why not?" asked Bede. C stammered and did not answer. . . .

The novel continues with C's private thoughts:

> What he was thinking was that converts always seemed to him rather tiresome, and never quite the same as real Catholics; but then he reflected that Bede was very likely a convert himself, so he refrained from saying anything. It was not, however, necessary, for Bede poured out a stream of argument and exposition to the effect that Catholicism was the great reality; the only thing that mattered; the only thing that counted; the only creed a thinking man could adopt; the only solace that satisfied the needs of the human heart; the only curb to human passions; the only system that fulfilled the demands of human nature and into which factors such as love and death fitted naturally; the unique and sole representative of the Divine upon earth.

While in Paris in 1899, Baring attended a low Mass in Our Lady of Victories where the devotion of the worshipers deeply moved him. He was further awed while attending a solemn Mass in St. Peter's in Rome in 1902 marking a jubilee of Pope Leo XIII. The experiences led to his eventual reception into the Church by Father Sebastian Bowden at the Brompton Oratory. Baring was always reticent in talking about his conversion and reduced the process to a single line in his 1922 autobiography, *The Puppet Show of Memory*. Nonetheless, he would call his conversion "the only action of my life which I am quite certain I have never regretted."

Esteemed for his wit and sociability, Baring, a great linguist, was at the same time an incisive observer of persons, places, and values. Dorothy

Parker, herself a famous wit and commentator on people's foibles, expropriated from Baring to point up the folly of attaching undue importance, never mind meritocracy, to the possession of great wealth. "If you would know what the Lord God thinks of money," said Baring, "you have only to look at those to whom he has given it."

*B*ASIL THE GREAT, saint (c. 329–379). A celebrated Eastern theologian, Basil belonged to a family of saints. His grandmother, mother, father, two brothers, and a sister were all sainted, the most famous being St. Gregory of Nyssa, his brother. Basil founded his own community and a rule that regulates the lives of monks of the Eastern Church to this day.

When Basil was archbishop of Caesarea, the Arian heresy, which denied the divinity of Christ, was rampant. Emperor Valens was an Arian, and he vigorously persecuted in its behalf. Threatened with confiscation, exile, torture and death, Basil and his diocese were spared by his eloquent plea:

> Well, in truth, confiscation means nothing to a man who has nothing, unless you covet these wretched rags and a few books; that is all I possess. As to exile, that means nothing to me, for I am attached to no particular place. That wherein I live is not mine, and I shall feel at home in any place to which I am sent. Or rather, I regard the whole earth as belonging to God, and I shall consider myself as a stranger wherever I may be. As for torture, how will you apply it? I have not a body capable of

bearing it, unless you are thinking of the first blow you give me, for that will be the only one in your power. As for death, this will be a benefit to me, for it will take me the sooner to the God for whom I live.

✍ The reprieve did not silence Basil. He fought the rapacity and oppression of corrupt officials, excommunicated those involved in "white-slave" trafficking, and constantly admonished the well-to-do. Addressing niggardliness among the latter, Basil said:

> You refuse to give on the pretext that you haven't got enough for your own needs. But while your tongue makes excuses, your hand convicts you—that ring shining on your finger silently declares you to be a liar! How many debtors could be released from prison with one of those rings? How many shivering people could be clothed from only one of your wardrobes? And yet you turn the poor away empty-handed.

But Basil also had an admonition for the poor:

> You are poor? But there are others poorer than you. You have enough to keep you alive for ten days—but this man has enough for only one. . . . Don't be afraid to give away the little that you have. Don't put your own interests before the common good. Give your last loaf to the beggar at your door, and trust in God's goodness.

*B*EA, Augustin (1881–1968). Born at Riedbohringen, Baden, Germany, Bea entered the Jesuit order in 1902 and was ordained in 1912. He went to Rome in 1924 as supervisor of the studies of Jesuit graduate students. He became confessor to Pope Pius XII *(q.v.)* and was the main author of Pius's 1943 biblical encyclical, *Divino afflante Spiritu.* He was named a cardinal in 1959 and subsequently director of the Secretariat for Promoting Christian Unity.

Bea played a prominent role in Vatican II, helping to draft several documents, including *Dei verbum,* the *Constitution on Divine Revelation.* He was remarkable for his open-mindedness and spirit of ecumenism, and for many, these qualities stood as a counterpoint to the conservativeness of Cardinal Ottaviani *(q.v.),* head of the Holy Office. During the council, a familiar sight about Rome was the advertising poster of British European Airlines, or BEA. Progressive wits, supporters of Bea, seized on the coincidence of his name and the airline's acronym and jested that the sign offered ideological as well as flying advice: "Travel with BEA."

*B*EECHING, Paul Q. (1928–). Professor and writer, Beeching has passed from formal Catholicism to what might be called a benign apostasy. He has been a member of the faculty at St. Louis University, University of Missouri, and Connecticut State University. He recorded his spiritual odyssey in *The Education of an American Catholic.*

Although Beeching has resisted what he calls "reconversion," he remains an astute observer of all things Catholic and what it is to be Catholic in the modern age. He passed on one story, which he said was "surely apocryphal" but which others found no reason to describe as such. It concerned a Jesuit who visited Mexico back in the 1950s and observed young couples going to the cathedral one Sunday morning.

As each man approached the church doors he handed his senorita through into the nave and then stood on the stairs smoking a small cigar, occasionally looking in to see how things were coming along at the altar. This happened again and again until quite a crowd was assembled "before the temple." Intrigued, the priest went down into the plaza. "Good morning, gentlemen." "Good morning, Father." "I see you escort the ladies to mass and then wait outside." "That's right," they said. "You don't go in the cathedral yourselves?" "No, not generally." "Well, that's puzzling. Aren't you Catholics?" The men looked at him in consternation. "Of course we're Catholics," they said. "But we're not *fanatics!*"

*B*EETHOVEN, Ludwig van (1770–1827). Beethoven was born a Catholic, and although not an observant believer, he did take the sacrament on his deathbed. Certain paradoxes seemed at work in Beethoven so far as the Church was concerned. He never went to confession, for instance, but he did urge his nephew to go. Beethoven was something of a pantheist. He saw God in all things and frequently called on God for peace or solace.

Formal Catholic or not, Beethoven today figures prominently in the Catholic liturgy. The chorale from his Symphony in D Minor is now a

LUDWIG VAN BEETHOVEN

favorite hymn at Mass, under the title "Joyful, Joyful, We Adore Thee." And, of course, there is Beethoven's glorious *Missa Solemnis,* his solemn Mass. The *Missa* is regarded as one of Beethoven's noblest and most profound compositions. He prepared painstakingly for its writing, delving into church music, obtaining copies of chorales used in monasteries, examining Palestrina's music, even checking the accuracy of Latin translations so that no linguistic nuance would escape him. Pleased with the results, he wrote at the head of the score, "From the heart—may it in turn go to the heart."

    Beethoven left behind short sentences he had written down on occasion pleading for divine support. But he did not expect God to do his work for him. Once, a young composer, completing a piano score of *Fidelio,* jotted at the end of it, *"Fine,* with God's help." When the notation came to Beethoven's attention, he scratched underneath, "O Man, help yourself."

*B*EHAN, Brendan (1923–1964). Irish playwright and revolutionary, Behan was as famed for his antics as for his literary gifts. His plays, beginning with *The Quare Fellow* of 1954, were highly autobiographical and drew on his experiences with the Irish Republican Army. He also wrote several books of nonfiction.

    Behan was notorious for his behavior, and drunk or sober, he stood in awe of no one. On a visit to England, he found himself once in the company of the bishop of Knaresborough. "What's your f . . . ing business, Mac?" inquired Behan of the bishop. "Not as profitable as yours,

I'm afraid," said his lordship. Always appreciative of a witty rejoinder, Behan shook the bishop's hand warmly.

ᗍ A hopeless alcoholic, Behan was constantly in and out of hospitals for the cure, as well as for a succession of illnesses complicated by drink. On one such sojourn, he recovered consciousness to find himself being administered to by a nursing nun. "Bless you, Sister," said Behan. "May all your sons grow up to be bishops."

ᗍ Behan's irreverence bordered on the scandalous, but he cherished his Catholicism and would publicly drop to his knees on occasion to recite the Angelus. He dreaded dying without the sacraments and so gave specific instructions on how he wanted to meet his end. "When I die," said Behan with less than mock extravagance, "I want to die in bed surrounded by fourteen holy nuns with candles. I am a Catholic. A damn bad one according to some. But I have never ridiculed my faith. Even when the drink takes to me I find that when darkness falls I think of my prayers."

(At Behan's funeral, the speaker's tribute ended with a quote from Maurice O'Sullivan's *Twenty Years a-Growing*, which appeared originally in Gaelic: *Ni fheicfimid a leitheid aris*—"We shall not see his like again." The Gaelic seemed especially appropriate, Behan being a Gaelic speaker himself.)

𝓑ELLARMINE, Robert (1542–1621). An Italian born in the Tuscany town of Montepulciano, Bellarmine became a Jesuit at Rome in 1560 and ultimately one of the foremost polemical theologians of Catholic history. He was a major voice in Vatican diplomacy and in theological controversies with early Protestant reformers. A great scholar, he revised the Vulgate Bible and wrote two celebrated catechisms, one of which was used into modern times. Bellarmine was created a cardinal in 1598, canonized a saint in 1930, and named a Doctor of the Church in 1931.

Bellarmine, an austere man, was raised to the cardinalate by Clement VIII and, in keeping with his office, was obliged to occupy apartments in the Vatican. He did so, albeit reluctantly, and relaxed none of the austerities that had come to characterize his way of life. He limited his household and expenses to bare essentials and in winter denied himself the comfort of a fireplace. For sustenance, he lived on bread and garlic, the food of the poor. He even took down the draperies in his rooms to be made into clothing for the poor, remarking, "The walls won't catch cold."

As the chief spokesperson and defender of papal positions, Bellarmine acquired a celebrity throughout the Christian world, although in some places that celebrity spilled over into infamy and resentment. In England, for instance, some held him responsible for the Gunpowder Plot. Academic doctors organized college faculties against him, and from the pulpit he was belabored as a "petulant railer," "the head of the popish kennel of Monks and Mendicants," and "a furious and devilish Jebusite." Paunchy liquor jugs, with necks shaped in the grotesque effigy of a bearded man, were labeled "bellarmines," and doggerels made him the butt of jokes, such as this one: "First to breakfast, then to dine, is to conquer Bellarmine."

One of the paradoxes of Bellarmine's life was his ineffectiveness in handling the Galileo *(q.v.)* case. Galileo was a friend and, in fact, dedicated a book of his to Bellarmine. Bellarmine, in turn, was knowledgeable in astronomy and lectured to university audiences on the theory of the heavens, "philosophically and astrologically," including the topic of spheres and fixed stars. It was Bellarmine, of course, who counseled Galileo to write hypothetically on the earth's movement, since his theories were still unproven.

The advice was sound, so far as it went. In retrospect, however, it is apparent that Bellarmine, his real knowledge in the field notwithstanding, not only never fully grasped the theories of Galileo, but also failed to allow the possibility that these theories might be accurate. Many think that he could have taken contingency actions to head off the showdown that brought Galileo before the Inquisition. Some think that Bellarmine's practicality and a concern for tradition betrayed him and cite in support of that conclusion such Bellarmine comments as the following: "Men are so like frogs. They go open-mouthed for the lure of things which do not concern them, and that wily angler the Devil knows how to capture multitudes of them."

BELLOC, Hilaire (1870–1953). Born in France but English by definition, Belloc was historian, biographer, essayist, travel writer, poet, sometimes sketcher, indomitable controversialist, unblushing Catholic, and aggressive defender of the faith. He wrote reams of articles and more than 150 books. In fact, he was so prolific that he once suggested his books ought perhaps be numbered, like the streets of America. His works cover thirty-one columns in the giant catalogues of the reading room in the British Library.

✎ Belloc wrote at breakneck speed, disdaining footnotes and other niceties of academic scholarship. He was asked once why he wrote so much and on such a variety of subjects. "Because," he said, "my children are howling for pearls and caviar."

✎ As a Catholic apologist, Belloc sparred with one and all, including Anglicanism's Dean William Ralph Inge, for saying the Catholic Church was an "impostor" institution and no one could be both an Englishman and a Catholic. Belloc responded in an open letter that concluded:

> There wholly escapes you the character of the Catholic Church. . . . You are like one examining the windows of Chartres from within by candle-light but we have the sun shining through. . . . For what is the Catholic Church? It is that which replies, co-ordinates, establishes. It is that within which is right order; outside the puerilities and the despairs. It is the possession of perspective in the survey of the world. . . . Here alone is promise, and here alone is foundation. Those of us who boast so stable an endowment make no claim thereby to personal peace; we are not saved thereby alone. . . . But we are of so glorious a company that we receive support, and have communion. The Mother of God is also our own. Our dead are with us. Even in these our earthly miseries we always hear the distant something of an eternal music, and smell a native air. There is a standard set for us whereto our whole selves respond, which is that of an

inherited and endless life, quite full, in our own county. You may say, "all that is rhetoric." You would be wrong, for it is rather vision, recognition, and testimony. But take it for rhetoric. Have *you* any such? Be it but rhetoric, whence does that stream flow? Or what reserve is that which can fill even such a man as myself with fire? Can *your* opinion (or doubt or gymnastics) do the same? I think not! One thing in this world is different from all others. It has a personality and a force. It is recognized and (when recognized) most violently hated or loved. It is the Catholic Church. Within that household the human spirit has roof and hearth. Outside it is the night.

As a Catholic, Belloc conducted himself in church with a complete lack of self-consciousness. At his home parish in West Grinstead, he was known to interrupt the priest at the beginning of Mass by inquiring in a loud voice from the congregation what Sunday after Pentecost or other special day it happened to be, so that he could follow the liturgy in his missal. Once, while attending Mass standing at the back of a church where he was not known, Belloc was motioned to a seat by an usher. Belloc ignored the man. Three times the usher beckoned to him to sit down. Finally Belloc exploded, "Go to hell!" "I beg your pardon," the usher replied, "I didn't know you were a Catholic."

Belloc was indeed a Catholic. When he stood for Parliament in 1906, he knew his faith was an issue with voters. He met the challenge head-on in his very first campaign speech. "I am a Catholic," he said, rosary in hand. "As far as possible I go to Mass every day. As far as possible I kneel down and tell these beads every day. If you reject me on account of my religion, I shall thank God that he spared me the indignity of being your representative." Belloc was elected and served until 1910.

In his 1920 book *Europe and the Faith,* Belloc used the phrase: "The church is Europe: and Europe is the church." In its repeating, the phrase led to distortions and misunderstanding, which Belloc clarified in a 1936 letter to the *Catholic Herald:*

> I have never said that the church was necessarily European. The church will last for ever, and, on this earth, until the end of the world; and our remote descendants may find its chief membership to have passed to Africans or Asiatics in some civilization yet unborn. What I have said is that the European thing is essentially a Catholic thing, and that European values would disappear with the disappearance of Catholicism.

As a controversialist, Belloc filled lecture halls and silenced mighty opponents. His friend Chesterton *(q.v.)* testified to this, commenting on one of his appearances:

> The moment Belloc began to speak one felt lifted out of the stuffy fumes of forty-times repeated arguments into really thoughtful and noble and original reflections on history and character. When I tell you that he talked about (1) the English aristocracy, (2) the effects of agricultural depression on their morality, (3) his dog, (4) the battle of Sadowa, (5) the Puritan revolution in England, (6) the luxury of Roman Antonines,

(7) a particular friend of his who had by an infamous job received a political post he was utterly unfit for, (8) the comic papers of Australia, (9) the mortal sins in the Roman Catholic Church. . . . It lasted for half an hour and I thought it was five minutes.

❧ Belloc was a profuse and witty versifier, and quatrains of his—which had an evangelical dimension in their day—regale readers to this day in anthologies and books of quotations. Although the number of such entries has thinned down in recent editions, many survive. It is difficult, however, to find one that in the age of triumphal certainty was more of a favorite among Catholics than the following:

> Wherever the Christian sun doth shine
> There is always laughter and good red wine.
> At least I have always found it so,
> *Benedicamus Domino.*

Belloc wrote several versions of this quatrain, including one in his verse "Heretics All," which went as follows:

> But Christian men that live upon wine
> Are deep in the water, and frank and fine;
> Wherever I travel I find it so;
> *Benedicamus Domino.*

*B*ERNADETTE of Lourdes. *See* Soubirous, Bernadette.

*B*ERNANOS, Georges (1888–1948). French novelist and pamphleteer, Bernanos was a powerful force in contemporary French literature. During times of confusion and crisis, many regarded him as the conscience of his country. *The Diary of a Country Priest* (1936) made his name famous throughout the world. His play *The Dialogue of the Carmelites,* which Francis Poulenc made into an opera, cemented his reputation.

To develop the literary techniques of *The Diary of a Country Priest,* Bernanos began to write his own private journal, devoting an hour a day to it. Almost inevitably, therefore, he placed himself in his clerical characters. The curé de Torcy is especially thought to mirror aspects of Bernanos's persona. As an example, the curé de Torcy speaks Bernanos's thoughts about the Blessed Virgin:

> The Blessed Virgin knew no triumph and worked no miracles. Her son did not allow her to be touched by human glory, not even to be grazed by its huge and savage wing. No one has lived, suffered, and died in greater simplicity than she, more utterly unaware of her own dignity which, for all that, places her above the angels. . . . Naturally she holds sin in abhorrence, but she has no experience of it—and the greatest saints have had experience of sin, even the seraphic saint of Assisi. Only the Virgin looks at us with the eyes of a child; hers is the only truly child-like gaze which has ever rested upon our misfortune and our shame. If you want to pray well, you must feel it resting upon yourself. It's not an indulgent look—because indulgence has some bitter experience behind it—but it's a look of tender

compassion, of sorrowful surprise, of some inconceivable, indefinable feeling which makes her younger than sin, younger than the race to which she belongs, and although Mother by the grace of God, Mother of the graces that flow from Him; the youngest daughter of mankind.

*B*ERRIGAN, Daniel J. (1921–). Poet, editor, author, and Jesuit priest, Berrigan was an intensive activist in the civil rights and peace movements in the United States. His witness against the war in Vietnam resulted in frequent arrests and incarcerations, including a three-year sentence in a federal prison for removing and destroying (with homemade napalm) draft records at Catonsville, Maryland, on May 17, 1968.

In 1967, Berrigan flew to Hanoi with Professor Howard Zinn of Boston University, another peace activist, to secure the release of three captured American fliers. Neither the Jesuit order nor the U.S. government sanctioned the trip or extended any thanks on the successful completion of the two men's mission. Typically, the mission resulted in a book, for Berrigan kept careful diaries. Entitled *Night Flight to Hanoi*, its foreword contained a passage that would become a manifesto for Berrigan's action at Catonsville and ultimately the charter of American antiwar Catholic activists generally:

> Our apologies, good friends, for the fracture of good order, the burning of paper instead of children, the angering of the orderlies in the front parlor of the charnel house. We could not, so help us God, do otherwise.

As Berrigan approached sixty, he was asked by the editors of a Catholic magazine whether, given his forebodings about the future, he would bring a child into this world if he were a young person and just getting married. His answer was an unqualified yes.

> This is a most important sign of hope. Maybe it's an illustration of the old text from Romans about what true hope is. We have to decide if we want to embody the fact that we believe we have a future. And a child is the most beautiful way of doing that that I know of.

BERRYMAN, John (1914–1972). Berryman was born John Allyn Smith in McAlester, Oklahoma, and became John Berryman when his mother remarried after her first husband's suicide. As a poet, he would win the Pulitzer Prize, the Bollingen Prize, and a National Book Award, and would hold a number of distinguished professorships. But his life was full of turmoil, and it ended as tragically as it was lived.

Berryman's mother converted to Catholicism after her second marriage, and John and his brother, Robert Jefferson, were raised in the Church. Berryman's Catholicism was not the intense element in his life that it was for his mother, although in 1971 his religious feelings did intensify. During a hospital stay for alcoholism, he pondered converting to Judaism, but ultimately he re-embraced the Catholicism of his youth.

On January 7, 1972, seriously underweight and suffering from insomnia, hounded by misgivings and obsessed with his own father's death, Berryman jumped off a Minneapolis bridge to a frozen Mississippi River embankment more than a hundred feet below. After a Catholic funeral, he was buried in Resurrection Cemetery in Mendota Heights, St. Paul. Among his effects was a heavily marked copy of *A New Catechism: Catholic Faith for Adults*. Underscored was the passage: "As regards suicide, this is sometimes the result of complete hypertension or depressions and we cannot pass judgment."

*B*ONIFACE VIII, pope [Benedetto Gaetano] (c. 1235–1303). Boniface succeeded to the papacy under unusual circumstances: his predecessor, Celestine V, resigned, the only pope in history to do so. Boniface's reign was a controversial one, and although he was a noted reformer of Canon Law, he is remembered chiefly for his contentions with European powers, notably involving Philip IV of France, and for two bulls: *Clericis laicos*, protecting the clergy against paying any tax not leveled by the pope, and *Unam sanctam*, one of the strongest statements of papal prerogatives ever made.

    Boniface helped facilitate the resignation of Celestine V, an aged man and, in truth, an inept pope. The unusual circumstances of his succession, combined with avarice, lofty claims to power, and frequent exhibitions of arrogance, made him many enemies. One was Celestine himself, who reportedly prophesied, "You have entered like a fox. You will reign like a lion—and you will die like a dog." (Actually, Boniface died at the Vatican, but he was a man broken in body and spirit, with hardly a friend in the world.)

☙ Among the foes made by Boniface was the poet Dante, and Dante treated Boniface ingloriously in both the *Inferno* and the *Purgatorio*. In the *Inferno*, Boniface is called the "Prince of the new Pharisees." In the *Purgatorio*, he is the subject of the lament that "in his vicar, Christ was made a captive" and was "mocked a second time."

ORROMEO, Charles (1538–1584). An aristocrat by birth (his mother was a Medici), Borromeo received the clerical tonsure at twelve and was made a cardinal-deacon of Milan by his uncle, Paul IV, at age twenty-two. A holy man and a serious reformer, he was a leading figure at the Council of Trent and is said to have most perfectly mirrored the ideals of the Counter-Reformation. He was canonized in 1610.

☙ Borromeo's income was large, both as a member of a noble family and as head of a large archdiocese. He gave a large part of this income to charity and eschewed luxury and ostentation. He was most comfortable not in the robes of office, but in a tattered plain black cassock. On one occasion, someone proposed to have a bed warmed for him. Borromeo declined, saying, "The best way not to find a bed cold is to go colder to bed than the bed is."

☙ As archbishop of Milan, one of Borromeo's primary objectives was a reform of the monasteries, many of which he found profaned by gross abuses and thoroughly disordered, their clergy lazy and debauched. He acted strenuously to correct conditions, forcing orders to revise their constitutions and effecting the abolishment of one order entirely (the

Humiliati). He insisted that priests be clean-shaven, believing a beard smacked of worldliness.

Although the wisdom of that policy could be challenged (critics countered that a smooth chin was decadent and effeminate), not so other policies that aimed at developing a virtuous and capable clergy. He wanted his priests to be models of holiness, and when an exemplary priest was sick and dying, his concern for that priest was a matter of comment to everyone about him. Borromeo accounted cogently for his concern: "Ah, you do not realize the worth of the life of one good priest."

$\mathcal{B}$OSCO, John (1815–1888). Founder of the Society of St. Francis de Sales (Salesian Fathers), John Bosco ranks as one of the most lovable of priests. He is famed for his catechetical, vocational, and recreational apostolates among neglected boys, a work that began in the slums of Turin and spread throughout the world. He was canonized in 1934.

John Bosco's facility for working with the roughest of youths was legendary, imbued as it was with humor and great common sense. One day some youths greeted him with the "caw-caw!" sound, the jeer of anti-clericals against black-cassocked priests. John Bosco walked up to them with a smile and asked, "Who are you boys who are so good at imitating a crow?" When one of them suggested the priest buy them a drink, he readily agreed. They went to a tavern, where John Bosco treated the bunch. Soon they were all attending one of his oratories.

BRENDAN (c. 484–c. 577). One of Ireland's most widely known saints, Brendan was famed as a navigator, and his voyages a thousand years before Columbus took him perhaps as far as America itself. He founded a number of monasteries in Ireland, most notably that at Clonfert in Galway.

> Brendan lived into his nineties but saved to his deathbed the great lesson of his life: the art of a devout death. He was visiting his sister, Briga, abbess at Enach Duin (Annaghdown), and after celebrating Mass, he bade her, "Commend my departure in your prayers." "What have you to fear?" she said. "I fear," declared Brendan, "if I go alone, if the journey be dark, the unknown region, the presence of the King and the sentence of the Judge."

BROUN, Heywood (1888–1939). Journalist and wit, Broun achieved fame as a columnist for New York newspapers and as a member of the Algonquin Round Table, the glittering group of intellectuals who met regularly for lunch at New York's Algonquin Hotel. He converted to Catholicism just months before dying of pneumonia. At the time of his death, he was a columnist for *Commonweal*.

> Broun was consumed by causes: the Sacco-Vanzetti case, the Scottsboro Boys, the organization of the American Newspaper Guild. In 1937, he offered in his column a definition of a convert. He wrote in oblique context, but given the circumstances of his own career and religious life (he was converted in May of 1939 by Monsignor Fulton Sheen (*q.v.*) and died the following December), he could have been holding a mirror to his spiritual self:

There is no fury like that of a convert. Those who come in at
the eleventh hour have more steam in their punches for rounds
twelve to fifteen inclusive . . . and at that stage of a fight, I
think the regulation has to be, "Quit your kidding."

*B*ROWNSON, Orestes A. (1803–1876). One of the great intellectuals
and controversialists of the nineteenth century, Brownson moved from
Presbyterianism, to Universalism and its ministry, to Unitarianism, to
Transcendentalism. At one point he even organized his own church. Finally he
embraced Roman Catholicism. In 1838, he founded the *Boston Quarterly Review,*
which evolved eventually into *Brownson's Quarterly Review.* He was a strong voice
in national politics in behalf of liberal and radical causes.

A man of fiery opinions and impulses, Brownson was in a bookstore one
day and fell into a conversation with a Mr. Trask. At the time,
Brownson was a Unitarian minister; Trask, a crusader against tobacco.
Irritated by one of Trask's remarks, Brownson promptly knocked him
down. Bystanders protested, and Brownson graciously apologized to
Trask for his loss of self-control. The apology was accepted, but Trash
overdid his magnanimity, repeating once or twice again, "I forgive you."
Becoming enraged a second time, Brownson said: "I have knocked you
down and I have apologized for it. If you say anything more about for-
giving me, I will knock you down again."

Brownson's conversion to Catholicism in 1844 caused a sensation, and
cost his *Review* many of its Protestant readers in New England and

almost all of the South. Catholics, too, were surprised by his conversion, and because of his gadfly religious past, some were unconvinced that their Church had won any great prize. Asked some years after his conversion whether he found life among Catholics a bed of roses, Brownson did not hesitate to reply, "Spikes, sir—spikes!"

As a Catholic, Brownson agitated for reform in certain disciplinary matters of the Church, and this activity, along with his history of religious instability, provoked reports that he was on his way back to Protestantism. Brownson responded that he knew "the best that could be offered outside" and was staying a Catholic:

> Catholicity is not with us something to be put on or off, as it may suit the exigencies of the moment; nor is it something that is or can be stowed away in a dark corner of the mind, to be brought out only on certain festive occasions; it is our intellectual and moral life, and we can no more divest ourselves of it than we can divest ourselves of ourselves. It is the element in which we live, think, move, and have our moral and intellectual being.

(Brownson died in Detroit. Eleven years after his death, his remains were reinterred in a crypt in the lower chapel of Sacred Heart Church at the University of Notre Dame, in South Bend.)

Brownson was a visionary of sorts, often of an impractical kind. In the 1850s, he was linking America's destiny to Catholicism in a manner not to be dared again until the aftermath of World War II and the beginnings of the Cold War, when the ground was replowed by certain Catholic ecclesiastical patriots. The destiny of the nation, said Brownson, stood on the firm ground of "Catholicity" and the two— nation and Church—shared a common path. He framed the linkage thus in 1856:

> The Catholic Church . . . comes not to destroy the natural, but to fulfill—to purify, elevate, direct, and invigorate it. That is, she comes to give us precisely the help we need, and as our country is the future hope of the world, so is Catholicity the future hope of our country; and it is through Catholicity bringing the supernatural to the aid of the natural, that the present evils which afflict us are to be removed, and the country is to be enabled to perform its civilizing mission for the world.

*B*RUNO, Giordano (1548–1600). Italian philosopher and priest, Bruno was one of the most creative minds of the sixteenth century. He was also a wanderer, moving between many countries and states and establishing a reputation for intrigue, irreverence, and theological unorthodoxy. (He claimed that the Old Testament's Song of Songs gave him an erection.) Hauled before the Inquisition, he was burned at the stake in Rome's Campo dei Fiori. During the *Risorgimento* of the nineteenth century he was elevated to a sort of national saint, and a statue was erected in his honor on the spot where he died.

꧁ Bruno was an author of note and in England in 1584 produced his masterwork, *Cena de le Ceneri,* or "Ash Wednesday Supper." In it, Bruno attacked Oxford's professors, saying they knew more about beer than about Greek. More to the point, the book, in retrospect, seems to have summed up his philosophy of life:

> . . . not only he who wins is praised, but also he who does not die as a coward and a poltroon. Not only the one who gains the prize is to be honored, but also the other who has run so well that he is judged worthy and sufficient to have gained it, although he has lost. And they are contemptible who, in the middle of the race, give up in despair and, though last, do not go on to reach the finish with the best nerve and strength they have left. Let perseverance triumph, for, if the effort is so great, the reward will not be trivial. Everything worthwhile is difficult.

(Insisting toward the end of 1599 that he was penitent and would abjure any unorthodox opinions proved against him, Bruno changed his mind and refused to abjure anything. Pope Clement VIII then turned Bruno over to the secular arm for burning at the stake.)

*B*URKE, Edward (c. 1907–1975). A priest of the Archdiocese of Chicago with the rank of monsignor, Burke was a powerful chancery figure in the 1940s and 1950s as chancellor during the administration of Samuel Cardinal Stritch *(q.v.)*. He was later pastor of St. Bartholomew's parish on Chicago's North Side.

 An outgoing, bon vivant personality, Burke was at lunch one day with a group that included Saul Alinsky, the Chicago community activist. It was about the time the archdiocese, through a well-connected law firm, had persuaded Station WGN, owned by the *Chicago Tribune,* to suspend a television broadcast of a film about Martin Luther. Nicholas von Hoffman, an Alinsky protégé, had convinced Alinsky that this was a grossly stupid tactic, and Alinsky proceeded to hector, cajole, and badger Burke to rescind the ban.

Obviously irritated, Burke told Alinsky to stay out of it. "It's strictly between us and the goddamn Protestants," he said. They argued heatedly, and Alinsky's final pitch was to let the movie be broadcast, "with one proviso, that they show it backward so that Martin Luther will end up as a Catholic." Everyone at table exploded in laughter, except Burke, who finally said, "You son of a bitch, Saul." The archdiocese withdrew its opposition to the movie.

6

CARROLL, John (1735–1815). Born in Maryland, Carroll studied for the priesthood as a Jesuit in Europe and, after several years' ministry there, returned to the United States. In 1783, he was named superior of the Catholic missions of the thirteen states, with power to confirm. Six years later he became the first American bishop, heading the see of Baltimore. In 1808, he was raised to the rank of archbishop.

In 1785, Carroll filed his first report to Rome on the state of the Church in the United States and cited a condition, aspects of which, some fear, may be returning as a result of the current vocations crisis.

> As for piety, [American Catholics] are for the most part sufficiently assiduous in the exercises of religion and in frequenting the sacraments, but they lack that fervor, which frequent appeals to the sentiment of piety usually produce, as many congregations hear the word of God only once a month, and sometimes only once in two months. We are reduced to this by want of priests, by the distance of congregations from each other and by difficulty of traveling.

CATHERINE of Siena (1347–1380). The youngest of twenty-five children, Catherine became a Dominican tertiary at age sixteen. Her profound spiritual insights won her a large following of men, and this in turn caused unwarranted charges of scandal to be leveled against her. She carried the stigmata and left behind some four hundred letters and a famous mystical tract, *Dialogue.* The Church canonized her in 1461.

> Catherine of Siena was an imperious and sometimes difficult woman, who would lecture a pope as quickly as she would one of her male secretaries. She traveled to France, where she confronted Gregory XI and persuaded him to end the Avignon Captivity and return to Rome. Catherine was especially severe on the clergy, writing that "they have chosen for their table the public tavern and . . . become animals through their sins."

> Catherine lived in bellicose times, and much of her energy was expended battling war, injustice, and corruption. At the same time, much of her preaching was in fact a call to action. As she wrote in one of her letters: "It is through silence that the world is lost."

CHARLES II (1630–1685). Charles wore the British crown from 1660 to 1685. He had fled England after the Battle of Worcester in 1651, taking up residence in France, from which he returned at age thirty as king—and as a Roman Catholic. Although he would continue as a Catholic, his reign would not affect a restoration of the Catholic faith. Not that Charles made that a goal. He recognized the strong Protestant feeling of his subjects and was not prepared to imperil his crown by defying it.

✺ An idle and voluptuous man (he had no children by his queen, but kept a stable of mistresses by whom he had numerous progeny), Charles was also a man of good humor and democratic instincts. When William Penn, the Quaker, appeared before him wearing his broad-brim hat to petition a charter for the New World, Charles ceremoniously removed his own feathered hat as he listened. "But, Friend Charles, why hast thou taken off thy hat?" Penn inquired, interrupting his plea. "Because," Charles courteously replied, "it has long been the custom here but for one person to remain covered at a time."

✺ One of the mistresses by whom Charles had a child was Nell Gwyn, an actress noted for her charm in comic roles. In fact, she is reputed to have had two sons by Charles. After the birth of one, a distressed Nell Gwyn stood on a balcony, baby in arms, and threatened to throw the child off for want of a name. Charles, galloping past on his horse, shouted over his shoulder, "Spare the Earl of Burford."

*C*HESTERTON, Gilbert Keith (1874–1936). Prolific British author and one of the great controversialists of his age, Chesterton jousted constantly with government, the establishment, and individuals such as Kipling, Shaw, and Wells. He became a Catholic in 1922 but for years prior was a keen apologist for Christian theology. There was great merriment to Chesterton, but together with the fun, there was great seriousness and sense of purpose.

✺ Chesterton cherished the Catholic Mass and communion, but the profundity of the Eucharist caused awe and a certain fear. Once, when the

Eucharist was brought to his wife, Frances, in their home, he declared: "I am a simple man, and I am afraid when God comes to my house."

ᴄᴏ Chesterton was celebrated for his wit, which he often expressed in quatrains in which laughter was employed as a medium of knowledge, sanity, and belief. For example:

> And Noah he often said to his wife
> when he sat down to dine,
> "I don't care where the water goes
> if it doesn't get into the wine."

ᴄᴏ Chesterton was a frequent visitor to the United States. Conducting a class one day on Dante at Milbrook Junior College in California, he was interrupted by a student who had lost her place. "Where the hell are we?" she exclaimed. The class roared. Chesterton warmed to the ejaculation. "I rather like that phrase," he remarked. Then he continued:

> Good Catholic expression. A Catholic doesn't live in Milbrook or in England, but *sub specie aeternitatis*, and the question always is, where in hell are we? or where in heaven are we? or where in purgatory are we? We live in that spaceless, timeless commonwealth and the question is very important.

ᴄᴏ Chesterton wrote a number of detective stories in which the principal character was one Father Brown. Like so much else of which he wrote, the Father Brown stories were full of Chesterton as story and the moral often fit the crime. Hence, passages such as the following: "I'm afraid

I'm a practical man," said the doctor with gruff humor, "and I don't bother much about religion and philosophy." To which Father Brown responded, "You'll never be a practical man till you do."

Enrico, a "guest" at SS. Francis & Therese Catholic Worker House in Worcester, Massachusetts, startled everyone at the dinner table recently by announcing that the Bible told what kind of car God drove. He told his perplexed listeners that the information was in Genesis. "It says in Genesis that God drove Adam and Eve out of the Garden of Eden in a Fury. So, there it is. God drove a Pontiac."

The Catholic Radical, February/March 1995

CLARE, saint (1194–1253). Born of patrician parents in Assisi, Clare became a follower of Francis of Assisi *(q.v.)* and founder of a religious order of women, the Poor Clares, which she modeled on Francis's rule. Her influence was widespread and reached to the papacy itself.

> ✠ When Clare founded her order, the Church of St. Damien was made over to her by the Benedictines. One day Francis of Assisi arrived to take a meal with Clare and her nuns. Everyone at table was so spellbound by the sweetness of Francis's conversation about the things of the spirit that they forgot to eat. Night fell and when it did, the convent was lit with glorious light. Seeing it, the people in Assisi supposed that St. Damien's was on fire, so they rushed to save the church. There was no actual fire; rather, the fire was said to be that of divine love.

> ✠ Pope Innocent II happened to be in Assisi when Clare died, and he presided at her obsequies. Knowing Clare and having been deeply moved by her holiness, Innocent thought of interrupting the requiem Mass and canonizing her on the spot. Cardinals present dissuaded him, urging that the usual canonization process be held first. Two years later, Pope Alexander IV added her name to the roster of saints.

CLAUDEL, Paul (1868–1955). Claudel served in the French diplomatic service as ambassador, successively, to Japan, the United States, and Belgium. But he is remembered primarily as a poet and dramatist. On Christmas Day in 1886, Claudel, an indifferent believer, experienced a spiritual awakening while attending vespers in Notre Dame Cathedral, and his life of religious casualness was transformed into one of intense belief and conviction. Thereafter, a strong Catholic Christian symbolism marked his works.

   Claudel was said to be instrumental in the conversion or religious rebirth of several notable figures of the early century, among them the critic Jacques Rivière and the poet Francis Jammes. He was a friend of André Gide (whom he did not succeed in converting), and for twenty-five years the two carried on a lively correspondence. In a 1905 letter, Claudel confided to Gide the mission he felt as a writer:

> I attach absolutely no value to the literary quality of my work. Frizeau [a friend of Rivière and Jammes] was the first one who, brought back to God by my dramas, because he saw religion dominating everything in them, made me think: then I haven't written in vain. The literary beauty of my work has no other significance for me than that found by a workman who is aware of having performed his task well; I simply did my best; but had I been a carpenter, I should have been just as conscientious in planing a plank properly as I have been in writing properly.

COGLEY, John (1916–1976). A native of Chicago, Cogley evolved through the Catholic Worker movement and *Commonweal* as the most prominent American Catholic journalist of his generation. He edited *Center Magazine,* a journal of the Center for the Study of Democratic Institutions in Santa Barbara, and for several years was religious news editor of the *New York Times.* In 1973, he was received into the Episcopal Church and applied for ordination. He received the deaconate shortly before his death.

In 1960, Cogley served on the presidential campaign staff of John F. Kennedy *(q.v.)*, and was a principal architect of his crucial talk to Protestant clergy in Houston. Earlier he had ghost-written speeches for Chicago's colorful auxiliary bishop Bernard J. Sheil, most notably Sheil's denunciation of Senator Joseph McCarthy at the height of the anti-Communist frenzy of the 1950s. The speech, which Cogley wrote working alone one night at his kitchen table in New York, was delivered before a 1954 meeting of the United Automobile Workers and caused a national sensation.

The speech was widely reprinted, and Sheil was featured on network television, including Edward R. Murrow's program. Shortly afterward, Cogley was having a sociable drink one afternoon in Manhattan with Saul Alinsky, the Chicago community organizer. Cogley recalled their conversation: "He told me, in strictest confidence of course, that *he* had written the McCarthy speech for Bishop Sheil. Keeping the secret was most difficult for me under such circumstances."

CONGAR, Yves M. J., O.P. (1904–1995). One of the great theological minds of the twentieth century, Congar entered the Dominicans in 1925 and was ordained in 1930. His innovative thought on ecumenical and lay questions brought him under censure in the 1950s, but his reputation was rehabilitated in the 1960s and he helped lay the groundwork for Vatican II and many of its most important decrees. Pope John Paul II *(q.v.)* cited him as an inspiration and awarded him a red hat in 1994.

❧ An anecdote in an old Catholic Truth Society pamphlet has a priest remarking that the layperson in the Catholic Church had two positions: to kneel before the altar and to sit below the pulpit. A cardinal corrected the priest and added that the layperson's position was also to give. In 1957, Congar used that anecdote as a springboard for a prescient comment on the laity of today:

> In a sense that is still so, and always will be so. There will never be a time when lay men and women are not on their knees before the altar and sitting before the pulpit, and for a long time yet they will have to put hand into purse. Nevertheless, now and for the future they do these things in a different way; or at least, doing these things they feel differently about their position as a body in the Church.

CONNELL, Francis J. (1888–1967). A Redemptorist father, Connell taught moral theology at the Catholic University of America and from 1949 to 1957 was dean of its School of Sacred Theology. In 1946, he was elected first president of the Catholic Theological Society. He was a *peritus* (expert) for the American bishops at Vatican Council II, author of several books, syndicated columnist, and a frequent commentator on radio and television.

❧ In those intellectually immodest days when Catholic theologians functioned as answer machines, Connell, as one of America's best-known moral theologians, was often called upon by the media for the "Catholic" position on issues of moment. He stood in awe of no topic.

In 1952, when eyes turned toward space exploration, Connell was asked to comment on the possibilities of flying saucers and of inhabited worlds other than Earth. Connell listed four principal classes into which outer-space dwellers might fall: (1) They might have received, like earth persons, a supernatural destiny from God . . . might even have lost it and been redeemed; (2) God could have created them with a natural but eternal destiny . . . i.e., like infants who die unbaptized, they could live a life of natural happiness after death, without beholding God face to face; (3) they might be rational beings who sinned against God but where never given the chance to regain grace, such as evil angels of the Fall; (4) they might have received supernatural gifts and kept them, leading the paradisiacal existence of Adam and Eve before they ate the forbidden fruit.

Connell's bottom line was as follows:

> If these supposed rational beings should possess the immortality of body once enjoyed by Adam and Eve, it would be foolish for our superjet or rocket pilots to try to shoot them. They would be unkillable.

CONSALVI, Ercole (1757–1824). Italian cardinal and statesman, Consalvi was one of the Church's most noted diplomats. He arranged concordats or similar agreements with France, Bavaria, Hanover, Sardinia, the princess of the upper Rhine, and King Ferdinand I of the Two Sicilies, which restored a certain eminence to the Papal States, albeit a twilight one. At the same time, Consalvi did much to enhance Rome's stature as a center of art, being the patron of a number of noted artists, including Antonia Canova and Albert Bertal Thorvaldsen.

◖◗ As Pope Pius VII's secretary of state, Consalvi's major objectives were the reorganization of the Papal States and the resolidification of the allegiance of Europe to the papal throne. He functioned as a quasi-governor of Rome, reforming the currency, introducing free trade, restoring old monuments, and adding to museum holdings. So dependent was Pius VII on him that wags said that when the pope died, he would have to wait at the gates of paradise until Consalvi arrived from purgatory with the keys.

(Consalvi's last will and testament attested to the close bond that existed between himself and Pius VII. In the will, Consalvi directed that his possessions be sold and that the proceeds be used for the monument to Pius VII planned for St. Peter's. Executed by the Danish sculptor Thorvaldsen, the memorial is one of the basilica's famous memorials.)

◖◗ Consalvi served for years as Pius VII's representative in France and in 1810 was one of thirteen cardinals stripped of property and denied cardinalate dignity (whence the term "black cardinals") for refusing to attend Napoleon's wedding to Duchess Marie Louise of Austria, Napoleon's second wife. The disagreement between Consalvi and Napoleon was not novel. Nine years earlier, in the course of tense diplomatic negotiations, Napoleon said that if he did not get his way, he would destroy the Church. Responding laconically to this threat, Consalvi said that the clergy had been trying to do that for centuries and had not succeeded.

*C*OPLESTON, Frederick C., S.J. (1907–1994). A convert to Catholicism as a teenager, Copleston entered the Jesuits upon graduating from Oxford and was ordained in 1937. He achieved renown as a professor and author, specializing in the history of philosophy, and was awarded many honors, including the Queen's "Commander of the British Empire" in 1993.

Copleston belonged to a noted Anglican family: two uncles were Anglican bishops and his father, a judge, was active in the life of the Church of England on various levels. His uncle Reginald was bishop of Calcutta, and Copleston told of Uncle Reginald being a guest at dinner in Calcutta with his wife, Edith, who coincidentally was the daughter of Anglican Archbishop Trench of Dublin. Aunt Edith was notoriously absentminded and frequently forgot where she was. Turning to her husband across the dinner table, she declared, "We must really change the cook, my dear; this soup is quite tasteless."

Copleston's many books, including his nine-volume *A History of Philosophy*, established him as one of the most prolific writers in his field. But could one person produce all that work? Lecturing in later years in the United States, Copleston realized that some Americans believed the name *Copleston* on his books represented some sort of syndicate. He addressed their skepticism:

> If anyone is curious to know how I managed to write so much, the answer is, I suppose, that I did little else but study, lecture and write. Being celibate and having for most of my life no administrative post, I was able to devote a large part of each day to literary work. The syndicate idea was a figment of the imagination.

COUGHLIN, Charles E. (1891–1979). Born in Hamilton, Ontario, and educated at St. Michael's College, University of Toronto, Coughlin came as a young priest to the United States and was incardinated into the Archdiocese of Detroit in 1923. During the 1930s he enjoyed great renown as a radio priest and as publisher of the newspaper *Social Action,* but became a lightning rod of controversy as his messages turned anti-Semitic, isolationist, and pro-Nazi. He was silenced in 1942 through a combination of ecclesiastical and governmental pressures, and lived out his days at Royal Oak, Michigan, as pastor of the Shrine of the Little Flower, which he built and made famous.

ꙮ Coughlin enjoyed the patronage and unqualified support of Bishop Michael J. Gallagher, but not that of the prelate who succeeded on Gallagher's death in 1937, Archbishop (later Cardinal) Edward F. Mooney. The two locked in intense struggles centered on tactics and authority, and in some partisan eyes Mooney was "the Judas who turned Coughlin over to his enemies." Mooney died in Rome in 1958 while attending the conclave that elected Pope John XXIII *(q.v.).* It was October 25, Coughlin's sixty-seventh birthday. Coughlin heard the word back in Royal Oak. He was silent for a few moments, then said, "My Father has given me a birthday present."

ꙮ In 1976 on the fortieth anniversary of the completion of the Shrine of the Little Flower, Coughlin was honored by friends and some old associates. Among the speakers was Monsignor Edward Hickey, chancellor of the Detroit archdiocese during Mooney's tenure. Hickey looked back on the tumultuous years in Coughlin's life with an olive branch and an acknowledgment: "We think he made mistakes in economics and in his international relations. . . . We condemned his attitudes toward the Jewish people. But when the showdown came, what so edified us all was his obedience. . . . I used to say if the bishop had told him to stand on his head . . . he would have done so."

CUMMINGS, William T. (1903–1944). A Maryknoll Missions priest, Cummings was aboard an unmarked Japanese ship transporting prisoners from the Philippines to Japan when an American submarine sunk the ship on December 15, 1944.

An Army chaplain, Cummings survived Bataan and the dreadful "death march" that followed the fall of Manila in January 1942. In a field sermon that year on Bataan, Cummings uttered the phrase that would immortalize him and encapsulate the faith of GIs around the world: "There are no atheists in foxholes."

CURLEY, James Michael (1874–1958). Son of a hod carrier, Curley ascended the political ladder as Boston alderman, city councilman, U.S. congressman, three-time mayor of the city, governor of Massachusetts, and convicted felon (mail fraud). His favorite title was "Mayor of the Poor," a title that he bestowed upon himself. A colorful personality, Curley provided the model for Frank Skeffington, the protagonist in Edwin O'Connor's best-selling 1956 novel, *The Last Hurrah*.

Curley did not introduce dirty tricks to politics, but he certainly indulged in them. In the 1921 mayoral election, he stood against Fire

Commissioner John R. Murphy, sixty-six, a respectable "old-timer" with roots deep into a past era of Boston politics. Curley, who always preferred the frontal attack, derided Murphy as "an old mustard plaster stuck on the back of the people for fifty years." Sharing a platform with him, he rose after Murphy had reviewed his long career, squinted toward the audience, and croaked, "I don't see anybody here that I welcomed back from the Civil War."

For Curley, nothing was so sacred it could not be exploited, including religion. He charged that Murphy, a practicing Catholic like himself, had not only joined a Masonic order but had moved so he wouldn't have so far to walk to fashionable Trinity Church (Protestant) in Copley Square.

Murphy spent several nights on the stump denying the allegation. Curley's response was to revive the charge in a slightly different form: "Where was James M. Curley last Friday night?" he would ask. "He was conducting a political meeting in Duxbury. And where was John R. Murphy last Friday night? He was eating steak at the Copley Plaza."

In those days the observance of Friday abstinence was a hallmark of Catholic orthodoxy, and Curley played on the abstinence rule shamelessly. He sent squads of his followers to the saloons and into tenement districts spreading the rumor, "The counterman at Thompson's Spa [an eatery near City Hall] told me Murphy ordered a roast beef sandwich last Friday."

Curley won the election by fewer than 2,700 votes.

❧ As an early supporter of Franklin Delano Roosevelt, Curley hoped for a cabinet appointment when Roosevelt was elected president in 1938. When this failed to materialize, he aimed to become U.S. ambassador to Italy, partially so as to one-up William Cardinal O'Connell *(q.v.)*, with whom he was constantly dueling. O'Connell had an impassioned love for Italy, and Curley would have been the last person in the world he would want to see go there in a diplomatic capacity.

Instead of Italy, however, Roosevelt offered Poland, a post Curley turned down indignantly. "If Poland is such a goddam interesting place, why don't you resign the presidency and take it yourself?" he said to Roosevelt. Piqued, Roosevelt made public his offer, an action that caused Curley much discomfit, while providing sport for his detractors. One wag remarked that if Curley, a politician noted for his public-works projects, went to Poland, he'd probably pave the Polish Corridor. (The Polish Corridor was a narrow piece of land given Poland in the Treaty of Versailles to provide Poland access to the Baltic Sea.)

When *The Last Hurrah* first appeared, Curley considered suing Edwin O'Connor, its author, for libel. Because of the flattering attention it brought him, however, he came to like the book, particularly the deathbed scene, where a newspaper publisher present in the sick room murmured that if Skeffington had his life to live over, he would perhaps have done things differently. Curley told a lecture audience that if the same were ever said of him, he would reply as did Skeffington, "Like hell I would!" (Curley expressed the same sentiment in his autobiography, titled more felicitously, *I'd Do It Again!)*

CURLEY, Michael J. (1879–1947). Born in Ireland, Curley was ordained in 1904 and emigrated that year to Florida. In 1914, at age thirty-five, he was named bishop of St. Augustine and seven years later was appointed successor to James Cardinal Gibbons *(q.v.)* as archbishop of Baltimore. In 1939, he was designated first archbishop of Washington, D.C., retaining his post in Baltimore. (The Archdiocese of Washington was not separated from the Archdiocese of Baltimore until 1947.)

○ Curley's appointment to Baltimore was not well received, and he did little to help the situation. Not long after arriving in the city, he declared from the cathedral pulpit: "I have not come to Baltimore to be archbishop to Baltimore's first families." It was a comment that inevitably irritated Maryland's Catholic gentry, and that some were slow in forgetting. Nor did Curley mellow with the years. In 1936 as *ex officio* chancellor of the Catholic University of America (a position he held as archbishop of Baltimore), he introduced the new rector to the faculty, reading the papal brief of appointment. He added: "It is in Latin; for those of you who do not understand Latin, let someone translate it for you."

○ A man of quick temper and deep-seated likes and dislikes, Curley possessed a measure of brashness. This brashness betrayed him on a notable occasion. It was Sunday, December 7, 1941, and Curley, who was confirming in western Maryland, returned to his residence in Baltimore without having learned of the Japanese attack on Pearl Harbor. Soon after reaching his residence on North Charles Street, a reporter appeared and asked what he thought of the war in the Pacific. "War in the Pacific?" he remarked. "We have a war in the Atlantic and we might as well have one in the Pacific!" (When Curley became aware of the true situation, he issued an apology, one of the few times he publicly acknowledged having made an error.)

*C*USHING, Richard J. (1895–1970). A priest of the Archdiocese of Boston, Cushing was named an auxiliary bishop in 1939 and in 1944 became archbishop. He was elevated to cardinal in 1958 by Pope John XXIII. Cushing, a populist, was famous for his small regard for pomp and circumstance.

☙ In time-honored episcopal tradition, Cushing would pace about at confirmation ceremonies asking questions from the catechism of those in the class, thus going through the final formalities assuring that the youngsters were ready to receive the sacrament. By posing easy questions and glossing over blunders, he would quickly set the class at ease.

At one such ceremony, Cushing came upon Michael Cronin, son of Joe Cronin, then manager of the Boston Red Sox and later president of the American League. "Who made the world?" Cushing asked Michael. "God made the world," said Michael. "Who made the Red Sox?" Cushing countered. "Tom Yawkey," declared the youth, citing the current owner of the Red Sox. Cushing waited for the laughter to subside, then said: "You certainly know your catechism."

☙ During the 1950s, the Boston Celtics dominated professional basketball in the United States. One day, three of the most prominent members of the team—center Easy Ed Macauley, guard Bob Cousy, and manager Red Auerbach—were standing around waiting for Cushing to arrive to dedicate a new Catholic school gymnasium. Macauley and

Cousy, being Catholics, were at ease, but Auerbach, being Jewish, was in a quandary. "What do I say to him," asked Auerbach. "Do I kiss his ring? What the hell am I supposed to do?"

Suddenly, Cushing's chauffeur-driven big black Cadillac pulled up and out popped Cushing, resplendent in his episcopal red robes. He looked at one of his aides and said, "OK, I've got twenty minutes. Let's get this show on the road." Looking around, he spotted the three Celtics luminaries and called over, "Hi Red! Hi Cooz! Hi Ed!" Then, zip, he was on his way inside. Macauley, Cousy, and Auerbach fell into line and followed on in. Auerbach nudged Macauley and said, "Boy, that's my kind of guy!"

✺ In the 1940s, Jesuit Father Leonard Feeney became increasingly obsessed with the medieval idea of no salvation outside the Catholic Church and would conduct prayer meetings with his followers on the Boston Common, where he would spew contempt for Jews and mock Protestants. Feeney was an embarrassment, but more than that, he was a source of concern. It was, after all, the time when the world was being made aware of the full extent of the Nazi Holocaust. Cushing, who had a Jewish brother-in-law, summoned Feeney in 1949 to impose a canonical silence on him. Feeney marched in and said to Cushing, "In the name of the Blessed Virgin Mary, I accuse you of heresy!" Cushing would crack later, "What could I do? He beat me to the draw." (Feeney was excommunicated by Rome in 1953, but later reconciled.)

✺ Years after he had settled into the hierarchy, Cushing cracked to priests, "When you become a bishop, you're certain of two things. You'll never have a bad meal, and no one will tell you the truth."

During Vatican Council II, speculation was rife about the possibility of the Church changing its position on artificial birth control. The case for change was advanced most prominently by Dr. John Rock of Boston in a book entitled *The Time Has Come: A Catholic Doctor's Proposals to End the Battle over Birth Control.* Rock, developer of a synthetic progesterone that blocked ovulation ("the Pill," so called), took his argument in favor of the Pill to a hostile Rome, where one day he chanced upon Cushing on the street. "Johnny boy, Johnny boy, what have you done?" chortled Cushing. "You've gone and got the whole Vatican pregnant."

Cushing was an impatient participant in Vatican Council II. He complained about Latin being the language of the council and offered to pay for the installation of a simultaneous translation system. Midway in session two, in 1963, he packed up and returned home, saying his time could be better spent raising money for the missions.

During the third and fourth sessions, he was an important player in debate on the issue of religious freedom, but an earlier dismissive comment typified a general American attitude toward a council that would prove as memorable as any in history. "There is a tendency, nurtured by periodicals and other influences of public opinion, to expect dramatic, even miraculous results from the Council," Cushing said in *The Pilot,* the Boston archdiocesan newspaper. "This is not good theology."

Cushing possessed strong ecumenical impulses, noticeably toward the Jewish people. He had, in fact, a Jewish brother-in-law. In 1963, when the matter of the relationship of the Church to non-Christian religions was still before Vatican II, Cushing gave an interview which in some respects previewed the council on the subject:

> There shouldn't be any anti-Semitism in a Catholic book. Anti-Semitism is not only a violation of God's law of love, it is a falsification of the New Testament record. The Catholic Church does not teach that the Jewish people were cursed by God when their leaders rejected Christ the Messiah. The Catholic Church does not teach that the Jews are a deicide people because they put the Son of God to death on a cross. What the church does teach is that all mankind—Catholics included—put the Son of God to death on a cross, because it was the sins of all of us that brought Him down to this earth and turned Him toward the cross and put Him up on that cross. No one can despise the Jews for the death of Christ if he has his theology straight; if he wants to despise somebody for the death of Christ, he ought to despise the whole human race. When the Jewish leaders in Jerusalem handed Jesus over to the Romans for execution, they were only our agents in an action for which we are all responsible.

There's an old South Boston election-day cliché about voting early and often. Cushing returned from the 1963 papal conclave claiming to have topped that. He said he voted twice for Milan's Cardinal-Archbishop Giovanni Battista Montini in the decisive round in which Montini emerged as Pope Paul VI *(q.v.)*. As Cushing told the story, he was sitting next to a South American cardinal with no facility for language beyond his native Spanish. The man had no idea what was going on, Cushing declared. All he could say was, "Who? Who? Who?" So it was when it came time to vote, Cushing reached over, took the man's ballot, wrote down "Montini," and passed the ballot in along with his own. "It was just like being back in Southie," Cushing reminisced.

❧ In raising funds, there were few who could match Cushing. He could get money out of the proverbial stone—and often needed to, for his generosity frequently exceeded his means. He reveled in money roles and played on his reputation as a money machine, as when he arrived at a nuns' school for a very formal affair. Dignitaries were lined up on the stage and the audience was shoulder to shoulder with nuns in their uniforms of old, students, parents, and friends of the institute. Cushing stood alongside the reverend mother superior, and at a particularly solemn moment, he leaned over to her and mischievously whispered (his voice amplified for all to hear), "Get your hand out of my pocket!"

❧ As Cushing approached the mandatory retirement age of seventy-five, rumors circulated that John Cardinal Wright *(q.v.)*, once his secretary, then prefect of the Congregation for the Clergy in Rome, and a man with whom he had a sometimes ticklish relationship, was anxious to return to the United States and had his eye on Cushing's episcopal seat. "He may have his eye on it," Cushing quipped, "but I've got my ass on it."

D

DAMIEN, Father. *See* Veuster, Joseph de.

DAY, Dorothy (1897–1980). A left-wing social activist, Day converted to Catholicism in 1927 and, with Peter Maurin in 1933, launched the Catholic Worker movement. She spent forty-five years supervising soup kitchens, providing free shelter, and espousing voluntary poverty in the name of Christian charity through Catholic Worker houses across the United States, and a few abroad, spawned by her movement. Although she accepted the University of Notre Dame's Lactare Medal in 1972, Dorothy Day generally spurned honors.

- Dorothy Day was arguably the most influential lay person, male or female, in the history of American Catholicism, so not surprisingly, soon after her death there were those espousing her beatification cause. In fact, during her lifetime people spoke of her as a saint, one who had a halo over her head. The talk annoyed her. "Don't call me a saint," she remarked. "I don't want to be dismissed so easily!"

- Day's radical social and political side notwithstanding, she was decidedly conservative in church matters. In 1968, while free on bail after pouring blood on draft-board files in Catonsville, Maryland, the Jesuit antiwar activist Daniel Berrigan *(q.v.)* visited the New York Catholic Worker house of hospitality to celebrate Mass. Sensitive to Day's feelings, Berrigan conducted what he thought was a rather orthodox liturgy. It was not orthodox enough for Day. Later, she recalled:

> He used a loaf of French bread for the Host, tore off hunks with his hands, crumbs all over the floor. And later they were swept up and dumped into the garbage pail. If you really believe they had become the body of Jesus, as I do, literally—well, that was no way to treat the body of Our Lord. Those crumbs bothered me.

❧ Among the social injustices of concern to Day was the treatment of women in prisons, and so she was one of the first to join the "prison faculty" organized by the Institute of Women Today, a feminist organization based in Chicago. On visiting a West Virginia prison, Day and her colleagues encountered a skeptical elderly resident, who challenged their presence. "Why are you here?" the woman demanded. Day, with her long history of serving the poor, calmly responded, "We have come to wash your feet."

❧ Day, an anarchist at heart, did not vote, did not pay taxes, and submitted no Internal Revenue Service tax returns on the voluntary contributions that flowed in to the Catholic Worker movement. In fact, she never even applied for tax-exempt charity status, which unquestionably would have been granted.

In 1972, this negligence resulted in a demand by the IRS for $296,359 in back taxes and penalties. The IRS dropped its case under a barrage of outraged public opinion, which included a *New York Times* editorial. First, however, Day had begged her followers' prayers and understanding in her column in *The Catholic Worker,* the movement's newspaper:

> I'm sure that many will think me a fool indeed, almost criminally negligent for not taking more care to safeguard . . . the welfare of the lame, halt and blind—deserving and undeserving—that come to us. . . . Our refusal to apply for exemption status in our practice of the works of mercy is part of our protest against war and the present social "order" which brings wars on today.

*D*E SMET, Pierre-Jean, S.J. (1801–1873). A Belgian émigré to the United States, De Smet joined the Jesuits in 1821 and achieved fame as a missionary to the Indians of the Pacific Northwest and the Great Plains. He became a spokesman for Indian causes in Washington and Europe and helped negotiate pacts with the Indians, including the Sioux peace treaty of 1867. His books are a valuable source of the history of the West.

> De Smet was uneasy about the future of America's Indian tribes, and he worried about their eventual extermination as white settlers pressed West. "They are styled savages," he wrote in his journal of the Indians, "but we boldly assert that, in all our great cities, and everywhere, thousands of whites are more deserving of the title."

PIERRE-JEAN DE SMET, S.J.

DESMOND, Daniel F. (1884–1945). A priest of the Archdiocese of Boston, Desmond was named bishop of the Alexandria, Louisiana, diocese in 1933 and served as its ordinary for twelve years.

In the pre-ecumenical era, when the Mass was celebrated in Latin, the practice was for priests to say Mass daily, even if in private. Desmond told a Boston newspaper man of making a trans-Atlantic crossing once on a liner with a chapel set aside to accommodate priests. The chapel was overseen by a sexton, a layman who scheduled the Masses at fifteen-minute intervals, arranging the altar necessities for each and serving as acolyte, or altar boy, seriatim.

One morning, after the last priest on his list had said Mass, the sexton repaired to the dining room for breakfast, when a late-arriving diner commented that he had just passed the chapel and saw a clergyman vesting for Mass. Believing he had forgotten someone, the sexton rushed back to the chapel and entered as the celebrant at the foot of the altar was intoning, "I will go to the altar of God . . . " "The hell you will!" cried the sexton, knowing the Anglican vernacular when he heard it. "Not on this ship."

DE VALERA, Eamon (1882–1975). De Valera was born in New York City of a Spanish father and Irish mother and brought as an infant to Ireland. There he became one of that country's most prominent political leaders and statesmen of modern times. He led a party of insurgents in the Irish national rising of 1916. When the British captured him, his American birth saved him from execution, although not from imprisonment. He established and led the

Fianna Fáil Party and served as Ireland's prime minister between 1932 and 1948, 1951 and 1954, and 1957 and 1959; and as president from 1959 until 1973.

✎ De Valera's name and foreign birth led some of his enemies to question whether he was Irish. Oliver St. John Gogarty *(q.v.)* was not an admirer, but he settled the question of origin emphatically. "He's a Hibernian, all right," said Gogarty, reflecting on de Valera's ungainly figure. "He looks like something uncoiled from the Book of Kells." (The Book of Kells is a famous illuminated manuscript of the early Middle Ages whose ornaments include initials in the form of exotic elongated animals. Done by monks at the monastery at Kells in County Meath, the book has been at Trinity College Library, Dublin, since the seventeenth century.)

✎ Wit was not a particular forte of de Valera, but he did have one moment of verbal glory. Arrested once while speaking to a crowd in Ennis, County Clare, he was jailed for a year. Released from prison, he returned to the same platform from which he had been hauled away and began, "As I was saying before we were interrupted . . . "

✎ De Valera's long and effective leadership in Irish politics and the fight for Irish freedom earned him near-reverential status among many Irish-Americans an ocean removed from the give-and-take of Irish domestic affairs. In 1957, an American journalist remarked during an interview with de Valera that certain relatives of his in the States regarded him as a saint. "Over here we hold that honor until the person is dead," said de Valera.

*D*OZIER, Carroll T. (1911–1985). A priest of the diocese of Richmond, Dozier was named first bishop of the diocese of Memphis, Tennessee, in 1970. An outspoken progressive, he took an early position critical of U.S. policy during the Vietnam hostilities and was one of the first American bishops to question publicly the legitimacy of the Church's just-war theory, not only in terms of nuclear weapons but also in terms of modern conventional weapons.

    Dozier was installed as bishop of Memphis in 1971 and soon after scheduled a general-absolution ceremony for the city's mammoth sports arena. He thought perhaps a few hundred would show up; some fourteen thousand came. Awed by the response, he arranged for a second general-absolution ceremony, which a smaller, but nonetheless still huge, crowd attended.

The leadership of the American church frowned. So did Rome, which did not approve of general absolution except for emergency circumstances, such as existed in battle areas during World War II, and which it felt did not exist at the time in Memphis.

Dozier was summoned to appear in Rome before the Congregation for Divine Worship and Discipline of the Sacraments, where he was reproved and directed not to repeat the ceremony. Dozier returned to the United States, and his plane circled New York City in preparation for landing at JFK Airport on Long Island. An unchastened Dozier joshed to a friend, "I looked out the window, and I raised my right hand and absolved the whole city of New York—everyone, that is, except Cardinal Spellman! *(q.v.)*"

(Spellman was actually dead by that time, but Dozier's point was clear in terms of his feelings about the place and usage of general absolution.)

73

*D*UCHESNE, Louis-Marie-Oliver (1843–1922). Born at Saint-Servan on the Breton coast, Duchesne was ordained in 1867 after studies at the Sorbonne and in Rome. He became director of studies at L'Ecole des Hautes Etudes in Paris and, as scholar and author, was a leader in the use of scientific and critical methods in the teaching of history. In 1895, Duchesne, by then a domestic prelate, returned to Rome as director of the Ecole Francaise, a position he held until his death. He was elected an "immortal" of the French Academy in 1911.

In 1912, Duchesne's three-volume *Histoire ancienne de l'église chrétienne,* his masterwork, was placed by Rome on the Index of Forbidden Books, the action coming shortly after the history's appearance in Italian translation. Well aware that he and his book had been caught in the anti-Modernist frenzy that marked the last years of the reign of Pope Pius X *(q.v.),* Duchesne took himself on holiday to Egypt. One day while walking down a street in Alexandria, Duchesne chanced upon an old Parisian acquaintance. "Mon seigneur," the friend exclaimed, "what are you doing in Egypt?" "My dear fellow," replied Duchesne, "I am waiting for the death of King Herod."

E

EDGEWORTH, Henry Essex [l'Abbé Edgeworth de Firmont] (1745–1807). Born in County Longford, Ireland, son of Robert Edgeworth, a Protestant vicar, Edgeworth was taken to France at age four when his father converted to Catholicism, making the rest of the family Catholics as well. After studying at the Sorbonne, young Edgeworth was ordained a priest and became a favorite in the court of King Louis XVI, husband of Marie Antoinette. He died of the plague in Mittau, Russia, where he had joined the court of the exiled Louis XVIII.

When the archbishop of Paris fled the city at the outbreak of the French Revolution, l'Abbé Edgeworth de Firmont (the *Firmont* derived from an ancestral holding in Ireland) was vested with his powers. His own life at risk, Edgeworth was urged by friends to seek safety in Ireland or England. He declined, confiding in a letter to a priest-friend in London:

> Almighty God has baffled my measures, and ties me to this land of horrors by chains I have not the liberty to shake off. The case is this: The wretched master [Louis XVI] charges me not to quit this country, as I am the priest whom he intends to prepare him for death. And should the iniquity of the nation commit this last act of cruelty, I must also prepare myself for

death, as I am convinced the popular rage will not allow me to survive an hour after the tragic scene; but I am resigned. Could my life save him I would gladly lay it down, and I should not die in vain.

☙ On January 20, 1793, l'Abbé Edgeworth was summoned to the Temple prison to minister to "Louis Capet," Louis XVI, who was scheduled to die the following day. Edgeworth spent the night with Louis, celebrated Mass for him in the morning, and accompanied him in the carriage to the guillotine. There he recommended to the king that he allow his hands to be tied, saying, "Sire, in this new outrage I see only the last trait of resemblance between your Majesty and the God who will be your reward." When the ax was about to fall, Edgeworth is said to have called out the celebrated—but perhaps apocryphal—words, "Son of St. Louis, ascend to heaven."

(Edgeworth was allowed to leave the scene of the execution, but soon his own head was in demand. Dressed as an ordinary citizen and using the name Essex, he eluded capture. He fled to London, where William Pitt offered him a life's pension. Edgeworth chose instead to become chaplain to Louis XVIII in his exile.)

ENGLAND, John (1786–1842). A native of County Cork, Ireland, England was ordained a priest in 1809. He served there until coming to the United States in 1820 as bishop of Charleston, South Carolina, which then comprised both Carolinas and the state of Georgia. In 1822, he founded the

United States Catholic Miscellany, the first fully Catholic newspaper in the United States. He twice visited Haiti as apostolic delegate and had charge of East Florida with the powers of vicar-general.

❧ As a young priest in Ireland, England was an outspoken defender of Irish rights, and next to Daniel O'Connell, "the Liberator," his influence was the greatest in the movement that culminated in Irish Emancipation. He was deeply involved in the Irish elections of 1812. Defending his role, he said that in vindicating the political rights of his countrymen, he was asserting their liberty of conscience.

England also vociferously opposed allowing the British government a voice in the selection of Irish and English Catholic bishops. Because of this, he was transferred to the small village of Bandon in 1817. The antipathy of the times toward Catholics could be gauged from the inscription over the village gates: "Turk, Jew or Atheist may enter here, but not a Papist."

❧ Once in the United States, England quickly established himself as one of the most dynamic prelates the country had seen. He was famous as an orator and unqualified in his defense of American values. A month before he received his final citizenship papers in 1826, he was invited to address Congress, the first Catholic priest ever so honored. England recounted the experience in a letter to his friend William Gaston:

On the day I filled the Speaker's chair I was indeed a show, and all Washington must have thought so, for the throng was so great that the President [John Quincy Adams] found it difficult to get in, and when in, much more so to get a seat. Upon my arrival, nearly half an hour after, I found vast numbers returning without a hope of getting upstairs, so as even to see in,—and for once I must own I felt ashamed at hearing my own name proclaimed by my friends [Charles Eaton] Haynes and [James] Hamilton [representatives] of S.C. who formed my bodyguard, whilst in all the pomp of Prelacy I struggled through and heard the proclamation renewed still to make way for me to enter. If I could blush, I am convinced I then did, because I had some unusual sensation of heart and some unwonted glow *in* my cheek and *in* my forehead. When I was done I certainly felt a very extraordinary gratification at the intense attention with which I was heard, and that every face seemed to say "go on." But I thought two hours enough for them and for me.

F

ÉNELON, François de Salignac de La Mothe (1651–1715). A Sulpician father and eventually archbishop of Cambrai, Fénelon was one of the brightest and most controversial priests of his day. Tutor to the king's grandson, author of famous tracts, and member of the French Academy, his horizons at one time seemed limitless. He fell into royal disfavor, however, after appealing a judgment of his peers to Innocent XII, an action viewed as a betrayal of the rights of the Gallican church. He was ordered to leave court, return to Cambrai, and stay there.

The storm that raged about Fénelon was brought on by Quietism, a heresy of Spanish origins that was in some senses a counterreaction to the rigidities of Jansenism. Quietism centered on the principles of contemplation in complete spiritual tranquillity and absolute passivity. The soul was to resign itself to the devil's intrusions and not regard as sin untoward happenings, such as carnal acts performed alone or with others. Scruples and doubts were to be set aside, and the acts not even to be mentioned in confession, the soul thus overcoming the devil and acquiring a treasure of peace.

Fénelon was really a semi-Quietist, but his close association with Quietism's great apostle, Jeanne-Marie Bouvier de la Mothe Guyon, tarred him with the brush of easy morality. Disgraced and defeated, he put on a bold front and, with a sad touch of humor, warned friends who had the courage to remain close to him: "Be careful; I have the plague."

FITZGERALD, F. Scott (1896–1940). Born in St. Paul of Irish Catholic parents, Fitzgerald attended Princeton University en route to becoming a celebrated novelist and, together with his wife, Zelda, the embodiment of the so-called Jazz Age. His 1925 novel *The Great Gatsby*, published when he was only twenty-nine, is an American classic. There were several more books of fiction, short stories, essays, and movie scripts, but the wonder boy of *Gatsby* partied away his talent bit by bit, and his health altogether.

Fitzgerald married in the Catholic Church and had his daughter, Scottie, baptized as a Catholic, then at some point he abandoned Catholicism. This created a problem on his death. He had often said that he wanted to be buried with his father and family in St. Mary's Catholic Cemetery in Rockville, Maryland. Church authorities refused permission, however, reportedly because his writings were "undesirable" and because he had not made his "Easter duty."

Accordingly, Fitzgerald was buried in the nondenominational Union Cemetery across the road from St. Mary's. An Episcopalian priest presided. When told the identity of the deceased, he said it made no particular difference to him who it was. The author Dorothy Parker earlier spoke a most apt benediction, drawing a line from the fictional Gatsby's funeral: "The poor son-of-a-bitch."

It took thirty-five years and an ecumenical council, but Fitzgerald finally made it across the road into St. Mary's Catholic Cemetery. The petition for transfer of the remains was made by his daughter and granted by William Cardinal Baum of the Archdiocese of Washington, within whose jurisdictional area the cemetery was situated. On November 8, 1975, Fitzgerald's remains and those of his wife, Zelda, were reinterred with a graveside Catholic liturgy. Cardinal Baum issued a statement on the occasion:

> F. Scott Fitzgerald . . . was a man touched by the faith of the Catholic Church. There can be perceived in his work a Catholic consciousness of reality. He found in this faith an understanding of the human heart caught in the struggle between grace and death. His characters are involved in this great drama, seeking God and seeking love. As an artist he was able with lucidity and poetic imagination to portray this struggle. He also experienced in his own life the mystery of suffering and, we hope, the power of God's grace.

FOLEY, Thomas P. R. (1822–1879). Born in Baltimore, Foley was ordained a priest in 1846, and served as rector of the cathedral and as Baltimore's chancellor. He was secretary for the First Plenary Council of Baltimore in 1852, and notary of the Second in 1862. In 1870, he was named coadjutor and administrator of Chicago, when that see's bishop, James Duggan, was judged mentally ill. He never succeeded to the see, however, as Duggan outlived him by twenty years.

◖ One of Foley's great challenges in Chicago was to rebuild institutions of the diocese, including the cathedral, that had been destroyed in the Great Fire of 1871. Another was to encourage religious orders to locate there to minister to the enormous wave of immigrants flocking to the area. One such order was the Servants of Mary (Servites), an Italian community. Their coming seemed particularly welcome, for Foley deemed Italian immigrants "erratically observant" as Catholics. Once, after Father Austin (Agostino) Morini, one of the founding Servites in the United States, had preached a successful mission to a group of Italians, Foley remarked to him, "Now that they are all in the grace of God, drown them in the river before they lose it."

*F*ORGIONE, Francesco [Padre Pio] (1887–1968). Born at Pietralcina in southern Italy, the future Padre Pio entered the Franciscan Capuchins at age fifteen. His health being frail, he made it to ordination only after several interruptions in his studies. After parish work in Foggia, he was transferred to the small monastery of Santa Maria delle Grazie at San Giovanni Rotondo, where he became famed for holiness and for the possession of miraculous gifts, among them, it is said, the power of bilocation.

◖ The mainspring of Padre Pio's spiritual life lay in contemplating the sufferings and death of Christ, and so it was that at San Giovanni Rotondo he suddenly experienced the stigmata—the duplication of the wounds of Christ's crucifixion. For fifty years, he bled continuously from hands, feet, and side.

When the hospital for which Padre Pio was the inspiration and motivating force was inaugurated at San Giovanni Rotondo, among those present was Paul White, consultant to then-President Dwight D. Eisenhower. On meeting Padre Pio, White was so moved that when he finished his little congratulatory speech, he blurted out with uncharacteristic gaucheness, ". . . and congratulations, Father, on your wounds."

Padre Pio first experienced the stigmata in September 1918. Doctors and clergy viewed the happening skeptically, and there was considerable controversy as to whether his wounds were natural or supernatural in origin. The Vatican was especially discomfited and forbade him to say public Mass. It then began its own investigation. Rumors flew that Pio was to be transferred from San Giovanni Rotondo, and these sparked riots by townspeople, which resulted in fourteen deaths and eighty persons being injured.

In 1920, the Vatican decided to leave Padre Pio where he was, but it also imposed tight restrictions on his public activities that were to last thirteen years. Pope Pius XI finally lifted these restrictions in 1933, saying to Pio's archbishop, "I have not been badly disposed toward Padre Pio, but I have been badly informed about Padre Pio."

FRANCIS de Sales (1567–1622). Of French extraction, Francis de Sales served as bishop of Geneva. As preacher and writer, he was one of the giant figures of the Counter-Reformation. Two of his books—*Introduction to a Devout Life* and *Treatise on the Love of God*—have been spiritual-reading classics for more than 350 years.

❧ Believing that "a sad saint is a sorry saint," Francis infused his preaching with love and the spiritual insight that characterized his writing. He said:

> Just as Joshua and Caleb held both that the Promised Land was good and beautiful and that its possession would be sweet and agreeable, so too, the Holy Spirit by the mouths of all the saints and Our Lord by his own mouth assures us that a devout life is a life that is sweet, happy, and lovable.

❧ Francis de Sales wrote *Introduction to a Devout Life* in the form of letters to "Philothea," a compound of his mother's name and that of a friend. In the introduction, he outlined his spiritual philosophy:

> It is an error, or rather a heresy, to say that devotion is incompatible with the life of a soldier, a tradesman, a prince, or a married woman. It is true, Philothea, that a devotion purely contemplative, monastical, and religious, cannot be exercised in these vocations; but, besides these three kinds of devotion, there are several others proper to conduct to perfection those who live in the secular state. . . . Nay, it has happened that many have lost perfection in the desert who had preserved it in the world.

*F*RANCIS of Assisi (c. 1181–1226). Founder of the religious order that bears his name, Francis is revered as a peacemaker. A gentle man, he conversed with birds and animals, and when he died, larks reportedly collected around the roof of his house, raising a song to heaven. The first Christmas crèche is attributed to him.

❧ Francis's remarkable spirituality attracted legions of followers and made him a celebrity in his lifetime. He maintained, nonetheless, a conscientious humility. Invited to dinner once by Cardinal-Bishop Ugolino of Ostia, Francis arrived with a bag of crusts of black bread. Affronted, the cardinal protested that this ostentatious dieting shamed him. Francis replied, "My lord, I have done you a great honor, since I honored a greater Lord." He emptied his crusts on the table and offered them to the other guests. Some ate, in embarrassment; others carried off the scraps as souvenirs.

❧ Francis designated that members of his order be known by the name Friars Minor, desiring that they should be below their fellows and seek the last and lowest of places. When the order held its second general chapter in 1219, five thousand were present, among whom were some who felt that affairs of the order were conducted too haphazardly and should be organized in a more practical way. Francis was indignant and said:

> My brothers, the Lord has called me by way of simplicity and humbleness, and this is the way he has pointed out to me for myself and for those who will believe and follow me. . . . The Lord told me that he would have me poor and foolish in this world, and that he willed not to lead us by any other way other than by that. May God confound you by your own wisdom and learning and, for all your fault-finding, send you back to your vocation whether you will or no.

When some pressed that Francis seek a papal license so that members of the order could preach without obtaining permission from the bishop of each diocese, he responded:

> When the bishops see that you live holily, and attempt nothing against their authority, they will themselves entreat you to work for the salvation of souls committed to their charge. Let it be your singular privilege to have no privilege.

Francis advised his followers to strip themselves of every worldly possession, as had he. Walking on a country road one day with Giles, one of his first associates, he encountered a beggar woman. Francis was wearing only his habit, which he had made out of a peasant's discarded gown, with a bit of a rope for a belt. Giles, on the other hand, was wearing a coat. "Give it to her," said Francis as naturally as he might have commented, "It's a fine morning." And Giles was launched on the Franciscan way.

G

GALILEO, Galilei (1564–1642). Italian physicist and astronomer, Galileo championed and advanced the Copernican theory (in contradistinction to Ptolemaic theory) that the sun, not the earth, was the center of the universe. He was also a noted inventor, as of the telescope, the astronomical clock, and the thermometer.

With the discovery of the telescope in 1610, Galileo enlarged the world, to use his own words, "a hundred and a thousand times from what the wise men of all past ages had thought." One of the first vistas opened was Jupiter. Looking through the telescope one could see in the visual field a solar system demonstrated on a small scale. Traditionalists were unnerved and sought to debunk Galileo's discovery.

Francesco Sizi, a young religious zealot, fired the first salvo in a treatise entitled *Dianoia astronomica* (1610). It was all optical illusion, said Sizi. In an imaginary conversation with an Uncle Toby, he wrote:

> Why, Sir, are there not seven cardinal virtues?—seven mortal sins?—seven golden candlesticks in Moses?—seven heavens? "Tis more than I know," replied my uncle Toby.—Are there not seven wonders of the world?—seven days of creation?— seven plagues?

Sizi wasn't finished. He added that there were seven metals in alchemical theory and, more wondrously, that there were "seven windows in the head: two nostrils, two eyes, two ears, and a mouth." He concluded that therefore there could be no more than seven planets in the heavens.

Twice, Galileo was hauled before the Inquisition for his views on the nature of the universe. After his first trial, he was officially admonished not to "hold, teach or defend" Copernican doctrine. Robert Cardinal Bellarmine, S.J. *(q.v.)*, the age's most prominent theologian, further advised that if he ever addressed the subject again it would be well to do so *ex suppositione*—hypothetically. That was in 1616.

Galileo followed Bellarmine's advice literally. His next major work on astronomy, *Dialogo dei due massimi sistemi del mondo (Dialogue on Two Chief World Systems)*, published in 1632, thus took the form of a hypothetical conversation between characters named Salviati, Sagredo, and Simplicio. The first expounded the views of Galileo himself; the second was an eager and intelligent listener; the third, Simplicio, was the defender of orthodox Ptolemaic theory and a buffoon given to simplistic (as the name implied) and sometimes asinine views.

Galileo's enemies in the papal court persuaded Pope Urban VIII *(q.v.)* that Simplicio was a caricature of himself—which he might or might not have been, and more probably wasn't. In any instance, on April 12, 1633, the Inquisition again took Galileo into custody.

The problem Galileo posed for the Church was that his theories of the earth's movement around the sun contradicted biblical narrative and thus brought into question the accuracy of scriptural language and the

Bible itself. The formal accusation lodged against him in 1633, however, was of being in contravention of the decree of his 1616 trial and in defiance of the command of the Holy Office. His defense was a disavowal of his opinions and an expression of his own good intentions.

Under threat of torture, Galileo read a recantation in the Church of Santa Maria sopra Minerva. Rising from his knees after repeating the formula of abjuration, he stamped on the floor and was heard to murmur under his breath, *Eppur si muove!*—"But it still moves." (Some dismiss this story as sheer myth, but one source locates the words on a circa 1640 portrait of Galileo.)

In 1992, the Church formally acknowledged that Galileo had been wrongfully accused, and in 1994, the Vatican issued a postage stamp in his honor. The press widely reported both events, especially the former. The *Los Angeles Times*, for example, ran the following headline over the story: "It's Official! The Earth Revolves Around the Sun, Even for the Vatican!"

*G*ASPARRI, Pietro (1852–1934). Diplomat, cardinal, and scholar, once holding the chair of Canon Law at L'Institut Catholique in Paris, Gasparri returned to Rome in 1901 and served in various Curia posts before being tapped as Benedict XV's secretary of state. He continued in that post under Pius XI *(q.v.)*, and negotiated the Lateran Treaty of 1929 that settled the so-called Roman Question, ending tensions stemming from the takeover of the papacy's territory in 1870 by the new Italian state.

✍ Negotiations leading to the signing of the 1929 concordat extended over three years, and reached a turning point when Italian dictator Benito Mussolini proposed to grant the pope sovereignty over the Vatican buildings and gardens. "But you won't get the votes in the Chamber [of Deputies]," said Gasparri. "Well, then, we'll change the Chamber," replied Mussolini. "But if you change the Chamber without changing the electoral law, the public will vote back exactly the same Chamber, with the same deputies," Gasparri said. "All right," declared Mussolini, "then we'll change the electoral law." "With such a man," said Gasparri, "I knew I could do business."

There's the story of an anonymous but real-life bishop. The bishop, allergic to liturgical dance, was visiting a particular parish when a young woman appeared at the back of the church and came dancing and cavorting (liturgically) down the aisle and laid a lily at the feet of the bishop. The bishop turned and whispered to the pastor: "If she asks for your head on a platter, she can have it."

Michael T. Farrell
National Catholic Reporter, 15 December 1995

*G*HIBERTI, Lorenzo di Cicone (c. 1378–1455). A noted sculptor and worker in bronze, Ghiberti was the artist responsible for the bronze doors of the north and east sides of the baptistery of San Giovanni in his native Florence. He was also a writer on contemporary art and architecture.

≈ Ghiberti lived when Florence was in its time of greatest glory. Like many artists throughout the ages, he exulted in freedom from the constraints of having a fixed residence. The attitude fit the cosmopolitan principle, as valid then as ever, that wherever the learned person fixed his or her seat, there is home. "Only he who has learned everything," Ghiberti wrote in his autobiography, "is nowhere a stranger; robbed of his fortune and without friends, he is yet the citizen of every country, and can fearlessly despise the changes of fortune."

*G*IBBONS, James (1834–1921). Born in the United States but raised in Ireland, Gibbons returned to the United States for seminary studies and was ordained in 1861 as a priest of the Baltimore archdiocese. A leader in causes of social justice, he was instrumental in heading off papal condemnation of the pioneer labor union, the Knights of Labor, in the United States. His leadership, it is said, helped pave the way for Pope Leo XIII's encyclical *Rerum novarum*. He became a cardinal in 1886.

≈ Gibbons was named a bishop in 1874 only four years after the promulgation of the doctrine of papal infallibility. The issue of infallibility was still a thorny one, and the press regularly queried bishops about it. Once, on returning from a visit to Rome, a reporter met Gibbons with the question "Is the pope really infallible?" Playing on the Italian pronunciation of the letter *g* as *j*, Gibbons responded, "All I know is that he kept referring to me as Jibbons."

The Rev. Dr. Wing, minister of the leading Unitarian church in Baltimore, was a friend of Gibbons. One day, while taking their constitutional around the city's Mt. Vernon Square, Gibbons remarked that he and Wing each represented one tradition in the Church for which he had great respect. Asked to explain, Gibbons said that Dr. Wing represented freedom and he (Gibbons) authority. "What I do not understand," Gibbons continued, "are those namby-pamby Protestants who believe in neither."

GILL, Eric (1882–1940). Son of an Anglican clergyman and a convert to Roman Catholicism in 1913, Gill was one of the outstanding artisans of his time. He was especially famous for stone sculptures, which included war memorials and the stations of the cross in Westminster Cathedral. He was also a wood engraver, designer of typefaces, and illustrator. He wrote a number of books and established his own press, named for St. Dominic, for the printing of his publications and woodcuts.

Gill was received into the Catholic Church on his thirty-first birthday, attracted less by the splendors of Catholicism (he believed St. Peter's Basilica looked "exactly like the Ritz Palace Hotel" and should have its carvings hacked off) than by a belief that the Roman Church was the right answer to modern England and its new ideologies. He explained his reasoning:

Religion was the first necessity, and that meant the rule of God. If then there be God, the whole world must be ruled in his name. If there be a religion it must be a world religion, a catholicism. In so far as my religion were true it must be catholic. In so far as the Catholic religion were catholic it must be true! The Catholic Church professed to rule the whole world in the name of God—so far as I could see or imagine, it was the only institution that professed to do so. That fact in itself seemed conclusive, conclusive and sufficient.

After his conversion, Gill became a member of the Third Order of St. Dominic, and believing that work and prayer were one, he loosely modeled his crafts commune at Ditchling, later Capel-y-ffin and finally High Wycombe, along monastic lines. The formalities of faith were observed with the help of visiting priests or, as was more often the case, a priest-in-residence acting as chaplain of sorts to the group. Gill was not priest-struck, but rather was one of those benign anticlerics, so common to England, who ultimately convey the impression that clergymen necessarily know less about true religion than anyone else. Said Gill:

The clergy are in the position of men standing on the brink of a frozen pool and shouting to men drowning under the ice that they should take good deep breaths if they want to stay healthy.

Gill harbored a strong aversion to industrialism, arguing that it reduced workers to a subhuman condition without intellectual responsibility. To the objection that "a person can be a good Christian in a factory," he would reply, "Yes, and St. Agnes was a good Christian in a brothel—but there was no reason why she should stay there." (St. Agnes was a fourth-century virgin and martyr who was handed over to a house of prostitution for declining to renounce her faith. There a young man turned a lascivious look on her and was blinded. Agnes was subsequently put to death, probably by stabbing.)

Shortly before his death, Gill wrote his autobiography, which he called his *autopsychography,* and remarked, "I really ought to die now. I don't know how I shall be able to face the world after stripping myself more or less naked as I have done."

As it turned out, Gill had omitted the most startling detail of his life: an incestuous history with his sisters and his daughters. Fiona MacCarthy's revelations of the incest in a 1989 biography, *Eric Gill: A Lover's Quest for Art and God,* startled admirers and triggered reassessments of the man. Gill's friend and editor, T. F. Burns, spoke for the defense:

> In justice it may be hoped that the absolution which he often sought and found in the sacrament of reconciliation should now be extended to him by those who have been shocked and saddened by the intimate revelations of the diaries, mute witnesses to occasional folly and weakness, but never to malice. The diaries should in no way diminish the gratitude for Eric Gill's life and work of those above all who share his faith. There are few now living who can recall him as a tireless searcher for

truth and goodness in every aspect of life and above all as the humblest and most lovable of men. Let their witness be transmitted to the exclusion of what should only concern a man and his Maker.

*G*ODFREY, William (1889–1963). Born in Liverpool, Godfrey was ordained a priest in 1916 and, after a succession of posts in England, Italy, and with the Vatican diplomatic service, returned in 1953 as Liverpool's archbishop. In 1956 be succeeded as seventh archbishop of Westminster and two years later was raised to the cardinalate.

In 1938, Godfrey was appointed the first apostolic delegate to Great Britain, Gibraltar, Malta, and Bermuda and in that capacity hosted New York's Francis Cardinal Spellman *(q.v.)* on one of Spellman's wartime visits to England as military vicar of the armed forces of the United States. One evening he accompanied Spellman to a dinner being hosted by U.S. General Frank M. Andrews, at which a number of other generals and admirals were in attendance. In the course of the evening, one of the generals asked Godfrey, who was as English as John Bull, if he had ever been to America. Godfrey answered, "No." "I thought you had," said the general, "for you speak English so well."

*G*OGARTY, Oliver St. John (1878–1957). A doctor and noted throat specialist in Dublin, Gogarty achieved additional fame as a patriot, poet, essayist, conversationalist, and wit. He was a friend, but also something of a foil, to James Joyce *(q.v.)*, whose Buck Mulligan character in *Ulysses* was unflatteringly based on Gogarty.

    The Dublin of Gogarty's time was alive with wits and storytellers of genius—Wilde, Joyce, Yeats, Synge, George Moore, George Russell (whose pseudonym was AE), and Mahaffy, among others. Gogarty said he could not begin to count them all, adding, "Every man is a potential idler, poet or friend!"

    In Gogarty's day, the Catholic archbishop of Dublin forbade Catholics to attend Trinity College, Dublin, without special ecclesiastical permission. The interdiction seemed silly to Gogarty, and he lampooned it by telling a story of an edifying man who arrived at the pearly gates:

> St. Peter was about to admit him when his eye fell on his record with the one indiscretion against him. He had entered Trinity without his Archbishop's permission. St. Peter was in a quandary. He didn't know what to do. Just then he saw the Lord passing by and he put the question to Him. The Lord's reply was, "I'm a Trinity man myself."

*G*REENE, Graham (1904–1991). One of England's most prolific twentieth-century writers, Greene converted to Catholicism after an early flirtation with Communism and regularly infused his writings with Catholic themes. In later years, he distanced himself from aspects of the faith, describing himself as a Catholic agnostic. Nonetheless, Catholicism remained integral to his life and his work.

❧ Greene's brief Communist phase came during his time at Oxford. In his own words, it was in the nature of a lark; he hoped to get a free trip to Moscow and Leningrad. That lark would create problems for him later, however, vis-à-vis the United States, and in 1954, he was deported from Puerto Rico under terms of the McCarren Act. Greene developed a jaundiced view toward the United States. He vented this view in *The Quiet American*. The Puerto Rican incident he was surprisingly sanguine about, remembering it "with pleasure," but pleasure of a satirical sort. Said Greene: "Life is not rich in comedy; one has to cherish what there is of it and savor it during bad days."

❧ During a particularly tight financial time as a young writer, Greene answered an advertisement for a subeditor at the *Catholic Herald*. He took the train to London and was received by the *Herald's* editor "with humiliating condescension."

Two weeks later, he was invited back and traveled to London thinking he would be hired. Instead he was told by the editor, who was "more condescending than ever," that he was "too good for the job," that he "would never settle down." Greene remembered the experience bitterly. "I had too much pride and too little spirit left to ask him to return my railroad fare," he said, "and since then I have taken a biased view of Catholic journalism and Catholic humanity."

❧ Greene wrote a number of movie scripts, including that of *The Third Man*. Its most famous scene occurs on a ferris wheel in an amusement park, when Orson Wells, the antagonist, says to Joseph Cotten, the well-intentioned Holley, an old friend now tracking him:

> When you make up your mind, send me a message—I'll meet you any place, any time, and when we do meet, old man, it's you I want to see, not the police. . . . And don't be so gloomy. . . . After all, it's not that awful—you know what the fellow said: In Italy for thirty years under the Borgias they had warfare, terror, murder, bloodshed—and they produced Michelangelo, Leonardo da Vinci, and the Renaissance. In Switzerland they had brotherly love, five hundred years of democracy and peace, and what did they produce? The cuckoo clock. So long, Holley.

(The myth exists that Wells wrote the whole passage into the movie. Actually, it was only the last words. "The popular line of dialogue concerning Swiss cuckoo clocks," Greene declared, "was written into the script by Mr. Orson Wells." The rest was directly from Greene's own treatment.)

◖ Many consider *The Power and the Glory*, Greene's 1940 novel about a fugitive whiskey priest in Mexico, his best book. But the Holy Office, then headed by Giuseppe Cardinal Pizzardo, condemned it. Years later, at an audience with Pope Paul VI, the pontiff remarked that he had read *Stamboul Train* and was now reading *The Power and the Glory*. "Your Holiness is reading a book that has been banned by the church," Greene told him. "Who banned it?" asked the pope. "Cardinal Pizzardo." The pope shook his head from side to side. "Some parts of all your books will always offend some Catholics," Paul VI commented. "You should not worry about that." It was counsel, Greene said, he found "easy to take."

Greene often discussed his problems of faith and belief with Father Leopoldo Duran, a close friend during the last quarter-century of his life. Duran recalled a particularly poignant moment after breakfast on July 8, 1987: "Each day I have less and less faith," said Greene. Duran replied, "Yes, but you have often told me that with every passing day you find you have less 'belief,' but more 'faith.'" Greene was silent, then uttered what Duran said was the most perfect remark on the subject: "The trouble is, I don't believe my unbelief." (According to Duran, when faith seemed to have disappeared, Greene told God: "Lord, I offer you my unbelief.")

Greene was never bashful about entering theological controversy, and he could be counted on to offer a provocative insight or suggestion, as when the issue cropped up about referring to God in feminine gender.

> I feel like many others a certain uneasiness at changing references to God in the liturgy from He to She. Would it be a possible compromise . . . if in the liturgy we were to call God It (of course with a capital I)? After all, there is a hint of the indefinable and inexplicable in the word "it."

After Greene's death, the Boston College Library in Newton, Massachusetts, acquired his library and personal archives. The books, including Greene's copy of David Pryce-Jones's 1973 work about his friend Evelyn Waugh *(q.v.)*, *Evelyn Waugh and His World*, were copiously annotated throughout. Remarking on Waugh's attendance at Sunday Mass, Greene had jotted in the margin: "Evelyn considered that at the Sunday collection the correct minimum was the price of a cinema seat."

GREGORY the Great, pope (c. 540–604). Born into a patrician family, Gregory resigned as prefect of Rome to enter the Benedictines. He distributed his wealth, founded six monasteries on his Sicilian estate, served as nuncio to Constantinople, then was elected pope in 590. He is particularly remembered for popularizing the work of St. Augustine *(q.v.)*. Sainted, he is honored as a Doctor of the Church.

As pope, Gregory was deeply concerned with the conversion of Britain, an interest said to have carried over from his youth as a monk, when, passing through a marketplace, he noticed three blond, fair-complexioned boys for sale as slaves. Struck by their looks, he inquired of their nationality. "They are Angles or Angli," was the reply. "They are well named," said Gregory, "for they have angelic faces and it becomes such to be companions with angels in heaven."

Learning the three boys were pagans, Gregory asked what province they were from. "Deira," he was told. *"De ira!"* exclaimed Gregory. "Yes, verily they will be saved *from God's ire* and called to the mercy of Christ. What is the name of the king of that country?"

"Aella," he was told. "Then must Alleluia be sung in Aella's land." So impressed was Gregory by the boys' beauty, and so moved was he by their ignorance of Christ, that he set off with several of his monks to preach the gospel in Anglia, the Latin name for England. As word circulated among Romans about Gregory's decision, an outcry was raised and Pope Pelagius sent envoys to recall him to Rome.

(Venerable Bede told the story, but historians are now inclined to doubt its authenticity, partially because Gregory did not indulge in such punning even in his most informal writings.)

When Emperor Justinian and the Eastern Church first condemned *The Three Chapters* of Theodoret of Cyprus, Theodore of Mopsuestia, and Ibas of Edessa on suspicion that the writings favored the Nestorian heresy, the pope and many Western bishops refused to join in the condemnation. Most, however, changed their minds after Constantinople II (553), the fifth ecumenical council, which confirmed the condemnation. Nevertheless, the bishops of Istria on the northern end of the Adriatic held firm.

Pope Pelagius II, Gregory's predecessor, wrote two letters urging the recalcitrant bishops to abandon their stand. The bishops of Istria countered that they were only being constant to a position that had once been Rome's and that Rome, as the repository of truth, had no right to be changing its mind on such matters.

Pelagius turned for help to Gregory, at the time papal apocrisarius at the court of Constantinople. Gregory then wrote a letter, issued in Pelagius's name, maintaining that changing one's mind was not necessarily reprehensible. In this context, Gregory cited St. Paul's initial resistance to Christianity and St. Peter's insistence that Gentile converts be circumcised, a position he abandoned after St. Paul openly challenged him. Here are the pertinent words of Gregory's reply:

> Dear Brethren, do you think that to Peter, who was reversing his position, one should have replied: "We refuse to hear what you are saying since you previously taught the opposite?" If in the matter of *The Three Chapters* one position was held while truth was being sought, and a different position was adopted after truth had been found, why should a change of position be

imputed a crime to this see? For what is reprehensible is not to change one's position, but to entertain fickle opinions. If the mind remains unwavering in seeking to know what is right, why should you object when it abandons its ignorance and reformulates its stand?

Ecclesiastical tradition ascribes to Gregory the Great the compilation of the antiphonal system of church music known as Gregorian chant. For centuries, Gregorian chant was the most highly regarded standard of liturgical music in the Roman Church before slipping in vogue with the reforms of Vatican Council II—except in monastic settings. Then a curious thing happened. In 1994 recordings of the intricate harmonies and fancy alterations of Gregorian chant hit the best-selling "pop" music charts. The reasons apparently had less to do with the chant's devotional qualities than with its placid and soothing tones.

For instance, Sister Mary Johnson, S.N.D., of Emmanuel College in Boston, told of entering a New Age bookstore and hearing Gregorian chant playing on the intercom. She asked the saleswoman if she knew the recording's title. There was the following exchange: "It's New Age music," the saleswoman said, but admitted not knowing the title. She offered to get the tape. Returning with it, the saleswoman said, "It's Gregorian chant." Sister Mary smiled. "Do you know who Gregory was?" she asked the woman. The answer: "Some New Age composer, I guess."

Gregory the Great was no feminist, nor was he a misogynist. Although he accepted prevailing theories about women's secondary and submissive place in the world, he often affirmed their competence and sought out the friendship of women with power, such as the Frankish queen Brunhilde. And on one issue he signaled the beginnings of a historic shift in church attitude: the question of menstruating women and holy communion.

Menstruation is natural, he felt, a gift of God's grace in order that the human race may continue; it should not be held against women any more than any other "infirmity of nature" that humans suffer. May menstruating women therefore receive communion? Gregory commended them for choosing not to approach the sacrament at such times out of respect for tradition, then added, "Let women make up their own minds."

(The historic nature of Gregory's comment is accented when placed alongside words of St. Jerome, who wrote: "Nothing is so unclean as a woman in her periods; what she touches she causes to become unclean." Local synods of the time were also resolving that menstruating women were impure and that the sacraments must be protected from defilement by them.)

*G*REGORY X, pope [Teobaldo Visconti] (1210–1276). Gregory's was a mixed legacy. He convened the second Council of Lyons and temporarily mended the two-hundred-year-old rift with the Greek Church over the *filoque* clause (the double procession of the Holy Spirit from the Father and the Son), the Greeks being allowed to keep their traditional form. The new union was to last only seven years, however. Gregory was a strong reformer of the clergy but spent much of his time seeking to renew the crusade—for which he found little enthusiasm.

In the Middle Ages, the election of a new pope was not always the tidy process it is now. Rivalries and feuds complicated the process, sometimes leaving the papal chair vacant for an inordinately long time. The delay in Gregory X's case was two years and nine months, the longest in history. To avoid such a delay happening again, he issued the bull *Ubi periculum,* in order to regulate the conclave. The cardinals were to assemble in the papal palace ten days after the death of a pope, there to be locked in a room, where the election would be conducted. But that wasn't all:

> . . . if, God forbid, within three days from the time they enter the aforesaid room, the cardinals have not provided the Church with a pastor, they must for the period of five days immediately following, on each day, be content at their noon and evening meals with only one dish. If at the end of that time they have not provided a pastor, then they shall be served only bread, wine, and water till they have done so. During the time of the election, the cardinals may receive nothing from the papal treasury, nor from any other revenue source accruing to the Church from whatsoever source during the time of the vacancy.

The threat to deny food and funds worked miracles.

*G*UINEY, Louise Imogene (1861–1920). Daughter of an Irish immigrant father who was a Civil War general and hero, Guiney was born in Boston and schooled in elite Catholic academies and by private tutors. In 1901, she moved to England, where she solidified a reputation as poet, essayist, biographer, and short-story writer. She was known as "the laureate of the lost" for her research on neglected authors and is credited for the revival of interest in such writers as Henry Vaughan and William Hazlitt.

Guiney's love of England and its culture and her refusal to embody a specific ethnic identity upset some Boston Irish-American Catholics. They regarded her actions as a betrayal of her Celtic heritage, and one prominent adversary went so far as to protest the plans of a Catholic firm to publish her correspondence. Aware of the complaints against her, Guiney was dismissive. She wrote:

> If I am to be hyphenated, I am several kinds of a hyphen, with a Scots and a French near paternal ancestor, and all my English blood on Mother's side! but plain 'American' is my due, and suits me well enough. One of the oddest Irish qualities is this almost universal grabbism: they claim anything and everything which they think is the least creditable!

Guiney did not deny the virtues of the United States, and she frequently gave foreign friends little gift packets of neatly folded American flags. But she was more comfortable in England, loving "the velvety feel of the Past underfoot, like the moss of the forest floor to a barefoot child."

On the other hand, she was not without criticism of American Catholicism. (Its churches were "aesthetic nightmares"; its cemeteries, "atrociously pagan"; its liturgies, "supplanted by the dumb-shows of private devotion.") And she cast a caustic eye on the country itself.

"Whoever has a rage for origin, a lust for things at first-hand, is fore-doomed to chafe at a civilization that dates from this morning," she said in 1907, "and spends its energies on tasks far other than the effort to see life steadily and see it whole."

GUINNESS, Alec (1914–). Born in London, Guinness began an acting career after schooling at Pembroke Lodge and a brief stint as an advertising copywriter. His distinguished career on the stage and in films led to a knighthood in 1959. He served as a naval office in World War II and at age thirty-two converted to Roman Catholicism.

When Guinness decided to leave Anglicanism for Roman Catholicism, he told Rev. Cyril Tomkinson, an Anglo-Catholic vicar and dear friend from Guinness's early days of playing Hamlet at the Old Vic. It was Tomkinson, Guinness said, who opened up to him "the wide world of St. Augustine (q.v.) and Newman (q.v.)," together with the world of "Hooker, William Law, Bishop Gore [and] Archbishop Temple."

"Oh dear!" said Tomkinson, distressed but polite on hearing that Guinness was going over to Rome. "They will teach you to think me a heretic." "Surely not," Guinness declared. "Only schismatic." "Schismatic!" Tomkinson replied. "It sounds like something to do with motor-cars."

Guinness was received into the Catholic Church in 1956, the ceremony taking place at St. Lawrence's, Petersfield. After the ceremony, attended by only two or three friends, Guinness took himself home, went upstairs, and mused on the step he had just taken. The moments are recounted in his autobiography:

English Countryside

For a long time I stood looking at the lovely line of gentle hills which surround us on three sides; the Hangers to the north-west; Buster Hill to the south and Harting Down in the East. Some phrase of Newman *[q.v.]*, in garbled form, ran in my head—something about the line of the hills being the skirts of the Angels of God. Checking it up I find, "I say of the Angels,—every breath of air and ray of light and heat, every beautiful prospect is, as it were, the skirts of their garments, the waving robes of those whose faces see God." Such was my mood that day and I was more than content: now the trees we planted thirty years ago have grown tall, obscuring much of the view in the summer-time. In these latter days, like Roy Campbell, "I love to see, when leaves depart, the clear anatomy arrive." The winter hills nourish my faith. There had been no emotional upheaval, no great insight, certainly no proper grasp of theological issues; just a sense of history and the fittingness of things. Something impossible to explain. Pere Teilhard de Chardin *[q.v.]* says, "The incommunicable part of us is the pasture of God." I must leave it at that.

❧ Four days before the death of Pius XII *(q.v.)* in 1958, Guinness was presented to the pope as part of an audience for a dozen or so American plastic surgeons. Pius was pale and drawn and given to hiccups. Guinness did not grasp what the pope said to him—"I was desperately anxious for him to say nothing and get back to bed," he recalled—but he did catch the following exchange with the middle-aged couple next to him:

> They both kneeled to kiss the Fisherman's Ring, and then the man burst into loud sobs, the tears coursing down his face. The Pope patted him, took his hand, saying the Italian equivalent of "There! There!" and the man grasped his white cassock. The

108

wife explained her husband away with a motherly smile. I imagined her to be a woman who would not have permitted him to buy his own shirts, socks or underpants. "He's so moved, Your Holiness," she said. "It is such an honor to meet you. Isn't it, dear? He's always like this on great occasions. Aren't you, dear? Oh, he's very moved! And just think, Your Holiness—we've come all the way from Michigan!" The Pope mastered a hiccup. "Michigan?" "Sure, Michigan." "I know Michigan," the Pope said, and managing to free himself from the plastic surgeon's grip he raised a hand in blessing: "A special blessing on Michigan!" Those were probably the last words of English he spoke.

H

HADRIAN VI, pope [Adrian Florensz] (1459–1523). Born in Utrecht in the Netherlands, Hadrian was to be the last non-Italian pope until the election of John Paul II *(q.v.)* in 1978. His election was extremely unpopular, and his reception by the Roman people was hostile, the Romans being resentful of the choice of a northern "barbarian" to occupy the Chair of Peter. Actually, Hadrian was a learned man; he was also, unfortunately, narrow-minded and academic.

 Britain's Thomas Cardinal Wolsey *(q.v.)* was King Henry VIII's candidate to succeed Leo X, but Wolsey was not acceptable to Emperor Charles V. The choice then fell to Hadrian, who received the news in Spain. He went reluctantly to Rome and served unhappily. His reign was less than two years and his epitaph summed up his attitude toward his election: "Here lies Adrian VI, who thought nothing in life more unfortunate than that he became pope." (The pope's name was spelled both Hadrian and Adrian.)

HAYES, Helen (1900–1993). Born in Washington and a graduate of Sacred Heart Academy, Hayes made her professional debut as an actor at age six. She established her reputation on Broadway in her teens, was a leading lady at twenty, and thence went on to win three Tonys, two Oscars, and an Emmy for performances on stage, screen, and television. Meanwhile, she would write two novels and an autobiography. In 1979, Hayes was awarded the University of Notre Dame's Laetare Medal. She also received the Presidential Medal of Freedom.

In 1928, Helen Hayes married famed playwright Charles MacArthur. It was an irregular marriage ecclesiastically, and it separated Hayes from the Catholic Church for thirty years. My "cardinal sin," she would write, was "loving my husband more than anything in this or any other world." After "Charlie" MacArthur's death in 1956, Hayes reconciled with the Church. She recorded the reactions:

> There were just as many friends who disapproved of my return to the Church as ever deplored my leaving it. But more and more, I felt the need to give my faith a form once more. I knew Charlie would understand that even sturdy, dependable Helen was the frailest of creatures and needed strength to prevail without him.
>
> I reminded Charlie that it was going to have to take the whole Roman Catholic Church to replace him.

HEALY, James Augustine (1830–1900). Son of Michael Morris Healy, a prosperous Irish immigrant, and Eliza Clark, a black slave woman, James was born in Macon, Georgia, the oldest of ten children of his parents' union, eight of whom lived to adulthood. He graduated with the first class from Holy Cross College and went on to the priesthood, serving as chancellor and vicar-general of the Boston diocese, before being named second bishop of Portland, Maine, in 1875.

   Historians have faulted Healy for not being a leader on Afro-American issues, and although he was indeed more comfortable in white society, he was constantly and often uncharitably brought face- to-face with his roots. (When he was named to head the Portland diocese, Irish gossips spread the word, "Glurry be to God, the Bishop is a *Nee-gar!"*)

    The story is told that one Saturday afternoon Healy was hearing a young girl's confession at the cathedral, when she suddenly blurted out, "I can't tell you the rest of my sins." Healy reassured her that she could go on. "But it's something I said against the bishop," she reluctantly admitted, almost at the point of tears. "Well, now, my child, what did you say against the bishop?" he asked fatherly. "I said the bishop was as black as the devil!" the distraught girl said. "Oh, my child," Healy responded, "don't say the bishop is as black as the devil. You can say he's as black as coal, or as black as the ace of spades. But don't say he's as black as the devil!"

    Another time, a young boy wrapped up his confession by saying, ". . . and I called the bishop a nigger!" Healy drew the confessional curtain aside and said angrily to the startled boy, "Well, son, is there anything wrong with being a nigger? Take a good look at your bishop. Is there anything wrong with being a nigger?"

   Healy possessed a strong temper, and his relationships with Rome, individuals, and groups of the diocese were fractious on a number of occasions. The sisterhoods were not exempt. In time, however, he achieved a high level of cordiality with nuns and sisters, and he often visited with them in their communities. On one such visit, he lit a cigar in the convent's recreation room, and as clouds of smoke billowed up from his cigar, the sister next to him coughed. Healy inquired whether the smoke bothered her. Waving her hand to clear away the billow, she replied, "Oh bishop, I wouldn't have a cloud come between us for anything."

*H*EALY, Timothy Michael [Tim] (1855–1931). A native of Bantry, County Cork, Healy was active in the Home Rule movement, and entered Parliament in London as a disciple of Charles Stewart Parnell. He later broke with Parnell, to the great approval of the Irish Catholic clergy, which had turned on Parnell because of his involvement in a divorce scandal. Healy gave general support to the Home Rule measure of 1912, but furiously opposed partition. When the Irish Free State was erected ten years later, he became its first governor-general.

When word of the Easter Rising of 1916 in Dublin reached Lord Beaverbrook, the British press mogul, he immediately contacted his old friend Tim Healy for news of what was happening. "Is there a rebellion?" asked Beaverbrook. "There is!" exclaimed Healy. "When did it break out?" "When Strongbow invaded Ireland!" answered Healy. "When will it end?" "When Cromwell gets out of hell!" said Healy.

(As all Irish nationalists know, Strongbow, the second Earl of Pembroke, was a Norman who invaded Ireland in 1170. Cromwell was the seventeenth-century British leader remembered by the Irish for a cruelly punitive expedition into their country.)

HEBBLETHWAITE, Peter (1930–1994). Born at Ashton-under-Lyne, near Manchester, Hebblethwaite entered the English Jesuits in 1948, was ordained in 1963, but left in 1974, laicized and married. A distinguished journalist and author, he specialized in Catholic commentary and papal biography, producing definitive studies of John XXIII *(q.v.)* and Paul VI *(q.v.)*.

 A reformer of liberal bent, Hebblethwaite wrote many books about the Catholic scene. Although the books were frequently laced with criticism of the institution, there was never any doubt about his loyalty. Not to be a Catholic, he would say, would be "suicide" for him. Hebblethwaite kept a healthy arm's length from Rome, heeding with relish Monsignor Ronald Knox's bon mot: "Never go down to the engine room, you'll only feel sick."

 In a 1992 talk in Washington, Hebblethwaite explained his love for the Catholic Church, using as a counterpoint a comment of Father Hans Kung *(q.v.)*:

> Hans Kung says he loves the church not as a mother but as a family. I wonder what he means by this distinction. I suppose he is rejecting the idea of "Mother Church"—*the ecclesia Mater* which is part of tradition—on the grounds that it keeps us in an immature state, prolongs adolescence, implies dependence. A church made up only of brothers and sisters feels much more comfortable and democratic.

> Yet, whoever heard of a family that consisted only of coequal brothers and sisters? Is it not possible that in rejecting Mother Church and all fatherhood, including that of the Holy Father,

we are losing an essential dimension? The church exists not only horizontally in space, but vertically in time as tradition and handing on. There is a danger in throwing out not just the baby with the bathwater but the grandmother as well.

Mothers—literal ones—do not have to be perfect to be loved. What is required of a parent is that he or she be "good enough." We are disappointed when we do not find perfect faith, perfect hope and perfect charity in the church. But that is asking too much. We have a right to expect enough faith, enough hope and enough charity to sustain us as we stumble along our pilgrim way.

ᒪ Shortly before joining the paper as a correspondent, Hebblethwaite explained his journalistic philosophy in the *National Catholic Reporter:*

Is there no accountability, other than to God, in the church? There is need for constant evaluation of the church's policies, especially in its central administration. Who is to do it? Unofficially, the task is left to journalists, who put their heads on the block every time they write.

*H*ERR, Daniel Joseph [Dan] (1917–1990). Publisher, writer, and lecturer, Herr joined the Thomas More Book Shop in Chicago in 1948, after heroic service in World War II. The operation was a modest enterprise with a book club and a literary magazine, but Herr speedily transformed it into a major Catholic publishing and art center, reincorporating it as the Thomas More Association. He himself went on to become one of the principal arbiters of taste in American Catholic publishing.

With colleague Joel Wells, Herr compiled several Catholic-press anthologies. He also wrote a column in the Thomas More Association's literary magazine *The Critic*, where he regularly sat in judgment on Catholic publications. He was caustic, contending that there were too many Catholic publications—too many to support, too many to staff, too many to read. "With apologies to Churchill," he once wrote, "never have so many worked so hard to put out a product that is read by so few."

Many sensed that Herr was playing the part of the curmudgeon and that behind the mask was a deep affection for the Catholic press. Nonetheless, the following assessment of his became, for a time, something of an embarrassing catch phrase: "There is nothing basically wrong with the Catholic press in America," Herr said, "that an acute paper shortage would not cure."

In his column in *The Critic*, Herr frequently wrote of family and associates. In a column on burying the dead, he relayed his father's story of two maiden sisters who succeeded, against both odds of old and their pastor's reluctance, in getting a church burial for their reprobate brother. The pastor, having second thoughts about his decision, approached the casket as it entered the church and, with a sudden burst of anger, pounded it vigorously, exclaiming, "Twice in church, and both times they had to carry him in."

*H*ICKLEY, Dennis (1918–1994). Artist, architect, priest, and scholar, Hickley came to Catholicism through Anglicanism, the Communist Party, and Britain's Royal Engineers, in which he served as a captain during World War II. He entered the Catholic Church in 1948 and was ordained a diocesan priest in 1971. In 1981, he was named chaplain of Plater College at Oxford.

    Hickley was known as a cook and bon vivant, and it was said that "his huge saucepan was a potent weapon for pastoral care, when filled with boiling spaghetti and accompanied by a large bottle of plonk." His "ministry of the kitchen" was not always successful, however. On the occasion of the laying of the cornerstone of Holy Rood Church in Oxford, Hickley provided tea and cake for those at the ceremony. He had to rush the job, and the cake ended up overcooked. Afterward, an Irish priest was heard to say, "I feel I've eaten the cornerstone."

*H*ILDEBRAND, Dietrich von (1889–1977). Son of Adolf von Hildebrand, famous German sculptor, von Hildebrand was born in Florence. He converted to Catholicism in 1914, and as a philosopher became, over time, one of the strongest champions of Catholic positions on traditional sexual morality. Forced during the Nazi ascendancy to flee first Germany, then Austria, von Hildebrand made his way to the United States, where he joined the faculty of Fordham University in 1942. He continued as a prominent voice in Catholic intellectual circles before becoming disenchanted with the renewals of Vatican Council II.

❧ As a professor at the University of Munich in the 1920s, von Hildebrand had in his classes several students who were ordained priests. He made a point of treating them with special respect, letting them pass, for instance, through doors ahead of him. One day a colleague called him aside, saying, "Why do you let your students step ahead of you? You seem to forget that you are a Herr Professor."

"In no way do I forget it," von Hildebrand responded, "but I mean to pay tribute to the extraordinary dignity which priests have received." "But," the colleague retorted, "they are only students, and in so doing you offend against the dignity of your rank." Von Hildebrand answered, "You forget that their hands hold the body of our Lord; this fact explains my behavior."

*H*OPKINS, Gerard Manley (1844–1889). An English poet known for his remarkable and innovative use of diction and rhyme, Hopkins was born in Stratford, converted to Catholicism in 1866, and entered the Jesuits in 1868. He was ordained in 1877 and, after duties in Britain, went to Dublin as a fellow at the Royal University of Ireland and as an examiner and professor at University College, Dublin. He is best known for his poem "The Wreck of the Deutschland," although the fame of that poem and other works of his eluded him in his lifetime. He died believing himself a failure both as poet and priest.

❧ Catholic imagery and themes dominated Hopkins's poetry. Still he was from a different mold than other Catholics of the England of his time. His was a "Gallican" rather than the "ultramontane" Catholicism of most recusant English Catholic families. Nevertheless, he was an unqualified believer, and one of his deepest and most abiding hopes was the return of England to the Catholic faith.

This hope did not die easily. The intensity of his Catholic convictions was so strong in fact that religion was a closed matter between him and his family, none of whom followed him into the Catholic Church. As he would write to a friend: "Religion, you know, enters very deep; in reality it is the deepest impression I have in speaking to people, that they are or are not of my religion."

Two years after his conversion to Catholicism, Hopkins burned all his manuscripts and resolved to write no more. That resolve ended after the ship *Deutschland,* America-bound out of Bremen, sunk in a wild storm off the English coast on December 7, 1875. Among the casualties were five German Franciscan nuns, who were being exiled under the Falck Laws.

According to the *Times* of London, the nuns went to their deaths "hands clasped," the superior, "a gaunt 6 ft. high, calling out loudly and often, 'O Christ, come quickly!' till the end came."

The emotional account in the *Times* stunned readers, including Hopkins. He returned pen to paper and, in his new sprung rhythm, produced the poem that would be his masterpiece: "The Wreck of the Deutschland." The focus of the poem was the "tall nun's" faith and her vision of Christ at the heart of the storm, re-enacting the Passion. The theme was preceded by a personal statement in which Hopkins reflected on his own spiritual crisis and conversion. The Jesuit journal the *Month* accepted the poem, but withdrew it before publication for being too "daring."

*H*UME, George Basil (1923–). An English Benedictine, Hume was abbot of Ampleforth before being raised to archbishop of Westminster in 1976. A month later he was made a cardinal. As leader of English Catholicism, he combines a profound spirituality and loyalty of Rome with a disarming informality and aura of self-deprecation.

In 1983, Hume was making a presentation of the book *Searching for God*, which collected his weekly talks to the monks of Ampleforth, where he had once been abbot. He was asked, "Do you think your Ampleforth talks would have been published had you not become Cardinal-Archbishop of Westminster? And if not, what does this tell us?" Without a moment's hesitation, Hume responded, "They would certainly not have been published. What does this tell us? That being a cardinal is a good commercial proposition."

Journalists delighted in Hume's press briefings, which were generally informal and spiced with humor. The 1985 briefing before his departure for Rome for the Extraordinary Synod of Bishops called to review and evaluate the implementation of the renewals of Vatican Council II is but one example. Asked by a reporter why John Cardinal Krol, the conservative archbishop of Philadelphia, had been chosen as one of the Synod's three presidents, Hume, with mischievous misstatement, answered, "Cardinal Krol was chosen because he was a secretary at Vatican I." (Vatican I took place between 1869 and 1870.)

Asked at that same press briefing why the Vatican imposed a ban on the publication of position papers by national hierarchies, Hume said with a certain wistfulness:

Well, some places don't have such a responsible press as we have. When I see what the Italian press has made of some of my remarks, I begin to understand. I had only to say [recently] in Bruges that I favored the ordination of married men to the priesthood for some of them to report that I was on the point of getting married.

*H*UNT, George W. (1937–). Hunt entered the Society of Jesus in 1954 and taught in several Jesuit institutions before joining *America,* the Jesuit-edited weekly, in 1981 as literary editor. He was a visiting professor at Georgetown University in 1983–84, then returned to *America* as editor-in-chief in June 1984. He is the author of books on the works of John Updike and John Cheever.

On September 8, 1994, Hunt attended a three-hour breakfast meeting at the White House hosted by President Bill Clinton for leaders from various religious faiths in the United States. The president greeted each participant individually. When Hunt's turn came, Hunt identified himself as a Jesuit who had once taught at Georgetown University, the president's alma mater. He mentioned to Clinton that they had a mutual Jesuit friend, Father Otto Hentz, once Clinton's teacher and still a professor at Georgetown.

President Clinton beamed with pleasure and said: "You know, I think the most flattering event in my life happened there in my freshman year. Otto invited me out for a Coke at the Howard Johnson's nearby and, well into our conversation, he asked me whether I ever thought of becoming a Jesuit. I was actually struck speechless at the compliment, and then I had to tell him I was a Baptist."

*H*URLEY, Joseph P. (1894–1967). A native of Cleveland, Ohio, Hurley served in church diplomatic posts in Japan, India, at the Vatican Secretariat of State, and from 1945 to 1949 as papal nuncio to Yugoslavia, the first American to attain that rank. In the years after 1940, when on diplomatic assignment, he was concurrently bishop of St. Augustine, Florida. In 1950, he was given the personal title of archbishop by Pope Pius XII *(q.v.)*.

The St. Augustine see dates from 1857, when all of Florida east of the Apalachicola River in the panhandle was erected by Pope Pius IX *(q.v.)* into a vicariate-apostolic. In 1870, the area was elevated to the status of a diocese and continued as a single diocesan unit until 1958, when the see was split, the southern section becoming the diocese of Miami. On being informed of the split, Hurley was quoted as saying bitterly, "They've got the gold, and I am left with the history."

I

IGNATIUS of Loyola (1491–1556). Youngest of thirteen children, Ignatius was a soldier as a young man, his career ending when he suffered a serious leg wound fighting with the Spanish against the French at Pamplona. During a long convalescence, he took to reading lives of the saints and resolved to challenge their legacy and become a saint of comparable renown. This he would accomplish as founder of the Society of Jesus (Jesuits), the missionary and teaching order whose origins date from 1528.

In times of most blatant anti-Semitism, the Jesuit order had a reputation as a haven for Jewish converts. Ignatius's own secretary, Juan de Polanco, was said by detractors to be a "New Christian," as baptized Jews were called in Spain and Portugal, particularly those whose conversions were thought to be less than sincere. Ignatius was hardly troubled by such aspersions. "What a stroke of luck," he once said, "to be related to Christ our Lord and his holy Mother, the Blessed Virgin."

Ignatius's youth was "given over to the vanities of the world," but his conversion experience rendered him a mystic with a desire to enlighten the world. "Out of gratitude and love for Him," he declared, "we should desire to be reckoned fools and glory in wearing His livery."

*T*RELAND, John (1838–1918). Born in Kilkenny, Ireland, John Ireland was brought to the United States at age ten. He studied for the priesthood in France and was ordained in St. Paul, Minnesota, in 1861. He became St. Paul's first archbishop in 1888. One of the great controversialists of his day, Ireland gained the reputation of a liberal. He was a supporter of labor, a champion of racial equality, and a strong believer in the American doctrine of separation of Church and state.

Ireland was keenly interested in educational questions and, with Bishop John Keane of Richmond, headed the fight for a national Catholic university, realized in 1889 with the establishment in Washington, D.C., of the Catholic University of America. Keane became the university's first rector, and he and Ireland stayed in close touch about its fortunes. The idea of a university was not popular with conservative members of the American hierarchy, and they in turn kept a watchdog's eye on its operation. Ireland pressed continually for excellence and, in 1892, counseled Keane: "You must educate your professors, and then hold on to them— making bishops only of those who are not worth keeping as professors."

A man of fiery opinions, Ireland belonged to the Americanist wing of the hierarchy and, as such, was held in particular suspicion by ethnic groups anxious to hold on to old-world identities. German bishops and laity were especially hostile because of Ireland's explosive reaction to the idea that a German-American church should be set up in the United States, a move Ireland viewed as an attempt to "foreignize our country in the name of religion."

Some idea of the German-American antipathy toward Ireland may be garnered in the commentary offered by Arthur Preuss, a champion of German Catholicism, in *Review,* a monthly for "German born or of German descent." Preuss was commenting on a speech given by Ireland in 1901 on the investiture of John Keane as archbishop of Dubuque:

> Is it really necessary for the Catholics of these United States to be continually reminded that they must be Americans? . . . Msgr. Ireland's admirers love to compare him with St. Paul, who is the patron of his episcopal city. But whatever virtues he may have in common with the Apostle of the Gentiles, we nowhere learn that the latter made love of country the keynote of his exhortations. . . . [We] should prefer to hail him as a real-latter day St. Paul, preaching not America and her glories, but Christ and Him crucified.

With obvious distress, Ireland noted that their fellow Americans were not noticing the distinction and success of American Catholics by acceptance at the polls. Three weeks before the presidential election of November 1908, he challenged a large audience on the subject at the Hotel Jefferson in St. Louis. At the time his optimism must have sounded wildly extravagant:

> I urge on all Catholics to make yourselves fit for the highest offices in the country, according to your number. There are now 17,000,000 Catholics in this country, and they are not represented in its great offices as they should be. I have heard the statement that there will never be a Catholic President, this is all nonsense. When the right man is presented the United States will choose him and not discriminate because of his religion.

*J*AMES II (1633–1701). Son of King Charles I and Henrietta Maria of France, James succeeded to the throne of England, Scotland, and Ireland in 1685. A convert to Catholicism, in 1687 he issued a Declaration of Indulgence protecting the religious rights of all dissenters from the established Church of England. He was forced to flee to France, when English nobles—fearful of a Roman Catholic restoration—offered the throne to his son-in-law, William of Orange, a Protestant and, in the Byzantine politics of the time, an ally of Pope Innocent XI.

    James II sought to regain his throne, and with the help of a small force provided by King Louis XIV of France, he invaded Ireland in 1689. Thousands of Irish recruits rallied to his cause. An army of King William crossed from England and engaged the forces of James II at the famous Battle of the Boyne on July 1, 1690. Routed, James fled to Dublin, the first member of his army to reach its safe haven. He was met there by Lady Tyrconnell. "The Irish ran away," James II exclaimed, imputing cowardice to his recruits. Lady Tyrconnell countered, "I see Your Majesty has won the race."

*J*OAN of Arc (c. 1412–1431). A totally uneducated French peasant maid, Joan began hearing voices in 1425 that told her to seek out the

JOAN OF ARC

dauphin and tell him that God had sent her to lead the French armies against the English occupiers of France. She was seventeen when she persuaded the dauphin of the authenticity of her mission, whereupon she led the French forces to a series of stunning victories that made possible the crowning of the dauphin in the cathedral at Reims as Charles VII. Taken prisoner in 1430, she was brought to trial by the English and convicted and burned at the stake in Rouen on May 30, 1431. The Church canonized her in 1920.

    The trial of Joan of Arc stands as one of the most infamous legalistic exercises of the Middle Ages. She was condemned to death as a relapsed heretic and sorceress, after intense interrogations ingeniously contrived to trick and confuse—as, for instance, in demanding of her a declaration of the distinction between the Church Glorified and the Church Militant so that the examiners could seize upon her answer to allege she had rejected the *Unam sanctam* article of the Creed. The nineteen-year-old Joan was brilliant, and the candor and skill of her defense won the reluctant admiration even of her enemies. One English lord extended the supreme compliment: "This is a really good woman. If only she were English!"

JOHANNES, Francis (1874–1937). Born in Mittelstren, Bavaria, Johannes was brought to the United States at age six. Raised in the Midwest, he was ordained a priest in 1897 and engaged in pastoral work in St. Joseph, Missouri, before being elevated to the episcopacy as coadjutor of the diocese of Leavenworth in 1928. He succeeded to the see the following year. (The name of the Leavenworth diocese was changed to Kansas City in Kansas in 1947; in 1952 the see was accorded the rank of archdiocese.)

Johannes, who rose every day at 4 A.M. and retired at 8 P.M., was regarded by some, perhaps patronizingly, as something of a farmer, perhaps because he lived the farmer's clock and a life totally in sympathy with the farming community. In the early 1930s, he assigned a young seminarian of the Leavenworth diocese for studies at the North American College in Rome, the first he had ever sent there. In due course, Johannes himself went to Rome on an *ad limina* visit, and the young student, one Alexander M. Harvey, was assigned to show him around.

Harvey thought that, in the circumstances, St. Peter's would be a safe place to take the bishop. They entered through the basilica's front doors. After about fifteen minutes, Johannes spotted the Blessed Sacrament Chapel and told Harvey that he was going to say part of his office and Harvey could pick him up exactly fifteen minutes later. When Harvey returned, the bishop said that he was ready to leave.

Feeling that the bishop had not given St. Peter's a fair viewing, a few days later Harvey returned with Johannes. This time they entered through a different door with totally different vistas. After about fifteen minutes, Johannes turned to Harvey and said, "Well, Alexander, we certainly have seen St. Peter's, haven't we? I must say it is a magnificent building, but it is hardly suitable for normal parish activities."

*J*OHN XXIII, pope [Angelo Roncalli] (1881–1963). Of humble origins, Roncalli spent much of his priesthood in humble diplomatic postings until his appointment as apostolic nuncio to France in 1944. In 1953, he was named cardinal-patriarch of Venice and five years later was elected to the papacy. Almost seventy-seven at the time, he seemed to be a "caretaker" choice. John reigned only five years, but they were momentous ones, during which he convoked Vatican Council II and issued historic encyclicals on social progress *(Mater et magistra)* and world peace *(Pacem in terris).*

    Roncalli served two hitches in the Italian army—as a seminarian in 1901–2 with an infantry regiment as part of the nation's compulsory military service program, and as a young priest during World War I as a hospital orderly with the rank of sergeant. He was at Caporetto in the fall of 1917 when the Austrian army, strengthened by seven German divisions, dealt the Italians a stunning defeat. It was the greatest battle of the war on the Italian front. (A second person who one day would become world famous also figured in events at Caporetto: an oberleutnant with the Wurttembergische Gebirgsbataillon, Erwin Rommel, the "Desert Fox" of World War II.) The shock of the defeat at Caporetto brought about a revival of patriotism throughout Italy, with even *L'Osservatore Romano,* the Vatican newspaper, editorializing on the Catholic's duty to resist the enemy. Roncalli, the hospital orderly turned sometime chaplain, shared the nation's mood, but his journal bespoke a soberness about that one day would echo in his encyclicals: "We are all guilty."

    On hearing news of the death of Pius XII *(q.v.),* the pope he was destined to succeed, Roncalli mourned, but characteristically looked immediately to the future good of the Church. "Sister death came quickly and swiftly fulfilled her office," he wrote in his diary. "Three days were enough. On Sunday, October 9 at 3:52 A.M. Pius XII was in paradise." Turning ruminative, he continued: "One of my favorite phrases brings me great comfort: we are not on earth as museum-keepers, but to cultivate a flourishing garden of life and to prepare a glorious future. The Pope is dead, long live the Pope!"

As pope, John XXIII was full of surprises, beginning with his choice of the name John. Throughout history, John had been the most popular name by far with popes, but at the same time the papal Johns had proved an ignominious line and one that seemingly had come to an end in 1415 with the deposition of the "first" John XXIII, an antipope, on charges of simony, perjury, and grossest misconduct. The "second" John XXIII provided the following explanation for the resurrection of the name:

> The name John is dear to me because it was the name of my father, because it is the dedication of the humble parish church where we were baptized, and because it is the name of innumerable cathedrals throughout the world, and first of all of the blessed and holy Lateran Cathedral, our own cathedral.

A short, stocky man with a quick Roman wit, John XXIII possessed a delightful mischievousness. He was showing a visitor about the Vatican one day, and the visitor asked how many persons worked there. "About half," John replied.

John XXIII also showed little concern for protocol. Joseph Cardinal Martin of Rouen once apologized to him for calling him "Your

Eminence" instead of "Your Holiness." John answered that there was nothing to apologize for, all the more since he had changed his title so many times in his life: Don Angelo, Monsignor, Your Grace, Excellency, Eminence, Holiness. "But now," John said with a smile, "I'm through with changing titles."

John XXIII felt a special affinity toward the Jewish people, and one of his favorite stories was that of the son of Jacob being reunited with his brothers and tearfully exclaiming, "I am Joseph, your brother" (Genesis 45:4). He would tell Jews, "I am your brother. . . . We are all sons of the same Father."

A dramatic display of this fraternity occurred during the 1959 Good Friday liturgy in St. Peter's Basilica. Among the solemn prayers or supplications of the liturgy at the time was one for the "perfidious Jews" *(Oremus et pro perfidis Judaeis)*. When the prayer was intoned, however, John interrupted the service and demanded that the prayer be repeated without the offensive reference. Thus was the word *perfidis* excised—forever—from the liturgy.

On March 7, 1963, John XXIII met at the Vatican with Alexis Adzhubei, the editor of *Izvestia,* and his wife, Rada, who, significantly, was the daughter of Nikita Khrushchev, then premier of the USSR. The meeting was fraught with diplomatic significance. Pope John turned it into a quasi-family reunion, when he turned to Khrushchev's daughter and said, "Madame, I know you have three children, and I know their names. But I would like *you* to tell me their names, because when a mother speaks the names of her children, something very special happens."

She pronounced the names: Nikita, Alexei, Ivan. John said something nice about each name, reserving Ivan for the last. (Ivan is the Russian form of the name John.) When he came to Ivan, the pope said:

> That is the name of my grandfather, my father, the name I chose for my pontificate, the name of the hill above my birthplace, the name of the basilica of which I am bishop. When you get home, madame, give all your children a hug, but give Ivan a very special one—the others won't mind.

John XXIII died a painful, lingering death from stomach cancer at age eighty-one. A few days before his death, he drew himself up in bed and issued a message that was the summation of his life and his papacy:

> Today more than ever, certainly more than in previous centuries, we are called to serve man as such, and not merely Catholics; to defend above all and everywhere the rights of the human person, and not merely those of the Catholic Church. Today's world, the needs made plain in the last fifty years, and a deeper understanding of doctrine have brought us to a new situation, as I said in my opening speech to the Council. It is not that the Gospel has changed: it is that we have begun to understand it better. Those who have lived as long as I have were faced with new tasks in the social order at the start of the century; those who, like me, were twenty years in the East and eight in France, were enabled to compare different cultures and traditions, and know that the moment has come to discern the signs of the times, to seize the opportunity and to look far ahead.

*J*OHN PAUL I, pope [Albino Luciani] (1912–1978). Born in Forno di Canali (since 1964, Canale d'Agordo) near Belluna in the Dolomite Mountains, Luciani was the son of a migrant seasonal laborer who settled down as a glassblower. Ordained a priest in 1936, he was consecrated bishop of Vittorio Veneto in 1958 and transferred to Venice as its patriarch in 1969. He was named a cardinal in 1973. Elected pope August 26, 1978, he died suddenly thirty-three days later, the shortest reign in papal history.

One month before Luciani was elected pope, the first test-tube baby, Louise Joy Brown, was born in England. In 1987, the Vatican's Congregation for the Doctrine of the Faith would condemn virtually all artificial methods of human reproduction, including in vitro fertilization, the method used in the Brown birth. But in 1978, the birth of Louise Joy Brown was an occasion of thoughtful commendation, not condemnation, from the patriarch of Venice:

> As far as her parents are concerned, I have no right to condemn them. If they acted with honest intentions and in good faith, they could even be deserving of great merit before God for what they wanted and asked the doctor to carry out.

John Paul I died of a heart attack about eleven o'clock of a Thursday night while reading in bed. The death was not discovered until five-thirty the next morning. The dramatic suddenness of his death, coupled with the lack of an autopsy, spawned rumors of foul play. These subsequently grew into claims that John Paul I was done away with because he planned to clean up the Vatican Bank, demote important Curia officials, and revise *Humanae vitae,* the birth-control encyclical. The claims were never substantiated.

JOHN PAUL II, pope [Karol Wojtyla] (1920–). In 1978, Karol Cardinal Wojtyla of Kraków, Poland, became the first non-Italian elected to the papacy in more than 450 years. During the Nazi occupation of Poland, he worked as a laboror in a stone quarry. He studied in secret for the priesthood and was ordained in 1946. A distinguished intellectual, and professor as well as priest, he advanced quickly in the Polish hierarchy and distinguished himself at Vatican II and at the postconciliar synods. The papal conclave turned to him to lead the Church after the brief, one-month reign of John Paul I.

Wojtyla was on a camping trip in northern Poland when word reached him in 1958 that he had been named an auxiliary bishop in his home archdiocese of Kraków. He went to Warsaw, where he paid a visit to the primate's office, then booked a seat on the night train home. With several hours to kill, Wojtyla, in clerical garb, knocked on the convent door of the Ursuline Grey Sisters and asked if he might go to the chapel and pray.

Though a stranger to them, the sisters showed Wojtyla to the chapel and left him alone there. When he did not reappear soon, a sister looked inside and found him prostrate on the floor. In fear and respect, she withdrew. After a time, she looked in again and found him still prostrate. This time she approached. "Perhaps Father would like to have dinner with us?" she said.

The unidentified priest replied, "My train for Kraków doesn't leave until midnight. Allow me to stay. I have a lot to discuss with the Lord. Don't disturb me . . . "

As a young man in his native Poland, Wojtyla established himself as a playwright, poet, and linguist. He was also an avid outdoorsman, particularly as mountaineer, canoeist, and skier, sports he continued to indulge in after being raise to high office. As a cardinal, he was skiing once near the Czechoslovakian border when he was stopped by a military patrol. A Communist militiaman demanded his identity card and, on being shown his papers, exclaimed: "Do you realize, you moron, whose personal papers you have stolen? This trick will put you inside [prison] for a long time." Wojtyla finally persuaded the man of his identity, but not before the militiaman protested: "A skiing cardinal! Do you think I'm nuts?"

When Wojtyla visited the United States in 1978 as Pope John Paul II, an American priest at a symposium asked him when there might be women priests and married men priests. He answered with the words of a popular British song of World War I: "It's a long way to Tipperary, it's a long way to go." (He omitted the next line: "To the sweetest girl I know.")

No sooner was he pope than John Paul II planned a return visit to Poland. He wished to make that visit in May 1979 for celebrations marking the 900th anniversary of the martyrdom of Stanislaus, Poland's patron saint, but the Communist government put off the visit until June, fearful of a dangerous political fall-out.

The bishops of Poland countered by merely postponing the observances until later. In the meantime, John Paul issued his first encyclical, *Redemptor hominis,* a treatise on the human condition. It was as if he were setting the stage of his visit, an impression heightened by remarks made to the Polish bishops during a visit to Auschwitz, site of a notorious Nazi death camp.

> Can anyone on this earth be surprised that a pope who came from the archdiocese that contains this camp started his first encyclical with the words *Redemptor hominis,* and that he devoted it in full to the cause of man, the dignity of man, the threats facing man, the rights of man?

When John Paul broke his leg in a fall while getting out of the shower in 1994, he was rushed to the Gemelli Polyclinic, a Catholic teaching hospital on Rome's northern edge. It was his sixth admission to the hospital during his pontificate and the second in a year's time. The pope arrived by ambulance. To the hospital officials there he said, despite his pain, "You have to admire my loyalty."

One of John Paul's first public meetings following his discharge from the hospital after breaking his leg was with 114 of the world's cardinals assembled in Rome to discuss papal proposals for observing the year 2000. "It is good to be together," he quipped to them, "without having to hold a conclave." (Conclaves are assemblies of the College of Cardinals called on the death of a pope in order to elect a successor.)

In March 1995, John Paul II traveled to Trent in northern Italy to commemorate the 450th anniversary of the opening of the Council of Trent, the gathering of the Church's bishops called in response to the Protestant Reformation. Toward the end of the chilly, rainy day, John Paul joshed with the ten thousand young people present, saying: "Today you are wet and tomorrow you'll probably have colds and your mothers will blame me, so I'm going to leave before they can."

JOYCE, James (1882–1941). With two early works, *Dubliners* and *Portrait of the Artist as a Young Man,* Joyce established a reputation among discerning readers, but he was to stun the world with two later works, *Ulysses* and *Finnegans Wake.* These novels profoundly influenced modern literature. A native of Dublin, Joyce left Ireland in 1902 for life on the Continent. He died in Zurich and is buried there.

Joyce was born and educated as a Catholic, but abandoned the faith as a young man. He made sport of Catholicism and particularly of the Irish church, which he labeled "the scullery-maid of Christendom." Nonetheless, his writings brimmed with religious references, almost as if he had trouble escaping his past.

For instance, as a youngster, he was taught by a governess to cross himself when lightning flashed and to whisper the following prayer: "Jesus of Nazareth, King of the Jews, from a sudden and unprovided death deliver us, O Lord." Thunderstorms forever moved his imagination as a writer, particularly so in *Finnegans Wake,* and to the end of his life, he would tremble at the sound of one. Asked by a friend why he was so affected, he replied, "You were not brought up in Catholic Ireland."

At a party in Zurich, guests were invited onto a balcony to look at the stars, whereupon a priest who was present embarked upon a cosmological proof of the existence of God, adduced from the intricate order of the starry sky. Joyce interjected, in German, "What a pity that the whole thing depends upon reciprocal destruction." When a friend asked him, "What do you think of the next life?" Joyce answered, "I don't think much of this one."

Joyce's departure from Catholicism was not one of bitter denial, but rather of transmutation. Christianity had evolved in his mind into a system of metaphors. Still, he would regard it as a superior kind of human folly and one which, interpreted by a secular artist, contained obscure bits of truth. Asked in later life, "When did you leave the Catholic Church?" Joyce replied unhelpfully, "That's for the Church to say."

JULIAN of Norwich (1342–c. 1423). An English mystic, Julian lived as a recluse in a cottage in the churchyard of Saints Julian and Edward in Norwich. At age thirty, she began to experience revelations—what she called "shewings"—and these became the basis for a book, *Sixteen Revelations of Divine Love* (*Showings* in modern title). The book is the record of twenty years' meditations on her "shewings" and contains insights that have been compared to those of Teresa of Avila *(q.v.)*

Julian's meditations have been termed the most perfect fruit of later medieval mysticism in England, and today they have a special relevance for many both because of the feminine imagery brought to an understanding of God and for the theological justification presented for such an approach. Julian speaks of God as father and mother and offers this praise for the Motherhood of God:

> To the property of Motherhood belongs nature, love, wisdom, knowledge, and this is God. . . . The kind, loving mother who knows and sees the need of her child guards it very tenderly, as the nature and condition of motherhood will have. And always as the child grows in age and stature, she acts differently, but she does not change her love. . . . This work, with everything which is lovely and good, our Lord performs in those by whom it is done. So he is our Mother in nature by the operation of grace in the lower part, for love of the higher part. And he wants us to know it for he wants to have all our love attached to him; and in this I saw that every debt which we owe by God's command to fatherhood and motherhood is fulfilled in truly loving God, which blessed love God works in us.

JULIUS II, pope (1443–1513). One of the great activist popes of history, Julius initiated the construction of St. Peter's Basilica and, by his patronage, put the talents of Michelangelo, Raphael, and Bramante to work for the Church. He was also a warrior pope and personally led the papal armies into battle, risking death and inspiring troops with his courage. On his death, he was eulogized as the liberator of Italy from foreign domination, though of course the peninsula was as yet ununified.

✺ Michelangelo was commissioned to make a bronze of Julius, and his design called for Julius's right hand to be raised. The question then arose about what to put in the statue's left hand. Michelangelo suggested a book. "Nay, give me a sword," Julius remarked, "for I am no scholar." (Julius's rejoinder is also rendered, "Put a sword there, for I know nothing of letters."

Jesuit Father Peter Henrici, before becoming a bishop in Switzerland, told of a European bishop arriving in New York City. An aggressive reporter asked, "When you come to New York, do you go to a night club?"

The bishop, hardly an innocent, asked with mock naïveté, "Are there night clubs in New York?" The next morning, he was shocked to read the newspaper headline: "Bishop's First Question: Are There Night Clubs in New York?"

America, 1 October 1994

K

KELLY, James Plunkett [pseudonym: James Plunkett] (1920–). Irish novelist and playwright, James Plunkett Kelly worked in the drama departments of Radio Eireann and of Telefis Eireann as a producer and writer. His three-act play *The Risen People* was first performed at the Abbey Theatre in 1958. His first novel, *Strumpet City,* appeared in 1969 and its successor, *Farewell Companions,* in 1977. He is a member of the Irish Academy of Letters.

Once upon a time, some Catholics playfully claimed to be able to tell a Catholic from a Protestant just by looking at the person. James Plunkett Kelly had sport with this presumption in *The Risen People,* depicting a down-on-their-luck pair singing for money in the streets. Their shrewd strategy, an inexact science to be sure, went thus:

> If he looks fat, he's a Catholic. Of course, Protestants are sometimes fat, too, but they never look it. If he's thin, he could be either. If he's thin with a long face and a sharp nose, that's a Protestant. If he has a long face and a nondescript sort of nose, that's a Catholic trying to look like a Protestant.

KENNEDY, John F. (1917–1963). Son of the wealthy financier Joseph P. Kennedy, John Fitzgerald Kennedy moved from World War II hero, to congressman, to senator, to president of the United States, the first Catholic so elected. As president, Kennedy confronted the Soviet Union over missiles in Cuba, expanded U.S. involvement in Vietnam, launched the Peace Corps, and gave impetus to the civil rights movement by terming it a moral issue. Before completing a first term, he was assassinated—November 22, 1963—on a political visit to Dallas, Texas.

As a congressman in 1947, Kennedy declined under pressure from U.S. bishops to appear at a banquet in Philadelphia capping a fund campaign for an interdenominational chapel memorializing four chaplains who went down with the transport ship S.S. *Dorchester* in 1943.

The decision would return to embarrass him when he was running for the presidency thirteen years later, for it raised the same issue of the Al Smith *(q.v.)* campaign of 1928: the independence of the Catholic politician from Catholic religious leaders. Kennedy faced the issue squarely in a speech to the Greater Houston Ministerial Association on September 12, 1960:

> I believe in an America where the separation of church and state is absolute—where no Catholic prelate would tell the president (should he be Catholic) how to act, and no Protestant minister would tell his parishioners for whom to vote—where no church or church school is granted any public funds or political preference—and where no man is denied public office merely because his religion differs from the president who might appoint him or the people who might elect him.

I believe in an America that is officially neither Catholic, Protestant nor Jewish—where no public official either requests or accepts instructions on public policy from the pope, the National Council of Churches or any other ecclesiastical source—where no religious body seeks to impose its will directly or indirectly upon the general populace or the public acts of its officials—and where religious liberty is so indivisible that an act against one church is treated as an act against all. . . .

Let me stress again that these are my views—for, contrary to common newspaper usage, I am not the Catholic candidate for president. I am the Democratic party's candidate for president, who happens also to be a Catholic. I do not speak for my church on public matters—and the church does not speak for me.

*K*NOX, Ronald Arbuthnott (1888–1957). Son of an Anglican bishop (of Coventry and later of Manchester) and himself Anglican chaplain at Trinity College, Oxford, Knox converted to Roman Catholicism in 1917 and two years later was ordained a priest in his new denomination. A great wit and satirist, he wrote and preached widely, and many of his sermons, retreat notes, and spiritual exercises were published as books. He also wrote several popular mystery stories.

  One of Knox's first sermons was reportedly preached, in Evelyn Waugh's *(q.v.)* term, *coram episcopo*—in the presence of a bishop. Afterward, the bishop commented to Knox, "An interesting sermon,

Father, but it is a pity you had to read it." To which Knox retorted, "I am bitterly conscious of my disability, my lord. Only the other day a friend remarked, 'When I saw you go into the pulpit with a sheaf of papers I thought we were in for another of those dreadful pastorals.'" (Pastoral letters originate with bishops.)

In 1939, Knox left Oxford, where he served as the fifth Catholic chaplain since the Reformation, to devote himself to a new translation of the Bible from the Vulgate, a task begun at the behest of Arthur Cardinal Hinsley. The project took until 1948. The Knox Bible never achieved the success hoped for it, and Knox was particularly disappointed with the response of Catholic priests, who discovered a sudden regard for the authorized Douay-Challoner Bible. Concerning this, he remarked:

> The clergy, no doubt, search the Scriptures more eagerly, and yet, when I used to go round preaching a good deal, and would ask the Parish Priest for a Bible to verify my text from, there was generally an ominous pause of twenty minutes or so before he returned, banging the leaves of the sacred volume and visibly blowing on the top.

Knox was a private tutor of note, and one of his students was Harold Macmillan, a future prime minister of England (1957–1963). The arrangement was of limited duration, being ended by the Macmillan family for fear of Knox's Catholicizing influence. The fear might not have been misplaced. When Knox died, Macmillan attended the funeral as prime minister and was heard to remark wistfully, "I am too old to change now."

🕮 As Knox lay dying of cancer, he was watched over alternately by Mrs. Raymond Asquith and Lady Eldon, old and dear friends. For three days he was in a coma before showing a stir of consciousness just before what proved to be the end. Lady Eldon asked if he would like her to read to him from his translation of the New Testament. Faintly but distinctly he said, "No." He seemed then to lapse again into unconsciousness. After a long pause, however, came the words, barely audible, in the idiom of his youth: "Awfully jolly of you to suggest it, though." They were his last words.

*K*UNG, Hans (1928–). A Swiss native on the faculty of the state-run University of Tubingen in Germany, Kung came to international fame in the early 1960s with *The Council, Reform and Reunion,* a book urging wide-sweeping reforms in the Church. Although his critique startled Rome and brought his orthodoxy into question in many quarters, it proved a virtual blueprint for the debates of Vatican II.

🕮 *The Council, Reform and Reunion* was only the first of several books by Kung confronting traditional disciplinary, biblical, and dogmatic suppositions in the Church. Kung went on to raise questions about the gender of God (the "feminine maternal" element must be recognized in God as well as the "masculine paternal") and the infallibility of the pope (infallibility belongs only to God, while the Church's claim is rather to "indefectibility or perpetuity in the truth"), among much else.

Kung's theological daring eventually brought censure from Rome, which sought to remove him from the Catholic faculty at the University of Tubingen. In 1980, however, a compromise was reached that allowed him to remain on the faculty, but without his designation as a specifically Catholic theologian. Official pressures have continued since, so much so that some have wondered why he has bothered to remain in the Church. Kung has responded that he has received too much from the Catholic community of faith to be able to leave so easily, adding that despite all the "reaction and restoration" on the part of Rome there was even reason to hope:

> . . . because the church cannot put back all the clocks in the world; cannot hold up the world's development and return to the Middle Ages or the Counter-Reformation.

> . . . because the power of the Gospel of Jesus Christ will prove in the long run to be stronger than all human incompetence, fear, and insincerity and more forceful than all our foolishness, weakness, and cynicism.

> . . . To those opposed to renewal, I do not want to give the pleasure of my leaving; to the partisans of renewal, I do not want to give them the pain.

More from *Catholic Nonsense* by Philip Nobile:

On "Overpopulation"

But the Catholic Church long ago, perhaps without realizing it, solved whatever problem of overpopulation there might be. It stressed the fact that there is a state of celibacy. it encouraged men and women to marry and bring into the world large families; but out of those families it asked for a generous supply of priests, monks, and nuns who would vow themselves to continuous chastity. Their example inspired people of the world with the realization of the possibility of purity. At the same time the fact of their professional chastity kept them from increasing the world's populations. So without any preaching about crimes against nature and by example of pure lives lived by men and women, the Church removed any possible danger of overpopulation.

Daniel A. Lord, S.J.,
Speaking of Birth Control (pamphlet), 1946

L

A FARGE, John, S.J. (1880–1963). Son of the noted American artist John La Farge, Father John La Farge entered the Jesuits after graduating from Harvard. For thirty-seven years, he was an editor of *America,* a Jesuit journal, at the same time being deeply involved in social and interracial causes. He was a founder of the Catholic Interracial Council, and in 1938, Pope Pius XI asked him to help draft an encyclical on racism. Pius XI died, however, before it could be promulgated. La Farge was also a leader in the fields of liturgy and ecumenism.

World peace was one of La Farge's abiding concerns, so almost inevitably he was a founding member of the Catholic Association for International Peace, a group now defunct but influential in intellectual circles in the years after World War II when world Communism seemed in the ascendancy.

One of the association's first meetings was held at the Catholic Club in New York City. A distinguished member of Tammany Hall wandered into the club that day and, hearing noise upstairs, asked what was going on. La Farge told him it was a meeting of the Catholic Association for International Peace. "The Catholic Association for *what?*" groaned the Tammany man. "My Lord, what are we coming to?"

As a young priest, La Farge was traveling of an autumn evening on the rural trolley car that ran from Tiverton to Newport in his native state of

Rhode Island. Two other passengers were on the car, one a dour-looking old Yankee farmer, the other a jovial individual and apparently a Catholic. The apparent Catholic edged himself closer to the old farmer and, pointing to LaFarge, said, "D'you know what kind of a person that is?" The old farmer shook his head. "Well, I'll tell you," he said. "He's a dominus vobiscum; that's what he is, he's a dominus vobiscum. I have no use for him and he has no use for me."

The remarks, though uncomplimentary in tone, tickled LaFarge, for, he said, he was indeed a "dominus vobiscum." He explained:

> Turning to the people at the altar and passing the Lord to them, as it were, and awaiting their response was an expression of the desire to impart all that could be imparted of that Divine Sacrifice to everyone present. Every Mass I celebrate increases in me the desire to bring every detail of it to the knowledge of everybody.

La Farge's holiness was manifest, and he believed passionately in the Incarnation.

> I am not baffled by the thought that the Creator of the universe should choose to experience for Himself the littleness of His Creation. If God has created the world out of nothing, and it is thus wholly His, I do not see any basic contradiction in the idea that He should choose to identify Himself in some way with certain aspects of its lowliness. A king has the right and the privilege to drop in and take supper with any of his subjects. His action may be a surprise, and cause some scurrying around, as

happened in *Green Pastures* when De Lawd decided to sup with Ole Man Noah; but I see nothing incongruous in the idea.

*L*AW, Bernard F. (1931–). Born in Mexico and the son of a U.S. Air Force colonel, Law was educated at Harvard and ordained in 1961. He was raised to the episcopacy in 1973 as head of the diocese of Springfield-Cape Girardeau, Missouri. With his appointment to Boston in 1984, he leaped from a see of fifty thousand persons to one of more than two million. He was named a cardinal in 1985.

> Boston has long been regarded, with mock seriousness, as the most suitable place to live on God's earth. For instance, Ralph Waldo Emerson, the sage of Concord, said that on rising he would look upon this beautiful world and thank God that he was alive and lived near Boston. When Law was selected to go to Boston as archbishop, Archbishop Pio Laghi, then the apostolic pro-nuncio in Washington, congratulated him. "After Boston," Laghi jested with Law, "there is only heaven."

> On a pastoral visit to Quincy, a city south of Boston, Law was approached by a newspaper reporter suffering from laryngitis. The reporter croaked out her question in front of a crowd of people, and Law answered accommodatingly. Suddenly he interrupted a question from the struggling reporter and asked her if she would like him to bless her ailing throat. "Why not?" she replied. With that, Law reached out and clasped his right hand on her throat, invoking a blessing for improved health and voice. Then he smiled and said, "Make sure you write something nice."

*L*ENCLOS [l'Enclos], Ninon de (1620–1705). A celebrated courtesan during the gayest and most licentious years of seventeenth-century France, Lenclos evolved over time into a fashion and social leader. Her salon attracted royalty and the most prominent literary and political figures of the age. She was a benefactor of poets, including the young Voltaire *(q.v.)*, leaving him two thousand francs in her will to buy books. Her influence remained strong to the very end of a long and eventful life.

> As courtesan, Lenclos's activities continued for what one source termed "a preposterous length of time." She had a succession of distinguished lovers, among them La Rochefoucauld, Condé, and St.-Évremond. She was not only the mistress of the Marquis de Sévigné, but also of his son, Charles, and possibly of his grandson, the Marquis de Grignan. In 1656, friends sought to temper her enthusiasms by having her confined to a convent. However, other friends quickly rescued her. When she died, her tombstone was inscribed:
>
>> Here lies the body of Madam the Countess Ninon de l'Enclos who died at the age of 85. She was celebrated for her chastity in the closing years of her life.

*L*EO X, pope [Giovanni de' Medici] (1475–1521). A member of one of the legendary families of Renaissance Italy, de' Medici came to the papal throne at age thirty-seven and ruled for eight turbulent years before dying suddenly of malaria. He was a strong patron of the arts and of learning, but he was recklessly extravagant and left Italy in religious turmoil, northern Europe in theological disaffection, and the Vatican in deep debt.

❧ Leo was a devious politician and an inveterate nepotist, and one of his principal goals was to aggrandize his family and advance its fortunes beyond Florence. An easygoing, pleasure-loving man, he set the stage early for his pontificate, announcing to his cronies, "Since God has given us the papacy, let us enjoy it."

(Leo's "enjoyment" proved to be limited. Bedeviled by debt, he was once so desperate for money that he pawned the palace furniture. A German Augustinian father, whom he finally excommunicated in 1521, also bedeviled him. The man's name was Martin Luther.)

*L*IPSCOMB, Oscar H. (1931–). A native of Mobile, Alabama, Lipscomb studied for the priesthood at North American College and Gregorian University in Rome and was ordained in 1956 as a priest of the diocese of Mobile. In 1980, Mobile was elevated to the status of archdiocese, and Lipscomb was named its first archbishop, succeeding Bishop John L. May, who was appointed archbishop of St. Louis.

❧ Over the years, Mobile has been hit by devastating hurricanes, so much so that beginning in 1927, the diocese added a special Mass prayer to beseech God's protection against "the fury of the storm." When the revision of the liturgy in the 1960s did away with the so-called double oration at Masses, priests were asked to offer the Divine Praises each day for protection against storms.

The record of protection was remarkable until hurricane "Frederic" hit in 1979. Mobile's then-Bishop May was in Washington, D.C., for meetings when "Frederic" turned toward the Mobile area. He was able to get only as far as Atlanta on the night of the storm. Three months later he was transferred to St. Louis. There was no cause-and-effect relationship between the transfer and the storm, of course—St. Louis was a large promotion—but, as Lipscomb told the story, May did leave with one piece of cautionary advice for his successor: "Remember, Oscar, one hurricane and you're out!"

*L*USTIGER, Jean-Marie (1926–). Born in Paris, Lustiger was the son of Polish-Jewish parents who had emigrated to France after World War I. His parents were deported during the Nazi occupation. His mother died in the concentration camp at Auschwitz in 1943; his father survived and lived his last years with his son. The son, who was born Aharon (a name that still appears on his passport), survived the Nazis by hiding in a monastery in Orléans. He converted to Catholicism in 1940 and was ordained a priest in 1954. In 1979, he became bishop of Orléans and, in 1981, archbishop of Paris. He was elevated to the rank of cardinal in 1983.

Proud of his Jewish roots, Lustiger frequently draws on them in pleas to Jews and Christians to make common cause, not only for peace and understanding between people, but also because of the message about God and man to which the two faiths bear witness. "A Christian can't understand who he is if he doesn't understand what is a Jew," he declared during a visit to London in 1995. "And a Jew has to recognize that a Christian is someone other than a goy." (A goy is a Yiddish term, often used disparagingly, for a non-Jewish person; that is, a Gentile.)

More from *Catholic Nonsense* by Philip Nobile:

ON "THE THEOLOGY OF ATHLETICS"

Those who take part in athletics are often chaste without any great difficulty, and physical fatigue is known to calm the imagination.

J. Leclercqu,
"Temptation" in *The Pastoral Treatment of Sin,* 1968

MACAULAY, Thomas Babington (1800–1859). English statesman, poet, essayist, biographer, and historian, Macaulay was not a Catholic, but one of his images of the Catholic Church is forever a Catholic treasure.

As a historian and author of a five-volume *History of England,* Macaulay was a logical reviewer of Leopold von Ranke's *History of the Popes* when it was published in 1840. In a review-essay, Macaulay produced lines dear to Catholic loyalists:

> She [the Roman Catholic Church] may still exist in undiminished vigor when some traveller from New Zealand shall, in the midst of a vast solitude, take his stand on a broken arch of London Bridge to sketch the ruins of St. Paul's.

McAULEY, Catherine Elizabeth (1787–1841). McAuley was descended from a distinguished Irish Catholic family. Orphaned at a young age, she saw her siblings become Protestants. McAuley, however, clung tenaciously to the Catholic faith and, in 1831, founded in Dublin the Sisters of Mercy, an order of religious women dedicated to the works of mercy, including visiting the sick and imprisoned, managing hospitals, running homes for distressed women, and educating the poor.

McAuley and her associates were known in Dublin as the "walking nuns" because of their visits throughout the city in search of those in need. She placed enormous faith in the power of prayer and once said that "prayer could do more than all the money in the bank of Ireland." Ironically, in 1994, the Irish government placed Mother McAuley's portrait on its new five-pound notes. Sister Bonaventure, a spokeswoman for the order, said that McAuley would be proud.

> Now that she is on the banknote, she is out and about again. She appears on the lowest denomination of the notes and that is the one she would want to be on because that means she is in the pockets of the poor.

McCARTHY, Eugene (1916–). Professor, author, and poet, McCarthy served in the House of Representatives from 1949 to 1959 and in the United States Senate as a Democrat from Minnesota from 1959 to 1970. In 1968, his presidential candidacy, although unsuccessful, was a factor in President Lyndon B. Johnson's decision not to seek re-election.

When McCarthy visited New York, he frequently dropped by the offices of *Commonweal,* the liberal Catholic lay journal of opinion, and on one occasion in the early 1970s joined the editors for lunch at the Williams Club on Thirty-Ninth Street. Conversation focused on unrest in the Church and the departure at the time of large numbers of priests and nuns from the religious life and people of all ages, it seemed, from the pews. McCarthy, Catholic intellectual as well as liberal Catholic, was asked if he was still observant as a Catholic. "I've come this far," said he. "I'm not going to be shot down by a legalism."

cNABB, Vincent (1868–1943). Dominican scholar and preacher, McNabb was a native of northern Ireland and studied in Belfast, Gloucestershire, and Louvain. He was ordained in 1891 and was a leading figure in the Catholic revival in England in the first half of the twentieth century. To Belloc (*q.v.*), Chesterton (*q.v.*), Knox (*q.v.*), and others of the revival he was something of a prophet and saint, albeit a quirky one. His order conferred on him the highest Dominican rank, Master of Sacred Theology.

> McNabb worked energetically for social reform and confronted the intellectual issues of the day as a writer for *Blackfriars*, a preacher at Hyde Park Corner, and an author of some thirty books. He deplored city life and modern machinery, and as a writer refused even to use a typewriter. When someone once tried to persuade him how efficient the typewriter was, he replied with characteristic sharpness, "And the central heating in Hell is very efficient, too."

cQUAID, John Charles (1895–1973). Born in Cootehill, County Cavan, Ireland, McQuaid joined the Holy Ghost Fathers and, after studies at University College Dublin and in Rome, was ordained in Rathmines in 1924. He was a leading figure in Catholic secondary education in the country before being named archbishop of Dublin in 1940. McQuaid held that education must be denominational and in accordance with that view in 1944 decreed

Trinity College Dublin off-limits to Catholics without permission of their bishop, a ban he reiterated for twenty years in the reading of the Lenten regulations. He retired in 1972 and died the following year.

> The 1960s and Vatican II introduced a period of ferment in the Church, and McQuaid had difficulty coming to terms with the new ways. On returning from the final session of the council, he told his people to relax. "No change will worry the tranquillity of your Christian lives," he remarked.

> McQuaid belonged to the old school of Catholic prelates, and the folk-memory of many Irish journalists harbored instances of coercion, censorship, and intimidation. One such involved veteran Dublin reporter Maurice Liston. Liston once approached McQuaid at a public function and respectfully asked whether His Grace would like to check for accuracy his report of an address the archbishop had delivered earlier. McQuaid scanned the two-page script and said, "Is this what I said?" Assured that it was indeed a faithful account, McQuaid tore the script into four pieces and declared, "If this is what I said, then I hadn't intended saying it."

MANNING, Henry Edward (1808–1892). An Anglican divine for eighteen years and a widower, Manning became interested in the Oxford Movement and was converted and ordained to the Catholic priesthood in 1851. He was named the second archbishop of Westminster in 1865 and was a strong supporter of papal infallibility at Vatican Council I. He was created a cardinal in 1875.

Two other English cardinals of the time having written novels—Wiseman producing *Fabiola* and Newman (*q.v.*), *Callista*—the question arose whether Manning, who himself wrote widely, would complete the trilogy. Manning said no, although "not for lack of material." He rejected the notion of books for books' sake:

> A book can only last till Christ's coming, and will then be burned
> up. It is, like food and raiment, part of our humiliation. To found
> an order or to feed a flock is better than to write a library.

Manning was a rabid proponent of Temperance. It was, in fact, one of his most striking involvements in social politics. Nonetheless, he allowed wine at his table and commented that he did not mind a bottle in the cupboard, but to be "kept there and shake your fist at it!" His intensity prompted one pub owner to display Manning's characteristically emaciated features in his window over the heading "A warning to teetotalers!" In 1872, Manning took the total abstinence pledge. "And maybe your Reverence needed it?" suggested an inebriate he met on the street.

MARCINKUS, Paul C. (1922–). A native of Cicero, Illinois, Marcinkus served in the Vatican secretariat from 1952 until his resignation in 1990, holding a number of important posts and rising to the rank of archbishop.

For twenty years, Marcinkus served as president of the Institute for Religious Works, also known as the Vatican Bank. That leadership ended in 1989, in the wake of a scandal involving the collapse of an Italian bank with which the Vatican Bank had ties. Events surrounding the incident placed the Vatican on the defensive and forced an explanation of its monetary policies, the most succinct of which was offered by Marcinkus: "You cannot run the church on Hail Marys."

MARITAIN, Jacques (1882–1973). Born in Toulouse, France, Maritain was reared a Protestant and converted to Catholicism in 1906 along with his wife, Raissa. He held professorships in France, Canada, and the United States, taking a leave from his teaching career to serve as France's ambassador to the Vatican from 1945 to 1948. His American professorships included two stints at Princeton University, from 1941 to 1942 and from 1948 to 1960. He wrote more than fifty books.

   Many credit Maritain with being the most important modern interpreter of the thought of Thomas Aquinas (*q.v.*). As a philosopher himself, he drew, of course, on Aquinas, but also on Aristotle and scholars in such fields as anthropology, sociology, and psychology. He was a profound thinker and a devout Catholic.

   Writer Tim Unsworth recalls coming upon Maritain one morning in the 1950s in a small church on the tip of Long Island. It was the time when Catholics carried missals to Mass and frantically thumbed pages and flipped ribbons, seeking to stay abreast of the celebrant. Unsworth was one such Catholic. Maritain, on the other hand, sat quietly, his arm over the pew, absorbing the graces of the Mass. After Mass, Unsworth asked Maritain why he didn't use a missal. "Oh," he said, "I have most of that memorized. I just look at him and he looks at me."

It was through the influence of the famous French writer Leon Bloy, author of the novel *The Woman Who Was Poor*, that Maritain became a Catholic. Bloy, in fact, stood as Maritain's godfather at the baptismal ceremony. He would subsequently sum up Maritain's genius:

> [I have] read in the *Revue Thomiste* a paper by my godson Jacques Maritain, "The Two Bergsonisms." That I have little use for philosophy is well known: In my opinion it is the most boring way of wasting the precious time of our lives and its Hyrcanian dialect discourages me. But with Jacques Maritain things are strikingly different. . . . It never occurred to me that the shabby jacket of a philosopher could clothe such a strong arm. The arm is that of an athlete and the voice expresses a powerful lamentation. I felt at the same time something like a wave of sorrowful poetry, a mighty wave coming from very far.

MAXIMILIAN (274–295). According to Roman law, Maximilian, as the son of an army veteran, was obliged to enlist as a soldier in the Roman legions. Refusing because of his Christian principles, he was beheaded for impiety to the pagan gods. He is revered as martyr and saint.

Maximilian's case is unusual in that it is one of the few martyrdoms for which there exists an authentic, contemporary account of the trial that led to the judgment against him. Known as the *Passio* of St. Maximilian, it is a document heralded by Christian conscientious objectors. The document records the following exchange between the proconsul Dion and Maximilian:

Dion: You must serve or die.

Maximilian: I will never serve. You can cut off my head, but I will not be a soldier of this world, for I am a soldier of Christ.

Dion: What has put these ideas in your head?

Maximilian: My conscience and He who has called me. . . .

Dion: You are a young man and the profession of arms befits your years. Be a soldier.

Maximilian: My army is the army of God, and I cannot fight for this world. I tell you, I am a Christian.

Dion: There are Christian soldiers serving our rulers Diocletian and Maximian, Constantius and Galerius.

Maximilian: That is their business. I also am a Christian, and I cannot serve.

Dion: But what harm do soldiers do?

Maximilian: You know well enough.

*M*ERTON, Thomas (1915–1968). The writings of Merton—poet, author, Trappist monk—reflected a profound religious experience and in the post-World War II period gave a contemporary interpretation to Christian contemplative life. A convert, he was born in France of an American mother and a New Zealand father, raised in the United States, and educated at Cambridge University in England and Columbia in New York. His 1948 autobiography of his youth, *The Seven Storey Mountain,* became the single most famous memoir ever written by an American Catholic.

Merton joined the Trappists in 1941, after having been rejected by the Franciscans, and was ordained a priest in 1949. He reflected on receiving Holy Orders:

> My priestly ordination was, I felt, the one great secret for which I had been born. Ten years before I was ordained, when I was in the world and seemed to be one of the men in the world most unlikely to become a priest, I had suddenly realized that for me ordination to the priesthood was, in fact, a matter of life or death, heaven or hell. As I finally came within sight of this perfect meeting with the inscrutable will of God, my vocation became clear. It was a mercy and a secret which were so purely mine that at first I intended to speak of them to no one. . . . [Ordination] was a transfiguration of simple and usual things, as elevation of the plainest and most natural acts to the level of the sublime. It showed me that the charity of God was sufficient to transform earth into heaven.

The *New York Times* once commented that for some avant-garde Catholic intellectuals, Merton was stranded by his vocation in the medieval garde. His friends, who felt that he was a seminal writer of the twentieth century and possessed a clarity of vision like that of the child in the fable "The Emperor's New Clothes," fiercely disputed the newspaper's observation. Merton, in fact, applied the fable to contemporary society and his own place in it:

> Have you and I forgotten that our vocation, as innocent bystanders—and the very condition of our terrible innocence—is to do what the child did, and keep on saying the king is naked, at the cost of being condemned criminals? If the child had not been there, they would all have been madmen or criminals. It was the child's cry that saved them.

Merton weighed in intellectually on most of modern society's great problems—from race ("What there is in the South is not a Negro problem, but a white problem. The trouble is pathological"), to social justice, to the interior life, to war and peace. He was especially outspoken on the arms race and the ideological polarization between East and West. "One day," he wrote, "we are going to wake up and find America and Russia in bed together . . . and realize that they were happily married all along."

From his hermitage at Gethsemani, Merton counseled widely, and much of his counsel opened windows on himself. In 1967, he wrote to Jesuit Father Daniel Berrigan (*q.v.*) after his order had refused to give Berrigan permission to join in a Freedom Ride protesting the segregation of bus terminals in Jackson, Mississippi. Berrigan was thinking of resigning from the order, and Merton said the following:

Look, a lot of the monastic party line we are getting ends up by being pure, unadulterated—crap. In the name of lifeless letters on parchment we are told that our life consists in the pious meditation on scriptures and withdrawal from the world. Try anything serious and immediately you get the line "activist" thrown at you. I have been told that I am destroying the image of the contemplative vocation when I write about peace. Even after *Pacem in terris,* when I reopened the question, I was told: "That's for the bishops, my boy." In a word, it is all right for the monk to break his ass putting out packages of cheese and making a pile of money for the old monastery, but to do anything really fruitful for the Church, that is another matter, altogether.

An interest in Eastern mysticism consumed Merton's last years, but his loyalty to Catholicism was as clear as a profession he made earlier about Church and country:

I cannot be a partial American and I cannot be, which is even sadder, a partial Catholic. For me Catholicism is not confined to one culture, one nation, one age, one race. My faith is not a mixture of the Irish Catholicism of the United States and the splendid and vital Catholicism, reborn during the past war, of my native France. Though I admire the cathedrals and the past of Catholicism in Latin America, my Catholicism goes beyond the Spanish tradition. I cannot believe that Catholicism is tied to the destinies of any group which confusedly expresses the economic illusions of a social class. My Catholicism is not the religion of the bourgeoisie nor will it ever be. My Catholicism is all the world and all ages. It dates from the beginning of the world. The first man was the image of Christ and contained Christ, even as he was created, as savior in his heart. The first man was destined to be the ancestor of his Redeemer and the first woman was the mother of all life, in the image of the Immaculate Daughter who was full of grace, Mother of Mercy, Mother of the saved.

METTERNICH, Klemens Wenzel Lothar von (1773–1859). After successful ambassadorships, notably to Berlin and Paris, Metternich served as Austria's minister of state and then state chancellor. He was the guiding spirit of the Congress of Vienna in 1814 and 1815, and he so dominated the political arena from 1815 to 1848 that it became known as the "Age of Metternich." An inability to understand the nature of the new European nationalism, particularly in Germany and Italy, led to his downfall. He fled Austria, returned in 1851, and lived in retirement until dying in Vienna.

Metternich's policies depended on censorship, espionage, and the suppression of revolutionary and nationalist trends. His diplomacy extended from one end of Europe to the other, and if a certain cynicism did not tinge his politics, they did affect his personal suspicions. Once, when he was negotiating with the Russians, the Russian ambassador suddenly died. Metternich remarked, "I wonder what he meant by that."

✎ Metternich was not an evangelist of the faith, but he did believe in religion's place in the state. Apropos of the subject, he said:

> The downfall of empires always directly depends upon the spread of unbelief. For this very reason religious belief, the first of virtues, is the strongest power. It alone curbs attack and makes resistance irresistible. Religion cannot decline in a nation without causing that nation's strength also to decline, and the fall of states does not proceed in arithmetical progression according to the law of falling bodies, but rapidly leads to destruction.

✎ Inevitably, many of Metternich's dealings were with Napoleon, and predictably, the two clashed as Metternich sought to make Austria supreme in the Germanic confederation, while at the same time maintaining a check on the dynastic aspirations of the French emperor. Because Napoleon had married into Austria's royal family, he expected Metternich's support. Frequently spurned in this regard, Napoleon would depart meetings with Metternich with an oft-repeated farewell meant as a threat: "We shall meet in Vienna."

*M*EYER, Albert G. (1903–1965). Son of a German-American grocery store owner, Meyer was ordained a priest of the Milwaukee diocese in 1926, then named bishop of Superior in 1946 and archbishop of Milwaukee in 1953. In 1958, he was translated to Chicago as archbishop and was elevated to cardinal the following year. He served as one of the twelve presidents of Vatican Council II and distinguished himself as a forceful progressive.

One fall day in 1956, while archbishop of Milwaukee, Meyer took himself to St. Mary's Hospital for a flu shot. The doctor who administered the shot sponged Meyer's arm, pinched a fold of skin, and darted in the needle. The needle bent. "Excellency," said the doctor apologetically, "it seems that we have a rather dull needle here and we need to repeat the injection." With God-given restraint, Meyer answered, "Don't worry, doctor, one has to be thick-skinned to be an archbishop."

MINIHAN, Jeremiah F. (1903–1973). A priest of the Archdiocese of Boston, Minihan was secretary to Cardinal O'Connell (*q.v.*) and subsequently chancellor of the archdiocese and auxiliary bishop to Archbishop Richard J. Cushing (*q.v.*). A frequent visitor to Ireland, he died while on a visit to that country.

In 1966, Minihan was in Dublin with a group of Boston-area tourists for ceremonies marking the fiftieth anniversary of the Easter Rising by Irish patriots against British rule. On parade day, the bishop found himself on one side of O'Connell Street, Dublin's main thoroughfare, while his party was on the other. Minihan moved to cross the street, but was stopped by a policeman, who declared, "There will be no crossing over here."

Hoping to "pull rank," Minihan explained that he was Archbishop Cushing's auxiliary and was representing him at the event. The policeman was unimpressed. "I wouldn't care if you were the pope himself," he said, "you wouldn't be crossing here." Minihan replied musingly, "Sic transit gloria mundi" (So passes the glory of this world.)

MORE, Thomas (1478–1535). Scholar, tutor to the future King Henry VIII, lawyer, author, family man, and finally lord chancellor of the British realm, Thomas More was indeed "a man for all seasons." In his day, no British subject was more celebrated than he, but he was shut up in London Tower and finally beheaded for refusing to take the oath provided in the Act of Succession repudiating the pope, declaring Henry's first marriage null, and recognizing the offspring of Henry's second wife, Anne Boleyn, as heir to the throne. More was canonized in 1935.

- For fifteen months, More sat in London Tower and engaged in a duel of wits with emissaries sent to dissuade him from what many considered his great folly. Sharing that opinion was his wife. Once, after a particularly emotional outburst of hers, the imprisoned More calmly exclaimed, "Is not this house as nigh Heaven as mine own?" Deprived toward the end of all amenities, he scrawled messages to his family with charcoal, the only writing tool available to him. "Farewell, my dear child," said one such message, "and pray for me and I shall for you and all your friends that we may merrily meet in heaven."

- For himself, More's prayer was simple and direct; namely, "Give me thy grace, good Lord, to set the world at naught." The prayer seemed to have been heard for More went to his death proclaiming that he died "the King's good servant, but God's first."

- More was a celebrated wit and jested with one and all, including his executioner. " I pray thee see me safe up," said More while climbing the scaffold, "and for my coming down let me shift for myself." As he placed his head on the block, he reportedly told his executioner to take care not to cut his beard since it, at least, was innocent of treason.

MOTHER TERESA [Agnes Gonxha Bojaxhiu] (1910–). Born in Skopje, Yugoslavia, of Armenian ancestry, Agnes Gonxha entered religious life as a member of the Sisters of Loreto in Ireland. She went to India in 1929 as a teacher. But in 1950, moved by the plight of the poorest of the poor, she founded her own order, the Missionaries of Charity, to work in the slums of Calcutta. Her apostolate spread to twenty Indian cities, then to many parts of the world. In 1979, she was awarded the Nobel Peace Prize.

 The all-absorbing concern of Mother Teresa—she took her name in religion after St. Thérèse of Lisieux (q.v.), "not the big St. Teresa of Avila (q.v.), but the little one"—has been in "carrying out the will of God with joy," a task done so effectively as to win for her the accolade from the *New York Times* of being "a secular saint." Others have called her "a contemplative in the world." What is her secret? The first step toward holiness is "the will to become holy," she has said. "Everything depends on these words, I WILL or I WILL NOT."

 On a visit to the Boston area in 1995, the revered nun from the slums of Calcutta, who made the slums of the world her vocational concern, delighted an audience by recounting a dream she had had years before. In the dream, she had died and gone to heaven. She arrived at the pearly gates and St. Peter greeted her, exclaiming, "What are you doing here, Mother Teresa? There are no slums in heaven."

❧ Mother Teresa also told of an audience with Pope John Paul II (*q.v.*). She remarked to the pope that members of her Missionaries of Charity order were going to "adopt" priests in various cities for regular prayers. The pope blessed the idea, then added, "Make sure someone adopts me. I am just a priest myself."

*M*UNDELEIN, George W. (1872–1939). A native of New York and an auxiliary bishop of Brooklyn, Mundelein was named archbishop of Chicago in 1915 and a cardinal in 1924. The archdiocese greatly expanded under his leadership, and Mundelein's influence was felt nationally. He was a friend and adviser to President Franklin D. Roosevelt and is credited with labeling Adolf Hitler "an Austrian paperhanger."

❧ In June 1926, Mundelein hosted the International Eucharistic Congress in Chicago and staged an enormous spectacle that drew ecclesiastical dignitaries from all over the world, among them eleven cardinals. The event included a Holy Name Night in Soldiers' Field featuring one hundred thousand men, each with a lighted candle, and a concluding ceremony at the seminary founded by Mundelein, St. Mary of the Lake. The latter event became famous for a sudden rainstorm that sent the cardinals scurrying to save their silks.

A foreign churchman, dazzled by the pageant, exclaimed to a native Chicagoan how stupendous it all was. "What could outshine the congress?" he asked. To which the Chicagoan replied, "Cardinal Mundelein is making arrangements to hold the Last Judgment in Chicago."

MURRAY, John Courtney (1904–1967). A Jesuit theologian, Murray achieved renown as an authority on church-state relations and the Church's place in the pluralistic society. Murray's positions were progressive, even radical for their time. His endorsement of the relationship that existed between Church and state in the United States brought him under fire in Rome, and for a time, he was forbidden to write or lecture on the subject.

- "Disinvited" from Vatican II's first session, Murray attended the 1963, 1964, and 1965 sessions as a *peritus* under the sponsorship of Cardinal Spellman (*q.v.*) and became a principal architect of the council's landmark Declaration on Religious Freedom. But first there was the matter of clearing his draft through the Theological Commission headed by Alfred Cardinal Ottaviani (*q.v.*), an old Murray nemesis and an opponent of change of almost any sort.

  On November 11, 1963, the full commission met to review the text that would go to the council floor. Ottaviani presided, but almost blind, he did not recognize the distinguished, tall figure of Murray when he was introduced to make the formal presentation. Ottaviani leaned over to his neighbor, Canada's Paul Emile Cardinal Leger, to ask who was speaking. Fearful of what might happen if Ottaviani realized that the one addressing the commission was none other than John Courtney Murray, Leger replied simply, "*peritus quidam*" (one of the experts).

- In the concluding months before Vatican II's last session, at which a final decision would be made on the religious freedom issue, Murray sought to enlist the support of known opponents for the text. In an August 20, 1965, letter to Ireland's (and the Curia's) Michael Cardinal

Browne, one of the council's staunch conservatives and a longtime opponent of religious freedom, Murray expressed gratitude for being allowed to write a memorandum explaining the text, saying modestly, "My only function as a peritus is to explain, as best I can, the document to the Secretariat." Then he added, with sly humor:

> There is an old folk-ballad among us about a boy who was treed by a bear (it is of Negro origin, as many are). The refrain runs thus: "O Lord, if you can't help me, for heaven's sake don't help the bear."

Murray was under no illusion that the Declaration on Religious Freedom was a milestone of history. Although he felt that the document cleared up a long-standing ambiguity, it must be admitted, he said, that the Church was late in recognizing the validity of the principle. In voting for the document, council fathers took the position that they were speaking to the world beyond the Church, but Murray, realizing that the fact was otherwise, said:

> Inevitably, a second great argument will be set afoot—now on the theological meaning of Christian freedom. The children of God, who receive this freedom as a gift from their Father through Christ in the Holy Spirit, assert it within the Church as well as within the world, always for the sake of the world and the Church.

For years, Murray was a mainstay on the faculty of Woodstock College and frequently traveled as a lecturer. Once, on a speaking engagement to the Midwest, he was met at the airport by a young Jesuit scholastic whose job it was to drive him to the lecture hall.

As they zipped down the highway, the scholastic sought to make conversation by bringing up the cover story that had appeared on Murray in *Time* for December 12, 1960. Murray was unresponsive.

A silence settled in, and in an effort to break it, the scholastic mentioned a fellow Jesuit who had unsuccessfully applied to join the Woodstock faculty. "I understand," he said politely, "that Father X will not be going to Woodstock." "Yes," said Murray, "the faculty had a meeting about him and we decided that he was a son-of-a-bitch."

Murray paused and allowed the car to travel a silent hundred yards down the dark highway before concluding in the sinuous baritone for which he was noted, "But not *our* kind of son-of-a-bitch."

*M*URRAY, Philip (1886–1952). Born in Scotland of Irish immigrant parents, Murray left school at age ten and followed his father into the coal mines. In 1902, he emigrated to the United States, where he became one of the most influential American labor leaders of the twentieth century, being named president of the new Congress of Industrial Organizations (CIO) in 1940 and subsequently of the United Steel Workers of America. He held both posts until his death on a working trip to San Francisco.

As a passionate believer in Labor and in the rights of the working person, Murray figured prominently among the reformers of American capitalism, beginning in the 1930s. At the same time, he was a passionate believer in Catholicism. A French writer summed up Murray's relationship to his religion:

> [He] belonged to the Church more than to Labor and represented the [Catholic] hierarchy within the working-class movement. God always came into his speeches, and he did nothing without taking the advice of a Pittsburgh clergyman, [Labor priest] Charles Owen Rice [*q.v.*].

In the early days of the New Deal, John L. Lewis, the leader of the United Mine Workers, and President Franklin D. Roosevelt, later bitter enemies, got along fine, and Lewis was a frequent visitor at the White House and one of the social lions of Washington. Murray would have none of this; it was not his style. He often said he was more at home in the workers' kitchens than in the social whirl.

On one occasion, he accepted an invitation to a grand function. Owning no formal attire, he rented some for the occasion. Stepping into the hotel lobby, he discovered he was the only one in "soup-and-fish." Murray hurried upstairs and changed. Returning, he bumped into a friend, who, on seeing him in ordinary attire, said, "Phil, didn't I see you a little while ago all dressed up?" Murray retorted, "It must have been someone else."

(This story has several variations. During one presidential campaign, Franklin Roosevelt made remarks in New York that were the direct opposite to what he had said in Pittsburgh just a day or two before. Asked by aides how to explain this discrepancy to the press, Roosevelt said to deny that he was ever in Pittsburgh.)

❧ Enormous controversy surrounded a decision by Francis Cardinal Spellman (*q.v.*) to use seminarians as grave diggers in a 1949 New York cemetery strike and to lead them though the picket line himself. Monsignor Charles Owen Rice (*q.v.*) criticized Spellman publicly for his actions. Bishop John F. Dearden, then head of the Pittsburgh diocese, admonished Rice for this.

Soon after, Murray was in New York for a Labor convention, accompanied as usual by Rice. Spellman delivered the opening prayer, after which Murray led Rice over to Spellman and said mischievously, "Cardinal, this is my buddy."

❧ Murray's charm and rapport with workers was legendary. One day, a delegation from one of the steel locals, fired up with a complaint, came to see him at his headquarters in the Commonwealth Building of downtown Pittsburgh. A relaxed Murray put the men at their ease, and after talking awhile, they left, themselves relaxed and satisfied and singing the praise of Phil Murray.

When they got out on the street, one of the men said, "What did he give us? What did we get out of it?" Sheepishly they looked at one another and admitted that Murray had given them nothing. Still, they went home in a good mood. For them, it was a great day.

The late Archbishop Derek Worlock of Liverpool (1920–1996) reminisced at a mass of thanksgiving on June 29, 1995, marking the centenary of the laying of the cornerstone for Westminister Cathedral in London. He remarked on the perspectives of the Bentley masterpiece, the dusty crumbling tasseled hats of cardinals past, the stations of the cross of Eric Gill *(q.v.)*, and, finally, the confessionals, "each box with its distinctive design, adorned by notices proclaiming the great linguistic variety and prowess of the incumbent." Worlock recalled a story about the Westminster confessionals:

At this distance we must have sympathy for one such chaplain who, nearly exhausted after long hours of duty, found the curtain of his box pulled aside by a lady demanding to know if he were hearing confessions. "No, ma'am," came the exasperated reply in unmistakable English. "I am driving this bus to Willesden."

The Tablet, 8 July 1995

N

NERI, Philip (1515–1595). A native of Florence, Philip Neri spent most of his life in Rome and with such sanctity as to become known as the Apostle of Rome. Pope Gregory XIII assigned him and his followers a church in central Rome where Neri founded the Oratory. It became a center not only of devotion, but of talk, mirth, and culture. The musical form known as the oratorio is said to have originated there. He was sainted in 1622.

❧ As a priest, Philip Neri advocated frequent confession and communion, although as confessor there was nothing of the zealot in him. When an earnest penitent once asked for permission to wear a hair shirt, Philip responded, "Certainly, provided you wear it outside your clothes."

❧ Rome was an especially dissolute city in Philip Neri's time, but he did not withdraw from it or condemn it. His antidote was holiness and gaiety, above all gaiety. "I will have no sadness in my house," he told the young men who crowded to the Oratory. To scrupulous penitents, he advised: "Don't be forever dwelling on your sins. Leave a little something for the angels."

❧ Aware of his special insights, penitents, especially men, flocked to Philip Neri. He was chary of accepting women penitents, although he could not keep them entirely away. When a young widow kept confessing to him that she was tormented by impure thoughts, he counseled her, "Then tell the devil next time that you will denounce him to that dull ass of a Father Philip."

Philip Neri's fondness for laughter and pranks was complemented by a spirit of self-deprecation. Once he commented:

> One day perhaps you will see me with the public executioner behind me, whipping me, and you will say, "Good heavens, surely it's that Father Philip we used to think such a good little man."

At one point in his life, Philip Neri thought of joining Francis Xavier (*q.v.*) in his mission to the Indies. A Cistercian monk convinced him otherwise, saying to him, "Your Indies are in Rome." Philip Neri stayed put. When Francis Xavier was canonized in 1622, the Church also raised Philip Neri to the honors of the altar.

NEWMAN, John Henry (1801–1890). The most noted Anglican clergyman in the England of his time and a leader in the Oxford or Tractarian Movement, Newman created a sensation by converting to Catholicism in 1845 and being reordained as a Roman Catholic priest. At the invitation of the Irish bishops, he spent several years in Dublin, establishing a Catholic university system in that country, finally returning to England and life as an Oratorian in London and Birmingham. He was named a cardinal by Pope Leo XIII in 1879.

Newman was denounced as a traitor for his conversion to Roman Catholicism, with Prime Minister Gladstone himself raising the question of how Newman could be loyal both to the Queen and to the pope. Newman answered:

> When, then, Mr. Gladstone asks Catholics how they can obey the Queen and yet obey the Pope, since it may happen that the commands of the two authorities may clash, I answer that it is my rule both to obey the one and to obey the other, but that there is no rule in this world without exceptions, and if either the Pope or the Queen demanded of me an "Absolute Obedience," he or she would be transgressing the laws of human society. I give an absolute obedience to neither. Further, if ever this double allegiance pulled me in contrary ways, which in this age of this world I think it never will, then I should decide according to the particular case, which is beyond all rule, and must be decided on its own merits. I should look to see what theologians could do for me, what the Bishops and clergy around me, what my confessor; what my friends whom I revered; and if, after all, I could not take their view of the matter, then I must rule myself by my own judgment and my own conscience. But all this is hypothetical and unreal.

Newman was also held suspect in Rome, notably for views connected with the main business of Vatican Council I: the question of papal infallibility. While Newman believed in papal infallibility, he did not believe it should be formally proclaimed. After the council voted its definition in 1870, he declared:

We have come to a climax of tyranny. It is not good for a pope to live for twenty years. It is an anomaly and bears no good fruit; he becomes a god, he has no one to contradict him.

◖ While awaiting action by Vatican I on papal infallibility, Newman reflected that the Holy Spirit would keep the council from teaching error, but not necessarily from acting inopportunely. After papal infallibility was proclaimed, he invoked the principle so important to his thought—*securus iudicat orbis terrarum;* that is, if the definition met "the general acceptance of Christendom," then it would have "the ultimate guarantee of revealed truth" for that was "the broad principle by which all acts of the rulers of the Church are ratified." Newman spoke of this as the *sensus fidelium,* the sense of the faithful.

◖ Newman was an outspoken person, and many of his statements were shockingly liberal for their time. In 1861, he voiced a thought that would find its echo a century later:

I cannot help feeling that, in high circles, the Church is sometimes looked upon as made up of the hierarchy and the poor, and that the educated portion, men and women, are viewed as an encumbrance, as the seat and source of heresy; and as almost alien to the Catholic body, whom it would be a great gain, if possible, to annihilate.

◖ The Catholic establishment viewed with particular unease Newman's view on the development of doctrine. Applying the principle of life as the test of truth in religion, Newman argued that as in the body there are changes that are anything but corruptions, so in the Church there are changes in which old principles reappear under new forms. The Church "changes with them in order to remain the same." In a higher world it might be otherwise, Newman conceded, "but here below to live is to change and to be perfect is to have changed often."

🙰 A principle most cherished by Newman was freedom of conscience, and although his understanding of conscience troubled many Catholics in leadership positions in his day, it was sufficiently orthodox for Pope John Paul II (*q.v.*) to refer to it approvingly in his 1994 book, *Crossing the Threshold of Hope*. Newman's famous words on the subject were: "I shall drink to the Pope, if you please; still, to Conscience first, and to the Pope afterwards."

*N*OVAK, Michael (1933–). A native of McKeesport, Pennsylvania, Novak was a seminarian in the Congregation of Holy Cross, but left short of ordination. He became prominent in Catholic circles as a writer and scholar, and his 1982 book, *The Spirit of Democratic Journalism,* is said to have strongly influenced the thinking of Pope John Paul II. In 1994, he was awarded the Templeton Prize. In latter years, he has been a resident scholar at the American Enterprise Institute in Washington, D.C.

🙰 In the 1960s, Novak was a leading liberal in political and ecclesiastical causes, most notably as a writer covering Vatican Council II. By the mid-1970s, however, he had turned ideologically and was solidly in the neoconservative camp. Asked to define a neoconservative, Novak responded that a neoconservative was "a liberal with three teenage daughters."

Jesuit Father Peter Henrici, before becoming a bishop in Switzerland, told of a European bishop arriving in New York City. An aggressive reporter asked, "When you come to New York, do you go to a night club?"

The bishop, hardly an innocent, asked with mock naïveté, "Are there night clubs in New York?" The next morning, he was shocked to read the newspaper headline: "Bishop's First Question: Are There Night Clubs in New York?"

America, 1 October 1994

O 'CONNELL, Daniel (1775–1847). Irish statesman known as "the Liberator," O'Connell entered politics to oppose the Act of Union, which abolished the Irish Parliament in 1800 and amalgamated Ireland and England into a single "United Kingdom." He was named to the British Parliament in 1828 and seated over objections to his Catholic religion. He carved out a distinguished career as an orator and parliamentarian. In 1841, he was elected mayor of Dublin and in 1844 was convicted on charges of conspiracy for demanding an end of Irish union with England. The sentence was ultimately reversed, but he did serve time in prison and this broke both his health and his hold on the Irish people.

In Parliament, O'Connell joined the Whigs and agitated vigorously for reform. At the same time, he built up an Irish party whose support was wooed by English politicians. O'Connell used this advantage shrewdly to extract concessions, including acknowledgment from the government of the full citizenship shared by all the people of Ireland. This opened up such things as judgeships and other state appointments for Catholics as well as Protestants.

O'Connell's was not a narrow, partisan concern, however. He also spoke up for English Jews, and when offered the backing of persons who owned slaves in the West Indies if he would drop his support for abolition of slavery, he spurned them, saying: "May my right hand forget its cunning and my tongue cleave to my mouth if to help Ireland—even Ireland—I forget the Negro one single hour."

⚜ O'Connell died in Genoa, while en route to Rome. Throughout Europe, mourning was widespread. The famed French Dominican Jean-Baptiste Lacordaire preached the panegyric in the Cathedral of Notre Dame in Paris. His words summed up the inspiring and motivating force of O'Connell's life:

> To deny the rights of man is to deny the rights of God. . . . The rights of God and human rights form a unity. . . . Liberty is a work of virtue, a holy work and therefore a work of the Spirit.

O'CONNELL, William Henry (1859–1944). Rector of the North American College in Rome from 1895 to 1901, O'Connell moved from that post to bishop of Portland, Maine. In 1905, he served as special papal envoy to Japan's Emperor Mutsuhito and in 1906 was named archbishop of Boston, where he served for thirty-eight years, thirty-three as a cardinal. He ruled imperiously and lived splendiferously, wintering in Nassau and maintaining a summer home high on the rocks overlooking Marblehead Harbor on Massachusetts' North Shore. His comings and goings won him the sobriquet "Gangplank Bill."

⚜ Although O'Connell's Marblehead home was modest in comparison to his Nassau residence (which once belonged to Lord Dunmore, a colonial governor), he guarded it as a castle. Trespassers were prohibited and picnickers were ordered off the rocks that stood between the house and the ocean. One summer an ousted—and annoyed—picnicker returned with a sign that made a play on the opening of Psalm 24: "The world is the Lord's and the fullness thereof, but the rocks belong to the Cardinal."

In Boston, O'Connell built the archbishop's residence, an imposing mansion of Renaissance design. He filled it with marble chests, carved oak furniture, oriental rugs, *objets d'art,* and choice antiques. Each year on his birthday he would invite the press corps in for a news conference. It was ever a large Boston occasion. One year an obese reporter hurried in late and took a seat on the one chair remaining unoccupied, a delicate gilt antique. The chair collapsed under his weight. Snapped O'Connell: "Why didn't you bring an axe?"

O'Connell aspired for acceptance by Harvard, across the Charles River in Cambridge, but for decades he was kept at arm's length. In 1919, Harvard presented an honorary degree to Belgium's famed World War I resistance prelate, Desire Cardinal Mercier, pointedly snubbing O'Connell, by then thirteen years a cardinal and living within five miles of Harvard.

In 1936, when Harvard was observing its tercentenary, O'Connell thought it timely that he should receive an honorary degree on that auspicious occasion. The Board of Fellows at Harvard apparently thought otherwise. The following year, however, an honorary degree was tendered. O'Connell, now seventy-seven and nearly blind, accepted unhesitatingly and hurriedly scheduled a risky eye operation so that he would not go staggering and stumbling to receive the degree. His true feelings, though, were expressed privately: "It's too late."

ᴈ O'Connell did not conceal the antipathy he felt for his auxiliary bishop, Francis J. Spellman (*q.v.*). He was not consulted on Spellman's appointment as his auxiliary in 1932, and this was a slight O'Connell neither forgot nor forgave. He assigned Spellman, raised to the episcopacy at a ceremony in Rome, to a debt-ridden Boston parish and handed him the confirmation schedule.

O'Connell treated Spellman with utter disdain. When the surprise announcement was made in 1939 that Spellman was going to New York as archbishop, O'Connell remarked privately, "Francis is the perfect example of what happens when you teach the bookkeeper how to write."

ᴈ To insure that scholars would have all the essential information they would need to fix his place in history, O'Connell wrote a memoir, *Recollections of Seventy Years,* published in 1934. A crescendo of mounting achievements and details of ecclesiastical honors, it prompted one person to wonder aloud how a man born in 1859 could have memories reaching back to the age of five. To which a wag is said to have replied, "Children were very precocious in New England in those days."

O'CONNOR, Flannery (1925–1964). Born in Savannah and raised in Milledgeville, Georgia, O'Connor produced a slim but distinctive body of literature in a brief lifetime. She was recognized as one of the outstanding writers of her day, and won a number of prizes, including a posthumous National Book Award in 1971 for *The Complete Stories.*

❧ O'Connor's fiction grappled with the forces of good and evil, and although her characters and situations were often grotesque and bizarre, the stories themselves evidenced a profound sense of sin, free will, and the presence of the divine. She was accused of being Manichaean; her art, rather, affirmed the Incarnation. In a letter, she wrote:

> When I know what the laws of the flesh and the physical really are, then I will know what God is. We know them as we see them, not as God sees them. For me it is the virgin birth, the Incarnation, the resurrection which are the true laws of the flesh and the physical. Death, decay, destruction are the suspension of these laws. I am always astonished at the emphasis the Church puts on the body. It is not the soul she says that will rise but the body, glorified . . . flesh and spirit united in peace.

❧ Like her father, O'Connor suffered from disseminated lupus, and she battled the disease throughout her adult life before succumbing to it at age thirty-nine when the disease was reactivated by abdominal surgery for a benign tumor. She did not call attention to her suffering and, in fact, rarely mentioned it in her letters. There was, however, this moving observation:

> In a sense sickness is a place, more instructive than a long trip to Europe, and it's always a place where there's no company, where nobody can follow. Sickness before death is a very appropriate thing, and I think those who don't have it miss one of God's mercies.

Retrospectives, oftentimes unflattering, can follow any famous person's death, and Flannery O'Connor's was no exception. Letters in the O'Connor Collection at the Ina Russell Dillard Library at Georgia College, for instance, indicate an uncomfortableness with Afro-Americans, and these, coupled with her known reluctance to take a direct, public position on integration issues, have triggered certain reassessments.

O'Connor was not a segregationist, but she seems, in the words of one writer, to have possessed a "naive preference for a gradual change in race relations in the South, [and] a blindness to the fact that only government intervention could reverse the egregious injustice against blacks."

In responding to social critics, O'Connor would complain that northern "progress" was no blessing to the South. "We are being forced out not only of our many sins," she said, "but of our few virtues as well."

ONASSIS, Jacqueline Bouvier Kennedy (1929–1994). Born in Southampton, New York, Jacqueline Bouvier studied at Vassar and the Sorbonne before receiving a bachelor's degree from George Washington University in 1951. She worked as an inquiring photographer in 1952 at the *Washington Times-Herald*. After being widowed by President John F. Kennedy (*q.v.*) in 1963 and by Greek shipping magnate Aristotle Onassis in 1975, she was a book editor at Viking and Doubleday, New York publishing houses.

Hammersmith Farm, the home of Mrs. Hugh Auchincloss, the mother of Jacqueline Bouvier, lies within the boundaries of St. Augustin's parish in Newport, Rhode Island. In 1953, when Miss Bouvier was planning her marriage to then-Senator John Kennedy, the pastor of St. Augustin's was Father James A. FitzSimon. The pastor held that as parish priest it was his right under Canon Law to be the officiating priest at all marriages in St. Augustin's and, because he wanted no social or monetary distinction between wealthy and poor, that no nuptial Mass would be celebrated after 9 A.M.

Miss Bouvier explained that Archbishop (later Cardinal) Richard Cushing (*q.v.*) of Boston, a friend of the Kennedy family, had asked to officiate at the wedding and that the time be set at 11 A.M.

Father FitzSimon remained adamant, and Miss Bouvier said she would look elsewhere. She went to Father Walter Leo Flynn, pastor of nearby St. Mary's Church, who told her that her plans were totally agreeable with him and that his only request was that he be allowed to be at the altar during the ceremony. So it happened.

During the Kennedy presidency, when President and Mrs. Kennedy were in Newport, they always went to St. Mary's Church for Sunday Mass—for, as the newspapers so sentimentally reported, that was the church in which they were married.

The Bouvier-Kennedy marriage took place on September 12, 1953. Shortly afterward, "Jackie," as she was commonly called, arranged to audit Professor Jules Davis's American history course at Georgetown University's School of Foreign Service in Washington, D.C. Having become the wife of a senator, she obviously thought it wise to bone up on politics and history, and—who knows?—maybe prepare herself for her own original contribution to American history. A member of the class recorded her entry into Georgetown's academe:

> On her first day, this young, commanding and impossibly regal-looking lady surprised (and intimidated by her presence) our all-male class. She strode into our basement classroom in the Healy building and was seated next to me. . . . A friend of mine quickly scribbled a note on a piece of paper and passed it back to me. It said, "This is a sociological revolution!"

O'REILLY, John Boyle (1844–1890). A native of Ireland, O'Reilly worked as a printer in Drogheda and on the staff of the *Guardian* in Preston, England, before joining the British government's Tenth Hussars. He became involved in the Irish Fenian movement, was arrested, convicted of treason against the Crown, and sentenced to death. This was commuted to twenty-three years of penal servitude in Australia. He escaped from Australia on an American whaling ship and settled in Boston in 1869, where he achieved success as a romantic novelist, poet, and editor of the *Pilot*.

> O'Reilly was nineteen when he enlisted as a trooper in the Tenth Hussars. Paradoxically, the enlistment was an act of Irish patriotism: he joined up in a secret conspiracy to promote the fight for Irish freedom. Of course, the venture was risky, and O'Reilly was detected, convicted, and shipped off to Australia as a prisoner. He never regretted his action. Years later, he explained his motivation: "They said to us: 'Come on, boys, it is for Ireland'—and we came."

A renowned orator, O'Reilly was especially engaging in offhand speeches, as at his club where he would pile hyperbole upon exaggeration until he himself would dissolve in laughter. On one such occasion, a person in the audience challenged him by saying, "That is not right—that is Irish." "Sir," O'Reilly replied, assuming an air of Johnsonian dogmatism, "it is better to be Irish than right!" (In point of fact, O'Reilly became thoroughly American, and would tell his Irish audiences: "We can do Ireland more good by our Americanism than by our Irishism.")

As a liberal editor and reformer, O'Reilly crusaded against tyranny and injustice. He called for prison reform and denounced inhuman working conditions and injustices generally. He also spoke out strongly for the American Indian, for Jews, and especially for Afro-Americans. After eight blacks were lynched on suspicion of murder on December 28, 1889, in Barnwell, South Carolina, O'Reilly editorialized:

> The black race in the South must face the inevitable, soon or late, and the inevitable is—DEFEND YOURSELF. . . . Unless the Southern blacks learn to defend their homes, women, and lives, by law first and by manly form in extremity, they will be exterminated like the Tasmanian and Australian blacks.

To charges that he was inciting blacks to open rebellion, O'Reilly responded:

> We have appealed only to the great Catholic and American principle of resisting wrong and outrage, of protecting life and home and the honor of families by all lawful means, even the extremest, when nothing else remains to be tried.

193

O'REILLY, Mary Boyle (1873–1939). The eldest of four daughters of John Boyle O'Reilly (*q.v.*), O'Reilly was born in the Charlestown section of Boston and became a noted journalist and sociologist. She reported from Europe on World War I, and at one point, the Germans, suspecting that she was a spy, imprisoned her. O'Reilly lectured widely on her war experiences and was involved in a number of humanitarian causes.

᭢ Though not a rabid feminist, O'Reilly held views advanced for her time. One of her great concerns was the welfare of women, particularly the luckless and underprivileged, and she worked tirelessly on their behalf. In tracing fault, however, O'Reilly was no feminist loyalist. In fact, she held feminine peers responsible for much of the lot of disadvantaged women, accusing them in effect of hypocrisy:

> I think the reason for the misfortune and unhappiness which comes to so many women is in a great part due to other women. The woman of today who has made a mistake is too often condemned without a hearing from other women. There seems to be no charity and no pity and no desire to help them at such a time. For a woman who is thus ostracized there comes rarely a word of encouragement from their own sex.

᭢ O'Reilly idolized her father, John Boyle O'Reilly. Her home in Auburndale, Massachusetts, built of native Irish stone, was a shrine to his memory, and many of the father's loyalties and causes were also her own. So it is not surprising, perhaps, that when asked what she considered her "ideal American man," she replied, "My ideal is an Irishman— an old-fashioned, great-hearted man."

O 'SULLIVAN, Seamus. *See* Starkey, James Sullivan.

O TTAVIANI, Alfredo (1890–1979). Born in Rome, Ottaviani was ordained in 1916 and spent most of his priesthood in the Vatican Curia, most notably as secretary of the Sacred Congregation of the Holy Office, where he established a reputation as a tenacious watchdog of orthodoxy. He was created a cardinal in 1953 and was a major defender of traditionalism at Vatican Council II.

    The motto on Ottaviani's coat of arms read *Semper Idem*, "Always the same," and for some, that typified the spirit that animated the man. They believed that his roots were deep in the Council of Trent, the council called four hundred years before to meet the challenge of the Protestant Reformation. For many, that council remained a milestone of reactionaryism. One Vatican II story had Ottaviani hopping into a Roman taxicab and exclaiming to the driver, "Take me to the Council." The driver immediately headed for Trent.

    During the final session of the council, after the progressive trend had clearly been established, Ottaviani, who suffered from nearly total sightlessness, gave an interview to *Corriere della Sera,* a Milan newspaper. Observers praised his remarks for their admirable abnegation and faith:

> I am the policeman who guards the gold reserve. Do you think I would be doing my duty if I abandoned my post? Dear sons, seventy-five years is seventy-five years. I have spent them

defending certain principles and laws. If you tell an old police-man that the laws are going to change, it is clear that as an old policeman he will do what he can to see that they don't change.

But if they change anyway, God will certainly give him the strength to defend a new treasure in which he believes. Once the new laws have become part of the Church's treasure, an enrichment of the gold reserve, there is only one principle to go by: serve the Church. And this service signifies: to be faithful to its laws. Like a blind man. Like the blind man I am.

P

PADRE PIO. *See* Forgione, Francesco.

PASCAL, Blaise (1623–1662). Scientist and theological thinker, Pascal was one of the great young geniuses of his day. At eighteen, he invented a calculating machine, and he went on to become one of the founders of the science of hydrodynamics. His latter-day fame, however, rests largely on his letters and thoughts (*Pensées*), controversial in their day because of Pascal's Jansenist propensities, but now regarded as a strong defense of orthodox Christianity.

Pascal gave his name to history in a discourse rationalizing belief for the existence of God in a situation in which reason can decide nothing. The formulation came to be known as Pascal's Wager. It is set forth in discourse 213 of the *Pensées*:

> Let us then examine this point, and say, "God is, or he is not."
> . . . Since you must choose [between the alternatives], let us see
> which interests you least. You have two things to lose, the true
> and the good; and two things to stake, your reason and your
> will, your knowledge and your happiness; and your nature has
> two things to shun, error and misery. Your reason is no more

shocked in choosing one rather than the other, since you must of necessity choose. This is one point settled. But your happiness? Let us weigh the gain and the loss in wagering that God is. Let us estimate these two chances. If you gain, you gain all; if you lose, you lose nothing. Wager then without hesitation that He is.

*P*AUL VI, pope [Giovanni Battista Montini] (1897–1978). Vatican pro-secretary of state under Pius XII (*q.v.*), Montini was removed and named archbishop of Milan in 1954, reportedly in papal disfavor. One theory attributed the transfer to criticisms of papal nepotism and irregularities in church finances; another to disagreements with Curia conservatives on sociopolitical issues. In any instance, he was not named a cardinal until after John XXIII (*q.v.*) became pope in 1958. Montini played a noteworthy role in preparations for Vatican II and on John's death in 1963 was elected his successor. He saw Vatican II to its conclusion and for thirteen years thereafter steered the Church through its turbulent postconciliar period.

Paul VI did not keep a formal journal, but he frequently put his thoughts on paper, as in 1975 when he was seventy-five and beginning to weary. At that time, he wrote the following:

What is my state of mind? Am I a Hamlet? Or a Don Quixote? On the left? On the right? I don't feel I have been properly understood. I have had two dominant feelings: *Superabundo gaudio.* I am filled with comfort. With all our affliction, I am overjoyed (2 Corinthians 7:4).

(In many cultures, Shakespeare's Hamlet is a symbol of indecisiveness, notably for his long soliloquy of Act 3, Scene 1, beginning "To be or not to be . . ." Don Quixote, of course, was Cervantes's legendary tilter at windmills. It is said that John XXIII (*q.v.*) once taxed Montini with being *amletismo*, a Hamlet, but, according to Peter Hebblethwaite, biographer of the two men, "this term was not in his vocabulary.")

For nothing is Paul VI remembered more than *Humanae vitae*, his encyclical reaffirming the Church's traditional ban on artificial birth control. When it was released in 1968, there were immediate and indeed enduring repercussions worldwide. Paul sensed that the encyclical would receive a negative reception. "Don't be afraid," he is reported to have told Edouard Gagnon, the Canadian Sulpician, on the eve of the document's issuance. "In twenty years' time they'll call me a prophet."

PERCY, Walker (1916–1990). Trained as a doctor, Percy burst on the American literary scene in 1962 when his first novel, *The Moviegoer*, won the National Book Award. Five more novels and a wide variety of philosophical and occasional essays established him as one of the great writers of his generation and a shrewd chronicler of life in the New South.

In the 1940s, Percy, an agnostic out of liberal Presbyterianism, developed an interest in Catholicism. He explained this turn in his life to an incredulous friend: "If you take the claims of Christianity seriously, then it seems to me that Catholicism is where you have to end up."

Percy took religious instructions in New Orleans from a Jesuit priest and on December 13, 1947, was provisionally baptized a Catholic. That same day he made his first confession, together with his wife, Bunt, and a friend, Jidge Minyard Milazzo, members of the same instruction class. Bunt and Jidge approached the confessional experience with considerable apprehension, finding it the most daunting requirement of their new church. But not Percy; he was elated. "This is one of the main reasons I've become a Catholic," he told them. "If you think it so great," responded Jidge, "then why don't you go first?"

PIUS IX, pope [Giovanni Maria Mastai-Ferretti] (1792–1878). Pius IX succeeded to the papacy in 1846, and his thirty-two-year reign is the longest in history. He came to the papacy as a liberal, but within a few years was associated with reactionary positions. He issued the Syllabus of Errors in 1864, condemning not only liberalism and socialism, but democracy and pluralism as well. From 1869 to 1870, he presided over Vatican Council I, the council that produced the dogma of papal infallibility. He came to be viewed by history as the personification of ultramontanism, that is, the tendency to centralize the Church's power and authority in the pope and the Roman Curia.

When Pius IX announced plans in 1867 for a Vatican council, the world was mystified. There had been nineteen previous councils, but with no mass media of any kind, the councils took place in virtual secrecy. Further, with none having been held in more than three hundred years, few people had any real understanding of what a council was. Many wondered whether the council was a power grab.

One news report had England's Queen Victoria asking her prime minister, Benjamin Disraeli, if she should dispatch battleships to Italy. The *New York Herald* called the council "a revival of Middle Age sentiment," and *Harper's Weekly* ran a cartoon of Pius IX sailing in a creaky tub called "Ecumenical Council." The *New York Times* added that Pius IX was "a degrading influence."

In 1870, Pius IX solemnly promulgated Vatican I's most celebrated and controversial issue, the dogma of papal infallibility. Teased later by a visitor to the Vatican about what it felt like to be infallible, the pope responded wearily, "I do not know whether I am fallible or infallible. But one thing I am sure of, I'm *infallimento* [bankrupt]!"

When Royalist troops occupied the papal city of Rome in 1870, Pius IX issued his famous *Non possumus* and shut himself up in the Vatican buildings. The state offered a set of Guarantee Laws, providing the pope financial compensation and a guarantee of residency in the Vatican. Pius IX refused the terms, citing Article 5 which stated: "The Pope will continue to enjoy the habitation of the Vatican and the Apostolic Palaces."

The word *enjoy,* Pius IX contended, implied that these buildings did not belong to him, and hence a new government could eject him as a landlord could a tenant, should it so wish. Pius IX refused to set foot on the soil he regarded as having been illegally taken from him, and thus set himself up, as well as succeeding popes until 1939, as "a prisoner of the Vatican."

*P*IUS X, pope [Guiseppe Melchiorre Sarto] (1835–1914). Son of a post-man and a seamstress, Sarto rose from humble origins to become patriarch of Venice and pope. He was a deeply conservative pope, but at the same time an effective reformer, particularly in the field of the liturgy. He popularized the idea of frequent communion and encouraged wider use in churches of Gregorian chant. He was canonized in 1954.

Sarto was elected to the papacy in 1903, two days after the cardinal-archbishop of Kraków announced the veto of Emperor Franz Joseph of Austria against Mariano Cardinal Rampolla, secretary of state under Leo XIII. Sarto had not expected to be elected, and when an overwhelming majority of fifty-nine cardinals voted for him, he pleaded to be excused. At the persuasion of the cardinals he relented, however, saying he would accept his cross: *Accepto in crucem.*

An extremely generous person, Sarto as cardinal-patriarch of Venice pawned all his personal possessions in order to help the poor. Thus when it came time for him to appear on the balcony overlooking St. Peter's Square for the proclamation of his election as pope, he could muster nothing but a cheap tin cross because he had earlier pawned the silver episcopal cross. Some were troubled about this circumstance, but not the new pope. "No one will notice," Pius X said. "It looks quite like the real thing."

Pius X opposed the liberalizing movement known as Modernism and in 1910 introduced an anti-Modernist oath that for years was required of all priests teaching theology and the sacred sciences, as well as of those in pastoral ministry. On the other hand, his sunny nature and charm of manner prompted him to launch a modern social innovation at the Vatican: having guests at the papal dinner table.

For years, if not centuries, the custom was for popes to dine alone. That was not to be Pius X's style. He dined with relatives, friends, visiting priests, messengers, aides, workmen in his garden. When word circulated about such innovations, people began to call him a saint and attribute miracles to him. "So now it's miracles they want from me," said Pius on hearing the reports. "As if I didn't have enough to do already!"

◖ The outbreak of World War I is said to have hastened Pius X's death, which occurred August 20, 1914. Hostilities had broken out the previous month, on July 28. Reportedly one of the last acts of his lifetime was to refuse the request of the Austrian emperor to bless his cause. Pius X responded, "I do not bless war: I bless peace."

*P*IUS XII, pope [Eugenio Pacelli] (1876–1958). A native Roman, Pacelli was ordained in 1899 and served in a number of diplomatic posts, negotiating concordats with Serbia, Bavaria, Prussia, and Austria. He came to the papacy in 1939 and steered the Church through World War II and the early years of the cold war, not without controversy. His forty-one encyclicals covered a myriad of topics. Among those with great impact were *Divino Afflante Spiritu* on biblical studies and *Mediator Dei* on the liturgy.

◖ Pius XII's militant anti-Communism is said to have elicited the dismissive retort from the USSR's Josef Stalin "How many divisions does the

Pope have?" But it didn't end there. When Pietro Nenni, leader of the Italian Socialists, went to Moscow in 1950 to collect his Lenin Peace Prize, Stalin tauntingly remarked, "Does the Pope want war?" But the last word belonged to Pius XII. When Stalin died in 1953, Pius is credited with saying, "Joseph Stalin is dead. Now he will see how many divisions we have up above."

(Stalin's remark about the pope's "divisions" is also told in the context of Francis Cardinal Spellman (*q.v.*) of New York. Reportedly, during the Yalta Conference, President Franklin D. Roosevelt cited Spellman as a patriotic churchman and army chaplain. Whereupon, Stalin is supposed to have said, "And how many divisions has this cardinal of yours?")

*P*LUNKETT, James. *See* Kelly, James Plunkett.

*P*OWERS, J. F. [James Farl] (1917–). An important American Catholic writer of the twentieth century, Powers produced several collections of short fiction and two novels, one of which, *Morte D'Urban,* won the National Book Award in 1963. He contributed regularly to the *New Yorker.*

    Powers's writings were intensely Catholic, and he drew on a familiarity with rectory life to probe the workings of grace on priests and those in their care. He was especially deft in depicting housekeepers and other auxiliary characters of the Catholic scene, such as parish committee members and benefactors.

Himself a firm believer, Powers was asked by a interviewer once if he read the Bible. "Hardly ever," he quipped. "I'm a Catholic." On a more serious note, he said that "the later versions of the Bible are so incredibly bad in this country, it's hard to believe. . . . [The] Catholic Church has turned the Bible over to people with at least three tin ears."

*P*REUSS, Edward Friederich Reinhold (1834–1904). Born in East Prussia and raised as a Lutheran, Preuss arrived in the United States in 1869 and joined the faculty of Concordia Lutheran Seminary in St. Louis. In 1871, he converted to Catholicism, and from 1877 to 1902, he edited *Amerika,* the most important German Catholic newspaper in the United States.

For ten years, Preuss was a tutor at the University of Berlin, where he got caught up in the controversy agitating German Lutherans over liberalism and the new rationalism. Preuss believed that "the conversion of liberal Protestants to the genuine and original Lutheranism could be brought about solely by a thorough-going renewal of the literary fight with Rome."

Preuss made his personal point of attack the newly proclaimed dogma on the Immaculate Conception of Mary and in 1865 published a book attacking this "Romanish" teaching. Catholics largely ignored the book. When his defense of Lutheran orthodoxy on the question of justification alienated him from his colleagues, Preuss emigrated to the

United States. However, his misgivings persisted, and he began to see the history of Lutheranism as "either a tissue of most irrational occurrences" or simply as a "transition stage" between Catholicism and the outright apostasy of the rationalists.

Feeling he could no longer teach the theology of Martin Luther, Preuss resigned from Concordia and became a Catholic. This was in 1871. By coincidence the day he left Lutheranism forever was December 8—the feast of the Immaculate Conception.

Q

QUELEN, Hyacinthe-Louis de (1778–1839). A native of Paris, Quelen was ordained a priest in 1807 and, following the Restoration of 1814, rose through a number of prominent ecclesiastical posts to become archbishop of Paris. During the cholera epidemic of 1832, he transformed his seminaries into hospitals and personally ministered to the sick at the Hotel-Dieu.

As archbishop, de Quelen was inevitably caught up in the turmoil over restoration of absolute monarchy in France, and the House of Orleans held him in suspicion. On one occasion, Louis Philippe, the duc d'Orléans who was chosen king after the July revolution of 1830, said to de Quelen, "Archbishop, remember that more than one miter has been torn asunder." "Sire," replied de Quelen, "God protect the crown of the king, for many royal crowns too have been shattered." (The February revolution of 1848 led to the abdication of Louis Philippe. A republic was declared. Louis Philippe fled to England, where he died two years later.)

R

RICE, Charles Owen (1908–). Born in New York of Irish immigrant parents, Rice was reared in Ireland by relatives, a circumstance dictated by his mother's death of scarlet fever in 1913. He returned to the United States in 1920 and lived in Pittsburgh. He became a priest and monsignor of that diocese and achieved national prominence as a champion of labor. He was particularly influential in CIO affairs as a friend of its leader, Philip Murray (*q.v.*). He also involved himself deeply in civil rights, the peace movement, and radical causes generally.

In 1965, the pastor of Holy Rosary parish in Pittsburgh died. The parish was in the Homewood section, a community with a high concentration of Afro-Americans. At the pastor's funeral, Rice approached Pittsburgh's Bishop John Wright (*q.v.*) about succeeding to the post. Anxious to defuse any negative reaction on Wright's part to his apparent presumptuousness, he preceded his request with a story of a priest approaching an Irish bishop with a similar request under similar circumstances. "Milord," said the priest, "I'd like to take this man's place." "It's fine with me," the bishop replied, "if only the undertaker doesn't object."

Rice possesses a quick Irish wit adaptable to all occasions. In the early 1960s, when ice was first beginning to thaw between the various religions, the late Rabbi Marc Tanenbaum liked to quote Rice's definition of the "ecumenical smile": "I'm not sure it's not like the smile of a baby. You can't tell whether it's real or a gas pain."

☙ Rice was a close friend of Mike Quill, the colorful Irish-born head of the Transportation Workers Union (TWU), who was sometimes known as "Red Mike" for his support of the Communist line on foreign and domestic issues. When Quill died in 1966, he was buried from New York's St. Patrick's Cathedral, with the indulgence of Cardinal Spellman (*q.v.*), Quill being in an irregular situation with respect to the Church.

Rice officiated at the funeral Mass. Quill, a man with a heavy brogue, was full of Irish blather, not all of it as mean-spirited as it sounded. Rice told of being in conversation once with Quill when the subject of ecumenism came up. Quill quickly dispatched the subject with the following aside: "The auld people in Kerry used to say of Protestants, 'Be nice to the poor bashtards; sure they're all goin' to hell anyway."

☙ In one of Rice's parishes there was a cranky woman, church-going but critical of priests in general. Her husband did not attend church, nor was he known to make his Easter duty, details which in those days would disqualify a person from having a church burial. The woman seemed blithe, saying of Rice, "One nice thing about that dumb son of a bitch of a pastor we have now, he'll bury anyone, and I don't have to worry about my Benny."

*R*OBERTS, Thomas d'Esterre (1893–1976). An English Jesuit of strongly progressive views, Roberts resigned in 1950 as archbishop of Bombay, believing it was time for the Church to raise up native hierarchies in places such as India. Roberts attended Vatican II as titular archbishop of Sygdia, but never addressed the council—or, as he would have it, was never given the opportunity. However, he did speak often at paraconciliar meetings and won the reputation of an outspoken liberal with no patience for pomp and circumstance.

When debate on missionary activity was introduced at the third session of Vatican II, Pope Paul VI (*q.v.*) presided, the first pope since Trent actually to preside at a working session of a council. Before he could begin his address introducing debate, seminary students of the Ethiopian College, who had provided the choir for the opening Mass, enthusiastically continued to beat drums, clash symbols, and rattle castanets, while frantic secretaries vainly waved their arms at them. "I don't known what's going on here," said Roberts, "but I *think* they are getting ready to boil a cardinal."

During the last session of Vatican II, the Jesuits scheduled an immense open-air Mass at a house of theirs in a leafy Roman suburb. Forty concelebrants gathered in a wide arc around the altar, the best of the old and the best of the new combined in ineffable Jesuit fashion. Roberts was present, not as a concelebrant but in the front row of the congregation.

Over a glass of wine afterward, Roberts was chatting with John Horgan, a Dublin journalist. Apropos of nothing, Roberts remarked, "During Mass the devil tempted me." As Horgan sought to absorb the surprisingly confessional remark, Roberts added, "I resisted, of course."

Curiosity piqued, Horgan asked what he meant. "The devil came to me just before the consecration," Roberts explained, "and suggested that if I said the words of consecration a moment ahead of them, then none of them would have said Mass." He paused, and a Robertsian twinkle came into his eye. "And then," he said impishly, "the thought occurred to me that, if I did so, I would be able to collect all their stipends!"

✠ When Roberts returned to England after Vatican II, he was approached by a woman admirer who asked to kiss his episcopal ring. "You may kiss my ring, madam," he replied, "but I must warn you that it is in my hip pocket."

ROLFE, Frederick William Serafino Austin Lewis Mary [Baron Corvo] (1860–1913). A versatile, brilliantly original, but eccentric English novelist, Rolfe was born into a lower middle-class Protestant family and "zigzagged" through life as a teacher, historian, pamphleteer, musician, photographer, discreet blackmailer, and charlatan. He became a Catholic in 1886 and in 1904, under the pen name Baron Corvo, published *Hadrian the Seventh,* a wishful "autobiography" of an English layman suddenly raised to the papacy who would remake the world and the Church in his own image. The book, one of many by Rolfe, enjoyed great renown in its time and has become a minor, if curious, classic of sorts.

✠ Rolfe, who failed twice in attempts to become a priest, wrote to Britain's Herbert Cardinal Vaughan during Lent in 1899, informing him that he was going to the theater on Holy Thursday and this was likely to cause a scandal. (The cardinal had just interfered in what Rolfe thought would

be his ordination.) Rolfe's "meager but extraordinary" costume attracted considerable attention, including a lingering stare from an opulent-
ly dressed woman. As Rolfe was settling into his seat, he turned to his
host and said in a loud stage whisper:

> It is a pity that so many rich men have the incredibly bad taste
> to use their wives as sandwich-boards to vulgarly display that
> they have superfluous wealth which they have locked up in dia-
> monds. I wonder they don't realize that only jewelers can rec-
> ognize that the stones are real diamonds and not glass. If I had
> the misfortune to be a millionaire and married to one of these
> females, instead of bedecking her with jewels I would plaster a
> banknote on her back. Then there could be no mistake about
> my wealth.

Among those drawn into Rolfe's orbit by *Hadrian the Seventh* was Robert
Hugh Benson, the noted Anglican preacher and novelist, who also converted to Catholicism and, successful where Rolfe would not be, was
ordained. Benson wrote Rolfe that he was placing *Hadrian* "among the
three books from which I never wish to be separated," but that he
intended to paste together the "sordid" pages speaking of Socialists.
Rolfe responded, "Do not paste down these pages . . . for the complete-
ly sordid Socialists will still exist under your paste, and paste is a notable
nursery for microbes."

RUTH, George Herman ["Babe"] (1895–1948). Born in Baltimore and
raised an orphan by the Xaverian Brothers at St. Mary's Industrial

School there, Ruth became a star pitcher for the Boston Red Sox and later a slugging outfielder for the New York Yankees. He played twenty-two years in the major leagues and was one of the first five players named to the Baseball Hall of Fame. He is one of the legends of American sports.

Ruth was a man of gargantuan appetites and excesses, but the public loved him, and when he died of cancer at age fifty-three, his funeral at St. Patrick's Cathedral in New York City was a major event, with luminaries from all walks of life in attendance. Several of Ruth's Yankee teammates acted as pallbearers, among them third baseman Joe Dugan and pitcher Waite Hoyt. It was a hot, muggy August day, and as the coffin was being borne into the cathedral, Dugan said to Hoyt, "Christ, I'd give a hundred bucks for an ice-cold beer." Hoyt nodded and said, "So would the Babe."

SARANDON, Susan Abigail (1946–). A well-known actor of stage and screen, Sarandon was born in New York City and was graduated in 1968 with a degree in drama and English from the Catholic University of America. She received Oscar nominations in 1992, 1993, and 1995 for her roles in the films *Thelma and Louise, Lorenzo's Oil,* and *The Client,* and in 1996 won an Oscar for her role in the film *Dead Man Walking,* in which she played the role of a nun.

In an interview with *Buzz* magazine, Sarandon professed that she had never been shy about speaking out:

> I was asking all the wrong questions even back in the third grade. When the nuns explained how you had to be married in the Catholic Church or you weren't married, I asked, "Well, how could Joseph and Mary be married, since Jesus didn't come up with it until later?" They sent me out to stand in the hall. I was told I had an overabundance of original sin.

SCANLAN, Patrick F. ["Pat"] (1894–1983). A native New Yorker, Scanlan was a teacher at St. Peter's High School on Staten Island before agreeing in 1917 to become "temporary" managing editor of the *Tablet,* Brooklyn's Catholic weekly. That decision launched him on a fifty-one-year career, during which he propelled the *Tablet* and himself to national attention as champions of conservative causes.

◖ In 1923, Pat Scanlan figured in a critical condemnation of the Ku Klux Klan at a rally in Floral Park, Long Island, but it was as an opponent of big government and of Communism that he built a following. His anti-Communism led to unqualified support of Senator Joseph R. McCarthy in his search for Communists in government, and he rejected charges that McCarthy was on a witch-hunt. He posed a question to members of Congress: "If you don't like the way Senator McCarthy is going about the business of ferreting out evidences of communism, how do you propose to go about it?"

◖ Scanlan's love of faith and Church was as impassioned as his loyalty to country. His testament thereof was set down in the last of the more than 2,600 columns he wrote for the *Tablet* under the rubric "From the Managing Editor's Desk":

> In closing out these close to 51 years' identification here with the Holy Roman Catholic Church, our diocese and our paper, the writer realizes and recognizes what a wonderful power our faith is. It melts the heart to human kindness, smoothes the brow of immoral thoughts, drives degraded instincts to cover. It is boundless, fathomless, limitless. It is as much at home in the sweatshop of the laborer as the stately mansion of the rich; it aims at the peaks and it travels in the lowlands; it rides with prosperity and it walks with poverty. It makes man better, women purer, government stronger.

It gives nothing but good to life, takes away nothing but bad. It enables one to scent the beauty of the flowers, to hear the music of the birds, to enjoy the children at play. It gives one a philosophy of life, a reason for existence, strength for perseverance, a fire for enkindling love, a program for goodness and kindness which no other force or power can give.

SHEED, Francis J. ["Frank"] (1897–1981). An Australian of Irish ancestry, Sheed was educated at the University of Sydney and went to England in 1922 to practice law. He became a member of the Catholic Evidence Guild, a street-corner preachers' group, and met Maisie Ward (q.v.), one of its founders. They married, then founded Sheed & Ward, which became a leading publisher of Catholic books in the English-speaking world. Sheed was a best-selling author himself and much in demand as a lecturer.

The firm of Sheed & Ward blossomed by introducing to American Catholic readers many of the great Catholic thinkers and writers of Europe, among them Leon Bloy, Jacques Maritain (q.v.), Romano Guardini, Paul Claudel (q.v.), Christopher Dawson, Chesterton (q.v.), and Gill (q.v.). When the European well dried up, or was closed off by World War II, Sheed & Ward sought to develop a stable of American writers, and one of the early talents the firm picked up was a young priest, Fulton J. Sheen (q.v.), who would go on to become famous as a preacher, radio and television personality, and finally an archbishop.

God and the Intelligence, Sheen's first title with a Sheed & Ward imprint, was a "good" book, but the firm found his second book "slapdash" and fretted that he seemed to see no harm in lifting bits of other people's material. "He became sufficiently eclectic to turn up at least once in the *New Yorker's* 'Department of Funny Coincidence,'" Wilfrid Sheed noted on reflection in his memoir of Frank and Maisie, his parents. Nevertheless, added the son, Frank Sheed's comment to Sheen on the second book was probably prankish: "I'll publish it if you'll agree to put the whole thing in quotation marks."

One of the mainstays in the Sheed & Ward stable of writers was Monsignor Ronald Knox (*q.v.*), a talented and prolific best-selling author and someone with a sense of his self-worth, however shyly conveyed. Knox once boasted of being at a party with three of his current publishers. Sheed countered sweetly, "Belloc (*q.v.*) used to come with thirty."

SHEEN, Fulton J. (1895–1979). Born in El Paso, Illinois, Sheen was baptized John, but adopted his mother's maiden name and used it throughout his life. He was ordained a priest of the Peoria diocese in 1919 but made his mark as the first regular speaker on radio's *Catholic Hour,* beginning in 1930. By 1951, he was reaching an estimated thirty million people each week via radio and a television program entitled *Life Is Worth Living.* In 1966, he was appointed bishop of Rochester, New York. He resigned three years later with the personal title of archbishop.

In 1950, Sheen was named national director of the Society for the Propagation of the Faith and over the next sixteen years made it the principal Catholic organization of its type in the world, raising many millions of dollars for the missions. His fund-raising appeal extended across generational divides and included the very young. Sheen told of one six-year-old girl anxious to help the Propagation of the Faith Society, who put the following sign on her front lawn: "Lemonade—5 cents a glass." Many customers came back three and four times, and soon the lemonade was gone. Her mother asked the girl where she was getting all the lemonade. The girl answered, "From the cocktail shaker you had in the icebox."

Sheen's flamboyant, theatrical style virtually guaranteed a standing-room-only crowd when he preached and lectured. In 1953, appearing before a very large audience in Chicago, he apologized that some had to stand. "It reminds me of when I went up to Rochester some time ago to talk," he commented, "and I went into a barber shop in the afternoon." The barber said, "Are you going to this lecture tonight?" The unrecognized Sheen allowed that he was. "Well, you'll probably have to stand," said the barber. "You know, it's a peculiar thing," replied Sheen, "but every time I hear that man talk, I always have to stand!"

SMITH, Alfred E. (1873–1944). A product of New York City's swarming, polyglot Lower East Side, Smith rose from the humblest of beginnings to become a four-term governor of the state of New York and, in 1928, the first Catholic to be nominated for the presidency by a major American political party. Herbert Hoover overwhelmed him in that election, but with fifteen million votes, he polled more votes than any previous Democratic presidential candidate in history.

Smith dropped out of school after the eighth grade and ascended to political heights after a series of odd jobs, including a clerkship at the Fulton

Fish Market. He was forever proud of his origins. At the state constitutional convention of 1938, Smith battled mightily for public housing and
told of a committee that in 1892 had investigated tenement conditions
and predicted in twenty years they wouldn't be standing. Emotionally,
he added:

> They are there yet, forty-six years afterwards, and I know they are
> there because I happened to live in one of those tenement houses
> that was put down by the committee as being unfit for human
> habitation, and it's there yet and I know the people who live in it.

The 1928 presidential election turned into a bitter religious fight, which
reached an epiphany of sorts when a prominent Episcopal layman, Charles
C. Marshall, attacked Smith in the *Atlantic Monthly*. Citing Catholic documents, Marshall suggested a fundamental conflict between Smith's loyalty
to the Roman Catholic Church and the Constitution of the United States.

Smith would answer the attack on his Catholicism with a subsequent
Atlantic article, although one that was less his own than that of Father
Francis P. Duffy of "the Fighting 69th" of World War I fame. But his
immediate response to the Marshall attack was more characteristic of
Smith. "I never heard of these encyclicals and bulls and books that the
Atlantic author wrote about," he said. "They have nothing to do with
being a Catholic."

Smith's trademarks were a brown derby, cigars, and a quick wit. He moved
easily in wealthy Irish-American circles and visited frequently at the
Murray-McDonnell Irish-Catholic enclave in Southampton. One Murray
family had seven children, another eleven, and the McDonnells fourteen.

Invited one day at poolside to dive in, he demurred, saying, "I might swallow a baby."

SOUBIROUS, Bernadette (1844–1879). Eldest child in one of the poorest families in Lourdes, the fourteen-year-old caused a sensation in 1858 when she announced that while gathering firewood on common land near the river Gave, she beheld a vision of a woman no bigger than herself, dressed in a white robe with a blue sash knotted at her waist. This was the first of eighteen apparitions of the Blessed Virgin, who proclaimed on her sixteenth appearance, "I am the Immaculate Conception." The Church canonized Bernadette Soubirous in 1933, and the place of her apparitions became the world-famous shrine of Lourdes.

    Bernadette entered the convent of the Sisters of Charity at Nevers in 1866, taking the name Sister Marie Bernard. Bernadette's health had always been frail, and it did not improve with the strict and oftentimes harsh regimen of convent life. She accepted her lot with equanimity, saying with devout resignation, "The Virgin used me as a broom, to remove dust. When the work is done, the broom is put behind the door and left."

    Bernadette's frailty often forced her to bed. One day a visiting nun came to her room and, finding her in bed, asked sarcastically what she was doing. "I am doing my job," Bernadette replied. "Oh," said the nun, "and what might that be?" "My job," said Bernadette, "is to be ill."

    The continuing miracles at Lourdes made a great celebrity of Bernadette, and there was a constant stream of visitors wishing to see the woman whom the Virgin Mary had favored. She did her best to dodge as many as she could. One day she was reproved by a superior for not wanting to receive a bishop. Wasn't she aware, the superior commented, that there was a forty-days' indulgence for kissing a bishop's ring. "Jesus, Mary and Joseph, I give you my heart and my soul!" Bernadette intoned. Then, turning to her superior, she remarked, "There, that gives me one hundred days." And with that she slipped away.

SPELLMAN, Francis J. (1889–1967). Protégé of Pope Pius XII and confidant of President Franklin D. Roosevelt, Spellman was the most prominent American churchman of his day. As cardinal-archbishop, he developed the New York archdiocese into one of the premier sees of Catholic Christendom, serving also as military vicar to the American armed forces, a high-visibility office that took him to the outposts of the world during World War II and the cold war that followed, occasionally on secret missions for Roosevelt. He was a rabid anti-Communist and ecclesiastical traditionalist, qualities that trapped him into frequent controversies.

Ordained a priest for the Archdiocese of Boston, Spellman rose to the hierarchy in 1932 as auxiliary bishop of William Cardinal O'Connell (*q.v.*). It was an appointment that infuriated the unconsulted O'Connell. Spellman, an attaché in the Vatican Secretariat of State at the time, was ordained a bishop in Rome, then sailed to the United States from Genoa aboard the liner *Rex*. On the third day out, he received a cable of greeting from O'Connell: "WELCOME TO BOSTON. CONFIRMATIONS BEGIN ON MONDAY. YOU ARE EXPECTED TO BE READY."

In 1943, Spellman went on a six-month, forty-six-thousand-mile trip to Africa and Europe as military vicar, carrying travel orders reading "Personal Representative of the President of the United States." The mysterious nature of the trip stirred speculation that Spellman was a possible go-between for peace negotiations between Italy and the Allies and also that he had a hand in the downfall of Italian dictator Benito Mussolini.

At a jammed press conference on Spellman's return to the United States, a reporter sought to pin him down. "There have been some very persistent rumors," the reporter began. "There have been some very persistent reporters," Spellman interjected, heading off question and questioner and keeping his secrets intact.

When Spellman went to New York as archbishop in 1939, he found the archdiocese twenty-eight million dollars in debt, a problem he quickly corrected with deft fund-raising efforts, usually private in nature. A one-time aide provided a peek into his modus operandi: One day Spellman invited to lunch five of New York's wealthiest Jewish leaders, one of them Bernard M. Baruch, the statesman and financier.

Spellman wasn't eating his lunch, and Baruch remonstrated with him, asking what the matter was. Spellman, in what was described as "his simpering way," responded, "I spent $250,000 yesterday for a piece of property in Harlem where the kids could play and keep off the streets," and added that he didn't have the money to pay for it.

"Your Eminence," said Baruch, "do you mean to tell me that a man of your stature in this city is going to lose his appetite over $250,000 when you have five men around this table who can take care of that right now?" Baruch then said he was good for $50,000, and he went around the table asking the same of the others.

In five minutes, Spellman had five checks for $50,000 apiece. His appetite back, he polished off his lunch like a truck driver. At the end of the lunch, as he was leading his guests to the Madison Avenue door, he tugged his aide at the elbow and said, "They're sure a nice bunch of fellows."

꧅ Spellman was not lacking in a sense of humor, and sometimes it was directed at himself. For example, he knew his limitations as a preacher. Once he was asked to preach at the National Shrine of the Immaculate Conception in Washington, D.C., on the occasion of the anniversary of Pope Pius XII's coronation. The master of ceremonies offered to take Spellman's manuscript and place it on the lectern for him. "Oh, no you don't," said Spellman. "If I lose this we will have three Our Fathers and three Hail Marys."

꧅ As archbishop of New York, Spellman was especially proud of restoring the archdiocesan seminary, Dunwoodie, to academic ranking of the first class. Thus, in 1948, he was astonished when he read that St. John's, the archdiocesan seminary in Boston, had been granted authority to issue pontifical degrees, a privilege Dunwoodie did not have.

Spellman fired off a letter to Giuseppe Cardinal Pizzardo, prefect of the Congregation of Seminaries and Universities, saying:

> I can hardly credit the news as authentic, but if it is authentic, then I wish to make a protest as it will create an unfavorable impression in the Archdiocese of New York whose seminary is in every particular at least the equal of the seminary in Boston.

It was an indication of Spellman's influence in Rome that he could tell Pizzardo that then-Archbishop Richard Cushing (*q.v.*) should never have made such a request, "and if he did make such a request, it should be denied." An embarrassed Pizzardo pointed out that the matter was already public. A vehement follow-up protest from Spellman caused Pizzardo to reverse himself. Thus, due to Francis J. Spellman, a native son of the Boston archdiocese, Boston's seminary never issued a pontifical degree.

When the dust settled after the failed attempt by President Harry Truman to name the first American ambassador to the Vatican in 1951–52, Giovanni Battista Montini, the substitute secretary of state under Pius XII (*q.v.*) and the future Paul VI (*q.v.*), wrote Spellman faulting the inadequate response of the American church in defending Vatican interests.

Spellman bristled, but bided his time before letting his true feelings show. He did not have to wait long. In 1953, Italy was to have a crucial national election, and the Vatican requested that the Italian-American community be rallied to urge Italians to vote against the Communists. The irony was not lost on Spellman. Knowing the information would be passed on, he noted in a letter to Enrico Galeazzi, a confidant of Pope Pius XII:

> This situation is of particular interest to me since only two weeks ago I wrote to Monsignor Montini defending the Bishops of the United States and myself from the accusation of not supporting the Holy See in the United States, and here now the Holy See asks the Bishops of America to defend the Holy See in Italy!!!!!!!!!!!!

STARKEY, James Sullivan [pseudonym: Seamus O'Sullivan] (1879–1958). Irish poet, essayist, and short-story writer, Starkey was one of the first members of the Irish Academy of Letters and winner of its Gregory Medal. He founded the Theater of Ireland in 1905 and *Dublin Magazine* in 1923.

In Starkey's day, Dublin teemed with persons of wit, among them Oliver St. John Gogarty (*q.v.*), Oscar Wilde, and Robert Tyrrell, the Trinity College classicist who immortalized himself with the comment that there was no such thing as a large whiskey. In such company, Starkey held his own. One day, having upbraided a carpenter for some shoddy work, and including in his denunciation all carpenters in general, Starkey was reminded by the workman that Christ was a carpenter. Starkey retorted, "How about the scab that made the cross?"

STRITCH, Samuel A. (1887–1958). A native of Tennessee, Stritch went on to become bishop of Toledo, archbishop of Milwaukee, and, in 1939, archbishop of Chicago. He received the red hat in 1946. After eighteen years in Chicago, Stritch was named pro-prefect of the Sacred Congregation for the Propaganda of the Faith, becoming the first American ever appointed to head a Curia department. Aboard ship en route to Rome, he suffered an occlusion of the major artery of the right arm and underwent surgery immediately after his arrival in Rome. He suffered a stroke and died in Rome.

A man of deep concern for the unprivileged, Stritch was known as the "cardinal of the poor." The epithet derived from his tenure in Milwaukee during the height of the Great Depression. During the 1930s, Stritch focused major attention on the poor and the jobless, sharing the archdiocese's resources with less affluent dioceses across the country. He rescued many parishes from financial failure and led annual fund-raising campaigns for local charities. "As long as two pennies are ours," he would say, "one of them belongs to the poor."

On matters of race, Stritch was very much a man of the geography of his origins, with the result that his leadership as a bishop was less than forceful on the knotty racial issues of the 1940s and 1950s. Once when he was a young priest in Tennessee, an African-American woman approached him in tears, complaining that the church usher had insulted her. "Oh, my dear, what did he say?" asked Stritch. "He called me a n_____ lady," said the woman, speaking out the n-word that many find offensive. "But, my dear," responded Stritch, "you are a n_____ lady."

𝒯

TEILHARD DE CHARDIN, Pierre (1881–1955). Geologist, paleontologist, philosopher, theologian, evolutionist, writer, and Jesuit priest, Teilhard was born in central France and pursued a career as priest, researcher, and explorer worldwide. His theories about an evolutionary relationship between God and humankind startled Rome, and it is believed (with good reason, some feel) that he was one of the targets of Pius XII's (*q.v.*) 1950 encyclical *Humani generis* condemning new theological methods and attitudes. He died in New York, his "shelter out of France." He never fully achieved his lifelong quest to reconcile Christian beliefs with evolutionary principle and to project their final synthesis.

Teilhard's early writings on original sin, including assertions about the scientific impossibility of a historical Adam and a terrestrial Eden, caused great upset in Rome, and in 1925, authorities there insisted that he sign a set of propositions that included a statement of belief in the literal truth of Genesis: Adam, Eve, the forbidden fruit, and so on.

After much soul-searching, Teilhard agreed to sign the propositions, persuading himself that his act of submission would win God's approval and help in spreading his "gospel of research." His signing was "purely . . . a mechanical gesture and not a sign of intellectual assent." He had not changed his ideas, nor his sense of mission. As for the likelihood of a literal Adam and Eve, Teilhard confided to a confrere, Galileo-like, "I'm *not* so innocent as all that."

ᗢ Teilhard's was a lifelong struggle with ecclesiastical repression and censorship. (The substance of his work was published only after his death, and then only because he had the foresight to convey control of his papers to a person outside his order.) The blindness of the Church to a scientific and religious logic that he considered self-evident wore on him, and he poured out his anguish a few weeks before his death:

> How is it possible, "descending from the mountain" and despite the glory that I carry in my eyes, I am so little changed for the better, so lacking in peace, so incapable of passing on to others through my conduct, the vision of the marvelous unity in which I feel myself immersed? . . .

> As I look about me, how is it I find myself entirely alone of my kind? . . .

> Why am I the only one who sees?

ᗢ There was occasional speculation that Teilhard would leave the Jesuits because of all the suppression and rejection he experienced as a member of that religious order. On the occasion of his golden jubilee as a Jesuit, however, he commented that, if he were able to turn the clock back, he would do the same again.

Four months before his death, he would say something similar to Father Joseph Donceel, S.J., of Fordham University's faculty. Donceel asked Teilhard whether he was sorry he had ever joined the Society of

Jesus. Teilhard responded, "But if I had not been a Jesuit I would not have had these ideas. I picked them up in the Society."

Teilhard died on an Easter Sunday. Was that coincidence, or was his dying on the feast of the Risen Christ (the great symbolic feast of his science and his theology, the feast that in the Teilhardian principle of convergence conveyed to the universe its essential Christic dimension) a sign? In either case, Teilhard's death seemed the answer to a prayer, the prayer spoken in his book *The Divine Milieu*:

> [When] I feel I am losing hold of myself, absolutely passive in the hands of the great unknown forces that have shaped me, in those dark moments, grant, O God, that I may understand that it is You who are painfully parting the fibers of my being in order to penetrate the very marrow of my substance, and bear me away with You. . . . O divine Energy, ineluctable and vivifying Power, because, of us two, You are infinitely the stronger, it is to You that the role falls of consuming me in the union which should weld us together. Grant me, therefore, something still more precious than the grace for which all the faithful pray. It is not enough that I should die while communicating. Teach me to communicate while dying.

TERESA of Avila [Teresa de Cepeda y Ahumada] (1515–1582). A saint whose life is associated with visions and cloisters, few combined the contemplative and the activist life so perfectly as Teresa. Founder of the

Discalced Carmelites, she wrote several spiritual classics celebrated as uniquely feminine and holy, most notably *Interior Castle*. Canonized in 1622, she was declared a Doctor of the Church in 1970, the first woman to be so honored.

❧ Teresa was known for her practicality and her wit—demonstrated one day when one of her recalcitrant abbesses (Teresa founded upwards of fifteen convents) was being particularly tiresome. "Lord," Teresa prayed, "if I had my way that woman wouldn't be superior here." God is said to have answered in one of Teresa's visions just as wryly. "Teresa," God said, "if I had my way, she wouldn't be, either."

❧ Teresa cultivated a familiarity with God, and her prayers would take the form of conversational pieces. "God deliver us from sullen saints!" she would exclaim, and none was less sullen than she. Sometimes she would sound more like a scold than a worshipful religious, telling God, "No wonder you have so few friends when you treat the ones you have so badly."

❧ In Salamanca in 1570, Teresa took possession of a house that had been occupied by students ("Students are not very neat persons," she observed), and her Carmelite traveling companion grew apprehensive as night fell over the eerie place and the two of them there alone. Whenever a board creaked, the companion would imagine the worst, perhaps fearing it was the step of a student returning for his guitar or his gown. Finally she gave vent to words. "Mother," she said, "if I were to die tonight and you found yourself alone here, what would you do?" To which Teresa responded drowsily, "When that happens, sister, I will consider the problem. Now let us have some sleep."

THÉRÈSE of Lisieux [Marie-Françoise Thérèse Martin] (1873–1897). The youngest of nine children, Thérèse joined the Carmelites at age fifteen and lived a life of such sanctity as to make her one of the most popular saints of the early twentieth century. Her autobiography, *The Story of a Soul,* made her famous throughout the Catholic world. French soldiers carried the book with them into battle in World War I, both as an inspiration and as a blessing of sorts for their safety.

> As a child, Thérèse and her sister Celine were once offered old toys and dolls by an older sister, who had outgrown them. Celine humbly chose one doll from the box. Thérèse uttered her famous response: "I choose all!" The words became a motto for her life, and far from being an expression of greed, the cry was recollected by her years later as a way of saying "Nothing half-hearted for me—I will follow Christ with all my heart and soul."

> Like a political figure planning his or her career, Thérèse set out quite consciously not just to make it to heaven, but to be formally acclaimed a saint. She was neither daunted by the large odds nor discouraged by the seeming presumptuousness of her objective.

>> The good God would not inspire unattainable desires. I may then, in spite of my littleness, aspire to holiness. I cannot make myself greater; I must bear with myself just as I am with all my imperfections. But I want to seek a way to heaven, a new way, very short, very straight, a new path. We live in an age of inventions. The trouble of walking upstairs no longer exists; in the

SAINT THÉRÈSE OF LISIEUX

houses of the rich there is a lift [elevator] instead. I would like to find a lift to raise me to Jesus, for I am too little to go up the steep steps of perfection. Then I sought in the Holy Scriptures for some indication of this lift, the object of my desire, and I read these words from the mouth of the Eternal Wisdom: "Whosoever is a *little one*, let him come to me."

￼ Life in the Carmel was especially strict in Thérèse's time, and when she first entered, she made life additionally difficult for herself. She had, for instance, an attraction to mortification and would secretly devise ways of making her food tasteless. "I gave that up a long time ago," she subsequently told one of her sisters. (There were two sisters in the Carmel with her). "When food is to my taste I bless God for it; when it is bad, then I accept [it] . . . such unsought mortification seems to me the safest and most satisfying."

￼ Thérèse of Lisieux lived only twenty-four years—she died of tuberculosis—which makes her popularity the more astonishing. Some attribute that popularity to the promise made on her deathbed: "I will let fall a shower of roses—I will spend my heaven doing good upon earth." The Church canonized her in 1925.

THURSTON, Herbert, S.J. (1856–1939). Born in London and educated at Stonyhurst and the University of London, Thurston was a noted Jesuit author and scholar. He lectured widely against spiritualism, coedited the *Westminster Library,* and, from 1926 until his death, worked on a revision of Butler's *Lives of the Saints.*

    ✆ Thurston was active in the Bollandist Movement, a loose-knit association of scholars that studied and exposed the extravagant claims in hagiography, false devotions, and pietistic writings. Indeed, he was involved in the disparagement and dismissal of so many legends and pseudo-facts, as to make some people nervous about what might come next. When Thurston lay dying in London, the minister of the house came to his bedside for a prayerful farewell. Leaning over the bed, he whispered apprehensively, "Tell me, Herbert, is there a Trinity?" Thurston nodded yes. "Thanks be to God!" said the Jesuit colleague.

TOBIN, Sister Mary Luke, S.L. (1908–). A native of Denver, Sister Mary Luke Tobin served for twelve years as mother general of the Sisters of Loretto, a title changed to president during her term. She served also as president of the Leadership Conference of Women Religious and in that role attended Vatican Council II as one of fifteen women auditors from around the world and the only one from the United States.

    ✆ The news of Tobin's selection as a woman auditor for Vatican II reached her in mid-September 1964, when she was on the high seas. As fate would have it, she was en route to Rome, charged by the Leadership Conference of Catholic Women to put an ear to the ground on "what the bishops were saying about [sisters and nuns]."

In mid-ocean, a crewman summoned her to the radio tower. There an apprehensive Sister Mary Luke found not one, but three calls waiting. The first call she took was from the *New York Times*. "What do you think about being chosen as an auditor for Vatican Council II?" the *Times* reporter asked. "Pardon me! Did I hear you right?" responded Tobin. Her wonderment was understandable; never before in church history had women ever been included as auditors at a council.

The ship's communications officer later said that in all his years at sea it was the first time he had taken three messages for one person at the same time. (The other two messages were of congratulations.)

One of the conveniences for bishops attending Vatican II was a "bar" in St. Peter's Basilica, jestfully called Bar-Jona, where coffee and sweets were available during recess breaks of the daily sessions. (Bar-Jona was the surname of St. Peter—apostle, first pope, and, coincidentally, patron of the basilica in which the council was taking place.)

One day a veteran male auditor invited Sister Mary Luke to come along with him for coffee and a sweet in Bar-Jona. Tobin, it turned out, had once again broken precedent; she had sexually integrated the "bar." Inevitably, she mingled with the crowd and came to be introduced to several bishops. It was all very pleasant, and her friend invited Tobin to return the next day.

On the third day, however, a waiter of the catering detail politely intercepted Sister Mary Luke on her way to Bar-Jona and steered her behind a curtain to the rear of the basilica. There she found a small table very nicely arranged with a few chairs set around it. Another waiter appeared with coffee and cakes. Wags quickly labeled the special arrangement Bar-Nun.

ᕦ Tobin told of a Vatican II committee meeting during which a Dominican father proposed adding to the working document a sentence that would honor women. After a flowery presentation, he turned to the women auditors for their approval. He didn't get it. "Leave out the bouquets," Tobin quoted one of the women. "The only thing needed is what women expect: To be recognized and treated as the full human persons they are in the Church, equal in all things."

*T*OKLAS, Alice B. (1877–1967). A native of San Francisco, Toklas settled in Paris as companion to the author Gertrude Stein, their home becoming famous as a salon for the most celebrated artists and writers of the early decades of the century. Toklas, who played "wife" to Stein's "husband," nurtured a literary career of her own after Stein's death in 1946, writing cookbooks and memoirs. She also lectured and engaged in journalism. She is buried in Paris, next to Stein.

ᕦ Toklas, of Jewish origins, claimed to have been baptized a Catholic as a child. Biographers have been unable to confirm that detail, but what is known is that Toklas took up the practice of the faith in 1957, reportedly to ensure a posthumous reunion with Stein.

Stein too was Jewish, and she shared an interest in Catholicism with Toklas. The two went on "pilgrimage walks" to famous shrines, including Assisi and Avila, and surrounded themselves at home with crucifixes, polychrome statues of saints, candlesticks, and other objects of Catholic ecclesiastical kind.

After Toklas returned or converted—as the case may be—to Catholicism, she asked Pablo Picasso what Gertrude might have thought of her action. Picasso replied, "Oh, she was there long before you."

*T*YRRELL, George (1861–1909). Born in Dublin into an intellectually renowned Protestant family, Tyrrell entered the Catholic Church in 1879 and the Jesuit order the following year. The order expelled him in 1906 because of his sympathy with "modernist" views. He became an outspoken critic of Pope Pius X's (*q.v.*) 1907 encyclical *Pascendi dominici gregis,* which condemned numerous propositions of Modernism and which acted as a Syllabus of Errors for the early twentieth century. Thereafter, Tyrrell was a virtual excommunicate, but he received the last rites before dying.

Tyrrell had a keen sympathy with the laity, particularly those trying to reconcile conservative elements in Catholicism with the principle of development and growth. When faced with the possibility of suspension from the clerical state, he wrote to William Ward (*q.v.*):

> For my own devotion I always preferred hearing to saying Mass, and to occupy the layman's part of the church, being too democratic even to enjoy the "superiority" of sacerdotal dignity. A Roman collar always chokes me, though I wear it still for propriety's sake.

𝒰

URBAN VIII, pope [Maffeo Barberini] (1568–1644). Elected pope in 1623, Urban was a vain, self-willed man who is said to have accepted the papacy chiefly as a temporal principality. He spent lavishly and practiced nepotism on a grand scale. He bore a hand in the condemnation of Galileo (*q.v.*), allowing the Inquisition to compel his abjuration because he believed himself to be caricatured in the *Dialogo*. On news of Urban's death, Romans broke into riotous jubilation.

 Urban's reign coincided with the Thirty Years' War, and he involved the papacy in its politics, but with such ineptness that, for years thereafter, the papacy ceased to be regarded as a serious political factor in events. At the war's final settlement of Westphalia in 1648, for instance, the papacy was entirely ignored. The downturn of fortune did not inhibit Urban, however. His cardinals were his nobility, and he honored them by ordering them to concede precedence only to crowned heads of state. In 1630, he suppressed the cardinalate title of "Illustrious and Most Reverend" and bestowed on them that of "Eminence."

 One of Urban's great concerns was for the defense of the Papal States, and he did much to render them formidable. He built Castelfranco on the northern frontier, fortified the port of Civita Vecchia, and strengthened Castel Sant' Angelo. The last he equipped with cannon made with bronze taken from the roof of the Pantheon. Romans punished this act of vandalism with the following pasquinade: *Quod non fecerunt barbari, fecerunt Barberini*—"What the barbarians will not do, the Barberinis will."

Religious orders were founded with specific purposes in mind, and inevitably those purposes have helped determine how members of the respective orders respond to specific challenges and crises. The truism has been demonstrated in the way a Franciscan, a Dominican, and a Jesuit allegedly responded to a blown fuse: The Francisan knelt in prayer; the Dominican discoursed on the theological qualities of light and darkness; the Jesuit changed the fuse.

Unknown

V

EROT, Augustin (1804–1876). Born and ordained in France, Verot came to the United States in 1830 as a Sulpician. After seminary and pastoral work in the Baltimore area, he was named vicar apostolic of Florida in 1857. In 1861, he was transferred to Savannah, Georgia, as its third bishop. In 1870, he returned to Florida as first bishop of the diocese of St. Augustine.

Verot was one of the hair shirts of Vatican Council I, vigorously opposing the idea of papal infallibility and absenting himself from the final vote on the doctrine, although accepting it once it was officially promulgated. He gave vent to other peeves at the council, including in debate on the schema on clerical life his upset over the poor choice of readings in the breviary from the homilies and writings of the Fathers of the Church. He rose and exclaimed, "I confess that I cannot read without distraction St. Augustine's explanation of the thirty-eight years the sick man at the Pool of Bethsaida had been in his infirmity."

"The Right Reverend speaker should speak with greater reverence of the holy Fathers," the presiding cardinal cried out. "Your Eminence," Verot replied, "I wish to speak with all reverence of the holy Fathers, but at times even Homer nods—*quandoque bonus dormitat Homerus.* Apocryphal stories and preposterous homilies, such as that in which St. Gregory asserts that the end of the world is at hand, should be eliminated." The presiding cardinal sighed: "The subject matter of the debate is clerical life. The speaker has given sufficient expression to his wish for a reform of the Breviary."

V EUSTER, Joseph de [Father Damien] (1840–1888). A Belgian missionary of the Fathers of the Sacred Heart and Mary (Picpus Fathers), de Veuster took the name in religion of Damien and in 1864 was sent to the mission field of Hawaii, where he became resident chaplain to the leper colony on Molokai. He was beatified in 1995.

    When Damien went to Molokai, the lepers had neither regular medical nor spiritual care. He helped them build houses; he dressed their sores and buried their dead. After twelve years, he himself contracted the disease. He conveyed the news at Mass on a hot Sunday in 1885. When time came for the homily, Damien doffed his chasuble against the heat and began his sermon, not with his customary "My brethren," but with "We lepers . . ."

    Having heard good and bad tales about Damien, Scottish novelist and essayist Robert Louis Stevenson visited the lepers' colony on Molokai shortly after the priest's death. Catholics wanted to erect a monument to Damien; Protestant missionaries, then in fierce competition with Rome, spread tales that he took leprous women to bed. Stevenson traveled on a steamer with a group of nuns. Greatly impressed by their "moral loveliness," he thanked his fellow travelers for the good they did him. Of Damien, Stevenson wrote:

He was a European peasant, dirty, bigoted, untruthful, unwise, tricky, but superb with generosity, residual candor and fundamental good humor: convince him that he had done wrong (it might take hours of insult) and he would undo what he had done and like his corrector better. A man with all the grime and paltriness of mankind, but a saint and hero all the more for that.

(Fanny Osbourne, Stevenson's wife, would later write: "Father Damien was vindicated by a stranger, a man of another country and another religion from his own.")

*V*OLTAIRE [François-Marie Arouet] (1694–1778). Philosopher, historian, dramatist, man of letters, Voltaire enjoyed in his time an intellectual renown that was unrivaled not only in France, but throughout Europe. He was born and educated a Catholic, but grew into one of the great baiters of organized religion, assailing the Church, its institutions, clergy, and influence on current events. Legends of eventual remorse and of a deathbed recantation circulated widely, but the reality is that Voltaire died the scandalous skeptic he was most of his life. He was hurriedly interred at the Abbey of Scellieres in Champagne in order to beat the local bishop's interdict barring a Christian burial.

   Voltaire mocked such details of faith as the inspiration of the Bible and the notion of a chosen people, yet he was in fact a deist who believed that there existed a Supreme Being who ordered the universe. His dinner guests once launched an attack on the existence of God. Voltaire halted the conservation and sent the servants away. He then said, "Now, messieurs, you may continue talking against God, but as I don't wish to wake up tomorrow with my throat cut, it is better that my servants not hear you." One of the guests proceeded to dispute the notion of God as the foundation of morality, saying that wives who were religious were as likely to deceive their husbands as those who were not. Voltaire replied, "I know one who was held back by the fear of God, and that is enough for me."

✸ As often happens in the instance of one who lapses as a Catholic, the question is asked, "What other religion have you joined?" The question was asked of Voltaire, who is said to have responded, "I have lost my faith, monsieur, not my reason."

✸ A young man is said to have once approached Voltaire seeking advice on starting a new religion. "I would advise," said Voltaire, "that you first get yourself crucified, then rise on the third day."

✸ Voltaire wrote more than twenty-thousand letters during his lifetime, employing the letter as an instrument against *l'infame,* a name he applied to superstition, ignorance, injustice, oppression, and enemies of reason generally. He aligned himself with the victims of fanaticism. In the latter context, the most famous quote attributed to him may be apocryphal: "I disagree with what you say, but I will defend to the death your right to say it."

(The sentiment is a paraphrase from a line in a letter to a French abbé: "Monsieur l'abbé: I detest what you write, but I would give my life to make it possible for you to continue to write." A biographer gave wider currency to the sentiment in revised terminology. But apocryphal or not, the sentiment is in keeping with the spirit of Voltaire.)

As with other philosophers of the Enlightenment, Voltaire did not reject the idea of God so much as he did mysterious doctrines that were abhorrent to reason. He considered atheism "a monstrous evil" and as testimony to his own belief built a chapel at Ferney with the following inscription on the lintel: *Deo Erexit Voltaire* ("Erected to God by Voltaire"). And, of course, it was Voltaire who suggested, "If God did not exist, it would be necessary to invent him."

*V*ON LE FORT, Gertrud (1876–1971). Born in Westphalia, von Le Fort, a novelist and poet, was considered in her lifetime Germany's greatest woman writer. Her *Hymns to the Church* ranked with the poetry of Paul Claudel (*q.v.*), and her novels, uncompromisingly Christian, were published to great acclaim in several languages. She converted to Catholicism in 1925.

Von Le Fort's father, a Prussian officer whose family came originally from Savoy, had ordered that his daughter be brought up without any religion, but her experiences in life and love led her to Catholicism in midlife. The fact of her conversion was a phenomenon to her as to those around her, and she wrote of the circumstance in hopeful tones of a then-incipient ecumenical movement:

> The convert is not, as mistaken interpreters sometimes think, a person who emphasizes the painful denominational split, but on the contrary some one who has overcome it: his most real

experience is not that of another faith to which he goes over, but that of the unity of the faith which submerges him. It is the experience of a child who realizes that his own most personal religious possession—the central Christian faith of Protestantism—as well as coming from the bosom of the Mother Church, is also preserved and protected in the bosom of the Mother Church. There is . . . a sudden recognition that the cleavage in faith is less a cleavage of belief than a cleavage of love, and that the theological conquest of the former can never succeed if it has not been preceded by the conquest of the latter.

W

WALKER, James J. [Gentleman Jimmy] (1881–1946). Born in New York City of immigrant Irish parents, Walker was twice elected the city's mayor, after serving in the state assembly and state senate. In Albany, Walker sponsored a wide range of liberal social legislation, and as mayor initiated some of the city's most famous construction projects, including the Queens-Midtown Tunnel, the Triborough Bridge, and West Side Highway. During his second term, charges of corruption were leveled against him, and there were rumors that Governor Franklin D. Roosevelt was going to remove Walker from office. He rendered the proceedings moot by abruptly resigning and moving to Europe.

ꟼ Fascinated by Broadway, Walker as a young man preferred writing songs for Tin Pan Alley than practicing law, the profession for which he had been educated. One song of his—"Will You Love Me in December as You Do in May"—proved an enormous success and became a sort of ballad for the age. Walker married twice—first to a musical-comedy and vaudeville entertainer then to a British actress—and he was divorced twice. He drifted from the Catholicism of his birth but in 1944 underwent a spiritual transformation. At a 1946 communion-breakfast of the Catholic Traffic Guild in New York (he was living again in the United States) he bared his soul:

James J. Walker

247

The glamor of other days I have found to be worthless tinsel, and all the allure of the world just so much seduction and deception. I now have found in religion and repentance the happiness and joy that I sought elsewhere in vain.

In 1912, Walker married Janet Allen, his first wife, at St. Joseph's Church in Greenwich Village. He was two hours late for the wedding. As the bride came down the aisle, the organist intermingled strains of "Will You Love Me in December as You Do in May" with "Here Comes the Bride." An ex-pugilist named Mike O'Toole was sitting next to another of Walker's friend, "Rubbernose" Kennedy. "What's this they're playing? What's the chune?" asked O'Toole. "It's thick in the head, ye are," said Kennedy. "Don't you know it's Jimmy's song?" "I know Jim's song," replied O'Toole. "But this sounds mighty slow-like." "It's a church you're in, man," said Kennedy. "It's Jimmy's own tune, but they're playing it in Latin."

Walker's enormous popularity was rooted in qualities admired during the Jazz Age by fun-loving contemporaries. He was, in many respects, the political celebrity-counterpart to novelist F. Scott Fitzgerald (q.v.)—playboy, free spender, dapper dresser ("Beau James," he was called), first-nighter, prizefight goer, sidewalk favorite. Toots Shor, the famed restaurateur, delivered the generation's eulogy. As he viewed Walker's remains at Campbell's Funeral Home, Shor burst out: "Jimmy! Jimmy! When you walked into the room you brightened up the joint."

When life was a lark, Walker was asked what he expected to encounter on reaching the pearly gates. He allowed he didn't know what to expect but, drawing on his legal background, ventured that if there was no one there with a sense of humor, he's going to "ask for a change of venue."

WALSH, William Thomas (1891–1949). Born in Waterbury, Connecticut, Walsh was educated at Yale and worked as a reporter for newspapers in Waterbury, Hartford, and Philadelphia. He entered teaching and was a professor at Manhattanville College of the Sacred Heart in New York City before retiring to devote himself to writing. The University of Notre Dame awarded him its Laetare Medal in 1941.

Walsh wrote a number of books, including several biographies of historical Catholic personalities. In 1937, his biography of King Philip II of Spain appeared, and a bottle of champagne was uncorked in the Walsh home to celebrate a favorable review of the book in the Sunday *New York Times*. Father Leonard Feeney, S.J., literary editor of *America* and a popular versifier, arrived at the door and was invited to join in a toast. When Feeney's glass was empty, he was asked if he would like more. He held out his glass and said, "Fill up two."

WARD, Mary Josephine ["Maisie"] (1889–1975). Spouse of Frank Sheed (*q.v.*) and the other half of Sheed & Ward, the publishing house, Maisie Ward was born on the Isle of Wight. In 1919, she helped found the Catholic Evidence Guild and over a long lifetime was involved in such activist programs as the Catholic Worker, the French priest-worker movement, and subsidized housing programs in England and the United States. She wrote a number of books, including biographies of Chesterton (*q.v.*), Newman (*q.v.*), and Browning, and an autobiography, *Unfinished Business* (1964).

> ✍ Maisie Ward was born into a distinguished English Catholic family, and traditionalist Catholic values suited her fine. Predictably she "fumed about this and that" in the post-Vatican II Church, but "very much in her own way." She couldn't stand, for instance, the new practice of chewing the communion host instead of letting it dissolve in one's mouth. Her feeling for the True Presence was "powerful." She often told a story that had shocked her since childhood about a woman who had spilled consecrated wine on her dress. The Anglican minister consoled the woman by saying, "Never mind, my dear, the new cleaning methods will get it out completely." Maisie Ward's outrage was still fresh at each retelling. "Of course the woman became a Catholic immediately," she said.

*W*ARD, William G. (1812–1882). Oxford educated and trained originally as a mathematician, Ward evolved as a philosopher. He became part of the Oxford Movement and was received into the Catholic Church in September 1845, one month before Newman (*q.v.*) himself. A frequent contributor to the *Dublin Review*, published in London, he became its editor in 1863 and, as such, was a strong defender of papal authority and a subtle critic of the "Experience School" exemplified in the writings of John Stuart Mill and Alexander Bain.

> ✍ In 1844, while still an Anglican cleric, Ward published *The Ideal of a Christian Church,* a controversial work arguing that ethical concern was

the center of genuine religion and advocating a policy of gradual assimilation of Catholic doctrine as a means of paving the way for corporate reunion between Rome and Canterbury. Written hurriedly, the book was rambling and difficult. It was also intense and spawned the sobriquet "Ideal" Ward.

❧ Shortly after publication of *The Ideal of a Christian Church*, steps were taken to "degrade" Ward, a Fellow of Balliol, by stripping him of his Oxford degrees (B.A. and M.A.), on grounds that the book was at variance with Anglican beliefs and made a mockery of his subscription to the Thirty-nine Articles, the statements of Anglican orthodoxy drawn up during the Reformation era.

The move made Ward, in effect, an academic contradiction: an undergraduate Fellow. He delighted in the paradox and would send out notes signed "W. G. Ward, Undergraduate." An expert mimic, he also entertained associates with a jingle that he would recite in tones imitating personages high in the Oxford establishment:

A system has now been devised
  Which cannot be evaded;
And those don't to it conform
  Will forthwith be degraded.

❧ In the intellectual furor following the publication of Charles Darwin's theories of evolution, Ward joined the great national public debate, taking a conservative position but with what has been described as "great openness of mind and readiness for logical adventure with lighthearted assurance in the certainty of Catholic truth." Questioned once about

Catholic doctrine on a point of conduct, he responded, "There are two views, of which I, as usual, take the more bigoted."

◖ Ward was prominent in the Metaphysical Society, one of the Victorian era's most famous debating societies. A debating opponent was the celebrated Thomas Huxley, champion of Darwin and the person credited with coining the term *agnostic*. Although debate with Catholics made Ward ill, he found controversy with skeptics and agnostics invigorating and took to inviting Huxley and other "desperadoes" to dinner.

On one occasion Ward, a man known for wit and good nature, was particularly censorious toward Huxley and the other guests. Huxley rose, walked to a window and looked out at the garden. Ward asked what he was doing. "I am looking in your garden for the stake, Dr. Ward, which I suppose you have got ready for us after dinner."

*W*AUGH, Evelyn (1903–1966). London born and Oxford educated, Waugh wrote books of biography, travel, and social and political study, but was most famous as a novelist of biting satire about life among the aesthetes and socialites of England. He converted to Catholicism in 1930 and, as a believer, was conservative to the point of being reactionary. When he died, a special dispensation was granted in order for the priest-celebrant to say his funeral Mass in Latin.

◖ *Brideshead Revisited*, Waugh's most famous book, appeared in 1944. Edmund Wilson, the eminent American literary critic, objected to the religious emphases of the book, which brought this rejoinder from Waugh:

He was outraged (quite legitimately by his standards) at finding God introduced into my story. I believe that you can only leave God out by making your characters pure abstractions. . . . They [modern novelists] try to represent the whole human mind and soul yet omit its determining character—that of being God's creature with a defined purpose. So in my future books there will be two things to make them unpopular: a preoccupation with style and the attempt to represent man more fully, which, to me, means only one thing, man in his relation to God.

Waugh's politics were Jacobite and his Catholicism Tridentine. He objected to renewals of Vatican II—and earlier to the modest changes that took place during the pontificate of Pius XII (q.v.). Once, during an audience with Pius, Waugh launched into some self-pontificating, only to be interrupted by the pope. "But Mr. Waugh," said Pius XII, "I too am a Catholic!"

(This story has many variations, one of which has Pius XII saying something of the same to Clare Boothe Luce when as U.S. ambassador to Italy in 1953 she pressed a point too energetically at an audience.)

Waugh was a literalist Catholic of rigid kind. On one of his frequent trips to the United States, he was to give a talk at Portsmouth Priory (now Abbey) in Rhode Island. It was during Lent, when the old fasting laws pertained. On the day of his talk, one of the priory's venerable monks died. Wishing to spare their guest the sight of the monk's empty place and overturned plate and cup as well as lugubrious refectory readings and the like, hasty plans were made for Waugh to dine elsewhere.

A family that was a longtime friend and benefactor of the priory was called, and the hostess quickly put together a meal of lobster bisque, followed by a standing rib roast with Yorkshire pudding. When the roast was served, Waugh turned to the hostess and said, "I am so sorry. I ate my meat at lunch time."

Friend as well as stranger experienced Waugh's acerbity. He once contacted Catherine and Harry Walston, English friends, proposing that he come to dinner on one particular evening at Newton Hall, their country home. Catherine Walston, who was carrying on a torrid liaison at the time with Graham Greene (*q.v.*), wired: "Must warn you I have 150 guests dining that night." Knowing exactly the real reason for the refusal, Waugh tersely cabled back: "Who? How? Why?"

By his own admission to the poet Sir John Betjeman, Waugh was "by nature a bully and a scold." He feuded with friends, quarreled with strangers, and generally conducted a rearguard action against modern life. But as he confided to his writer-friend Nancy Mitford, it might have been worse. "You have no idea," he said, "how much nastier I would be if I was not a Catholic. Without supernatural aid I would hardly be a human being."

WEIGEL, Gustave (1906–1964). Born in Buffalo, New York, Weigel entered the Jesuit order at age sixteen. By the time of his ordination in 1933, he held B.A. and M.A. degrees from Woodstock College and a doctorate from the Gregorian in Rome. A leader in the ecumenical movement, Weigel was a member of the Vatican Secretariat for Promoting Christian Unity at Vatican II and was responsible for briefing non-Catholic observers at the council. He was the author of several books and, in 1960, was the first Catholic to deliver a series of lectures at Yale Divinity School.

❧ While at Woodstock College in Maryland, Weigel underwent two operations for cancer and at one point was so gravely ill that a grave was opened in Woodstock Cemetery in anticipation of receiving his remains. In the meantime, another Jesuit priest died and the rector asked Weigel if he would yield his grave to the dead priest. "The proposition seems very unfair to me," responded Weigel, "but, oh well, since he is an old friend, he can have it."

❧ Weigel died between the second and third sessions of Vatican II. On January 3, 1964, he was in New York to lecture in the morning at Jewish Theological Seminary and in the afternoon at General Theological Seminary. He delivered the morning lecture and returned to the old America House at 106th Street, off Riverside Drive near Columbia University, for lunch.

Weigel was staying in the room next to Jesuit Father Walter M. Abbott (q.v.), and he came to Abbott's door. "Walter," he said, "would you do me a favor? I haven't made my bed. And I have a sore back. I'm going to soak my sore back before I go down for lunch. Would you do the bed for me?" Abbott said, "Sure," and Weigel went into the bathroom and drew a tub of water. Abbott heard the water running, made the bed, and went downstairs for lunch himself. Weigel never appeared. After lunch, Abbott and several others went looking for him. They found "Gus" Weigel dead in the bathtub.

*W*EST, Morris L. (1916–). An Australian, West derived his fame as a writer of popular best-selling novels of Catholic focus, several of which made their way into movies via Hollywood. His professional career began, however, as a professed religious and teacher in schools in Sydney's inner suburbs of the Congregation of the Brothers of the Christian Schools of Ireland.

In 1990, West looked back on his religious vocation and its slow erosion and wrote of the disappointment of losing a musical teaching assignment to another Brother. He protested to the Irish Brother Superior, who admonished him to go to chapel and beg forgiveness for his faults. The chapel visit produced a boyhood memory of a favorite aunt, who was to him a second mother. He remembered her telling him the following:

> Morris, darlin', never argue with the Irish! They're slippery as eels in a bucket and they've always got God on their side! So don't butt into their squabbles. Button your lip and walk away. You'll keep your dignity and save yourself a lot of heartache.

*W*HITFIELD, James (1770–1834). Born in Liverpool, England, Whitfield was trained as a priest by the French Sulpicians at their seminary in Lyons. He was ordained in 1809 and, after pastoral work in England, was brought to the United States by his old seminary rector, Ambrose Marechal, S.S., at that time coadjutor of Baltimore and subsequently its archbishop. Whitfield succeeded Marechal as fourth archbishop of Baltimore in 1828. In 1829, he convened the first Provincial Council of Baltimore and in 1833, the second Plenary Council of Baltimore, forerunners of the annual American bishops' meetings.

✍ The early American church was heavily stocked with French clergy, who fled the revolutionary disturbances in France after 1790. The French priests were not followed, however, by a proportionate number of the French Catholic laity. Rather, it was the Irish who flocked to the country, and this development triggered tensions in the hierarchy over which nationality group would dominate the American church.

Of the ten bishops in the United States in 1830, six were either French or French-sympathizers, two were Irish-born, and two were American-born. The English-born but French-trained Whitfield strongly favored the French ascendancy. When Cincinnati's bishop died in 1832, it was necessary for the bishops to consult about a successor. Whitfield confided the following to a friend, Bishop Joseph Rosati of St. Louis:

> If possibly a good choice can be made, let an American born be recommended and (between us in strict confidence) I do really think we should guard against having more Irish Bishops. . . . This you know is a dangerous secret, but I trust it to one in whom I have full confidence.

*W*ILLIAMS, Tennessee (1911–1983). Born Thomas Lanier Williams III in Columbus, Mississippi, Williams adopted the name Tennessee at age twenty-eight. A prolific writer, he achieved fame as a playwright, producing

twenty-four full-length plays and winning the Pulitzer Prize for two of them—
A Streetcar Named Desire (1947) and *Cat on a Hot Tin Roof* (1955). His plays
gave major shape to the American theater in the post-World War II era. Williams
died suddenly, choking to death on a plastic cap of the type used on a nasal spray
or eye solution.

> Williams first used the name Tennessee for a story he published under
> the title "The Field of Blue Children," and subsequently adopted the
> name officially. Over the years, he would offer several explanations for
> the name change: it was a reaction against earlier "inferior" work pub-
> lished under his real name; it was a college nickname; it was because his
> father was from Tennessee; it was distinction.

> Reared a high-church Episcopalian, Williams converted to Catholicism
> in 1968. He entered the Church one day after receiving the sacrament
> of extreme unction from a Jesuit priest when he was sick with the flu. At
> baptism, he took the names Francis Xavier. His brother, Dakin, an ear-
> lier convert, was instrumental in his conversion, although Tennessee
> Williams himself was thoroughly familiar with Catholic rites and beliefs
> from his high-church upbringing.
>
> For years, in fact, he kept a "small tacky statue" of the Infant of
> Prague standing on a penny in his various apartments. Williams was
> not much of a churchgoer as an Episcopalian, and he would not
> become one as a Catholic. He dismissed the notion of churchgoing,
> saying he figured the Lord would just as soon have him working
> as mumbling.

*W*ISEMAN, Nicholas Patrick Stephen (1802–1865). Born in Seville of Anglo-Irish parents recently settled in Spain for business purposes, Wiseman was educated at Ushaw College and the English College in Rome. He was ordained a priest in 1825 and held various academic posts in Rome before being sent to England as coadjutor to the vicar apostolic of the so-called Central District in 1848. He was also appointed president of Oscott College, near Birmingham, and developed it into a center for English Catholics. Wiseman befriended Newman (*q.v.*) and others of the Oxford Movement. In 1850, Pope Pius IX (*q.v.*) named him a cardinal.

Initially, Wiseman took his elevation to the cardinalate to mean that he was being recalled to Rome. In fact, the appointment was part of a careful plan by Pius IX for the restoration of the English hierarchy. Wiseman learned this on his arrival in Rome. He was to return to England as archbishop of Westminster. News of the "papal aggression" fired England with indignation. The *Times* of London thundered:

> It is the greatest act of folly and injustice which the Court of Rome has perpetrated since the Crown and people threw off its yoke. . . . Its only meaning is to insult the Church and Crown of England.

Casting about for the ultimate insult, the *Times* added:

> Dr. Wiseman is an English subject who has entered the service of a foreign power and accepts its spurious indignities. The elevation of Dr. Wiseman to the imaginary Archbishopric of Westminster signifies no more than to confer on the editor of

The Tablet [the English Catholic weekly] the rank and title of Duke of Smithfield.

When Wiseman returned to London with the red hat of a cardinal, mobs hooted at him and pelted his carriage with stones. Slowly but surely, however, he neutralized his critics, largely by means of his geniality and scholarship and a thirty-page pamphlet, *Appeal to the Reason and Good Feeling of the English People,* which persuaded his strongest enemies that their fears were unfounded. In time even the *Times* was won over. On Wiseman's death, the newspaper editorialized on the extraordinary popular demonstration accompanying Wiseman's funeral, declaring that it took place "amid such tokens of public interest, and almost of sorrow, as do not often mark the funerals even of our most illustrious dead."

WOLSEY, Thomas (c. 1475–1530). English cardinal and statesman—he served as lord chancellor—Wolsey was twice a candidate for the papacy. Although he doubtless would have accepted the position, his pre-eminence in the court of King Henry VIII and as diviner of English foreign and domestic policy mitigated any disappointment he might have felt. He fell from power on the issue of Henry's determination to divorce Catherine of Aragon in favor of Anne Boleyn, an effort to which he lent himself sensing that his very survival depended upon the king's favor.

Wolsey foresaw his fall and in 1529 surrendered offices and preferments, except that of archbishop of York. He retired there and for six months lived an exemplary life devoted to the duties of a bishop. Word circulated, however, that he had invoked the assistance of continental kings and the pope to prevent his fall and for this he was charged with treason. Slowly and as an invalid, he headed to London with the king's commissioners, knowing full well what to expect. He turned to one, "Master Kingston, I see the matter against me how it is framed; but if I had served God as diligently as I have done the king He would not have given me over in my gray hairs."

✍ Wolsey died en route to London. The end came at Leicester Abbey, where on arrival he told the abbot, "I am come to leave my bones among you." He was buried there the next day.

WOODRUFF, Mia (1905–1994). Woodruff was the widow of Douglas Woodruff, editorial writer for the *Times* of London, who became editor of the *Tablet* when it was restored to lay ownership by Arthur Cardinal Hinsley in 1936. The granddaughter of the first Lord Acton (*q.v.*), she was one of the colorful figures of English Catholicism.

✍ When Mia Woodruff's husband, Douglas, died in 1967, there was a memorial service in Westminster Cathedral, which many members of the hierarchy attended. A reception followed the service. Toward the end of the reception, Woodruff, her black widow's veil peeled back from her face, announced, "I have been kissed by more bishops than anyone since Lucrezia Borgia."

After the Allies liberated Rome in World War II, Mia Woodruff helped oversee the club for British servicemen run there by the Catholic Women's League. Monsignor Giovanni Battista Montini, the future Paul VI (*q.v.*), frequently dropped by in the evening to practice his English. One evening he said to Woodruff, "I don't understand how you operate; one couldn't organize Italian women like this. What's your secret?" "Englishwomen are natural nannies," she replied grandly. "They are used to clearing up messes. They have done this all over the empire. They take over when the chaps don't know how to cope."

WRIGHT, John J. (1909–1979). A priest of the Archdiocese of Boston, Wright served as bishop of Worcester (Massachusetts) and of Pittsburgh before being elevated to the cardinalate in 1969 and promoted to Rome as prefect of the Congregation for the Clergy. For years he was the highest ranking American at the Vatican, serving in the pontificates of Paul VI (*q.v.*), John Paul I (*q.v.*), and John Paul II (*q.v.*).

Widely respected as a scholar, Wright was a member of the Preparatory Theological Commission for Vatican Council II and was frequently back and forth between Rome and Pittsburgh for commission meetings. On returning from one such trip, he visited an aged, well-read friend in the hospital. "Those bishops working pretty hard over there?" inquired the friend. "Yes," replied Wright. The friend then looked Wright hard in the eye and asked in mock seriousness, "They going to do anything to cure my arthritis?" Wright commented later, "That's the way it was. Everyone thought of the Council in terms of his own interests."

A liberal on social and political questions, Wright was conservative on theological matters and issues of church discipline and tradition. For example, he was a bitter critic of priests who left the structures of the Church in the postconciliar period and married. Interviewed by the *Boston Globe* before leaving for Rome in 1969 to assume curial duties, Wright was asked about these priests. "In my opinion, what they need is to go to confession," he responded, "and that right away. . . . They gave their word. They should keep it."

𝒳

XAVIER, Francis (1506–1552). Born in the Spanish kingdom of Navarre, Xavier entered the University of Paris at age eighteen, and there met Ignatius Loyola (*q.v.*) and became one of the company of seven known as the first Jesuits. As a Jesuit, he went to the Far East, where his missionary efforts were legendary. The mark of his missionary zeal is discernible to this day, notably in Goa, India. He was canonized in 1622.

❧ Francis Xavier sailed to the Far East on his thirty-fifth birthday. Shortly before his departure, the king of Portugal presented him with briefs from the pope constituting him apostolic nuncio in the East. The king wished to bestow benefactions of his own on Xavier, but Xavier would have none except for some clothes and a few books. Nor would he consent to have a servant assigned to him. "The best means to acquire true dignity," he commented, "is to wash one's own clothes and boil one's own pot, unbeholden to anyone."

❧ Missionary work in the Far East was demanding—and difficult. Contrary to pious legend, Francis Xavier did not possess the gift of tongues, and he was forced to rely on translators to relay his messages; some misled him and his followers. His food was often of the poorest kind—rice and water—and his "bed" as frequently as not was the bare ground of a hut. His work was also fraught with personal danger. From the islands of the Malay Peninsula, he wrote to Ignatius Loyola (*q.v.*) of his trials:

> The dangers to which I am exposed and the tasks I undertake for God are springs of spiritual joy, so much so that these islands are the places in all the world for a man to lose his sight by excess of weeping. But they are tears of joy. I do not remember ever to have tasted such interior delight and these consolations take from me all sense of bodily hardships and of troubles from open enemies and not too trustworthy friends.

Y

*Y*EO, Margaret (1877–1941). Daughter of a prominent English family (her father was His Majesty's Inspector of Schools and an honorary canon of Canterbury Cathedral; her mother, the daughter of the bishop of London), Yeo converted to the "strange" religion of Catholicism in 1906. She wrote several novels, but her strength was in biography, where she combined scholarship with a keen dramatic sense.

Yeo's fascination with Catholicism, its personalities and culture, was consuming. Many of her biographies were of saints, and the very foundations of her home at St. Alban's were once part of a medieval abbey. In 1929, she went on a motor tour through Italy, focusing on out-of-the-way places where "nothing had changed for many thousand years." She reflected on the trip, saying:

> It seemed that only two things last in this world, the Catholic Church and the cultivating earth. Perhaps the drift away from these two is the major cause for the decadence of our materialistic, mechanistic "civilization."

❧ *Index of Names and Sources* ☙

Whenever possible, sources are provided for the anecdotes. Only names and titles are cited. Full bibliographical information is contained in the bibliography. Abbreviations used in the list are for the following:

BLS—*Butler's Lives of the Saints*
TCE—*The Catholic Encyclopedia* (1913)
DAB—*Dictionary of American Biography*
EB—*Encyclopaedia Britannica* (1913 edition, unless otherwise stated)
NCR—*National Catholic Reporter*

ABBOTT, Walter M.   Abbott to J. Deedy.

ACTON, Lord   *EB* and *Bartlett's Familiar Quotations*.

ALBERTI, Leon Battista   J. Burckhardt, *The Civilization of the Renaissance in Italy*.

ANDREW, Agnellus, O.F.M.   P. Bussard, ed., *The New Catholic Treasury of Wit and Humor* (NCWC News Service).

ANGELICA, Mother   **1.** & **2.** *Newsday*, 25 April 1994.

ANTHONY, of Padua   **1.** J. Coulson, ed., *The Saints*; **2.** Desmond O'Grady, as quoted in *The Tablet*, 4 January 1992.

AQUINAS, Thomas   **1.** J. Deedy, *The Catholic Fact Book*; **2.** T. Maynard, *Saints for Our Times*; **3.** J. McKenzie, *The Civilization of Christianity*.

AUGUSTINE   **1.** *Confessions*; **2.** K. Armstrong, *A History of God*; **3.** R. West, *Saint Augustine*; **4.** Anne Fremantle, *Saints for All Seasons*, ed. J. Delaney.

BARING, Maurice   **1.** M. Baring, *C*; **2.** M. Hoehn, *Catholic Authors*; **3.** Dorothy Parker, *Writers at Work*, ed. M. Cowley.

BASIL, the Great   **1.** J. Coulson, ed., *The Saints*; **2.** *BLS*.

BEA, Augustin	X. Rynne, *Letters from Vatican II.*
BEECHING, Paul Q.	*The Critic,* spring 1994.
BEETHOVEN, Ludwig van	**1.** & **2.** G. Marek, *Beethoven.*
BEHAN, Brendan	**1.** & **3.** U. O'Connor, *Brendan*; **2.** legend.
BELLARMINE, Robert	**1.** *BLS*; **2** & **3.** G. de Santillana, *The Crime of Galileo.*
BELLOC, Hilaire	**1.** & **6.** *Picture Post*, 17 May 1952; **2.** Frederick D. Wilhelmsen, "Hilaire Belloc: Defender of the Faith," in *The Catholic Writer*, ed. R. McInerney; **3** & **5.** R. Speaight, *The Life of Hilaire Belloc*; **4.** J. Deedy, *The Catholic Book of Days*; **7.** place mat, Abbey Press, St. Meinrad's, Ind., n.d.
BERNADETTE, of Lourdes	*See* Soubirous.
BERNANOS, Georges	R. Speaight, *Georges Bernanos.*
BERRIGAN, Daniel J.	**1.** & **2.** J. Deedy, *'Apologies Good Friends. . .'*
BERRYMAN, John	R. Kelly, ed., *We Dream of Honour.*
BONIFACE VIII	**1.** *EB* and P. Granfield, *The Papacy in Transition*; **2.** *EB.*
BORROMEO, Charles	**1.** & **2.** *BLS.*
BOSCO, John	T. Maynard, *Saints for Our Times.*
BRENDAN	*BLS.*
BROUN, Heywood	J. Gaines, *Wit's End.*
BROWNSON, Orestes A.	**1.** J. Roche, *Life of John Boyle O'Reilly*; **2.** & **3.** T. Ryan, *The Sailor's Snug Harbor*; **4.** Mark S. Burrows in *The Catholic Historical Review*, January 1990.
BRUNO, Giordano	*TCE* and J. Bossy, *Giordano Bruno and the Embassy Affair.*

BURKE, Edward — William A. Simpson reviewing *The Philosopher and the Provocateur: The Correspondence of Jacques Maritain and Saul Alinski*, ed. Bernard Doering in *Commonweal*, 20 May 1994, and Martin E. Martin in *Context*, 15 August 1994.

CARROLL, John — J. Ellis, *Documents of American Catholic History.*

CATHERINE, of Siena — 1. *Generation*, September 1983; 2. G. Markus, ed., *The Radical Tradition.*

CHARLES II — 1. & 2. H. Fairbanks, *Louise Imogene Guiney* and *EB*.

CHESTERTON, Gilbert Keith — 1. M. Ward, *Return to Chesterton*; 2. J. Deedy, *The Catholic Fact Book*; 3. J. Deedy, *The Catholic Book of Days*; 4. J. Foster, *Contemporary Christian Writers.*

CLARE, of Assisi — 1. & 2. T. Maynard, *Saints for Our Times.*

CLAUDEL, Paul — J. Foster, *Contemporary Christian Writers.*

COGLEY, John — J. Cogley, *A Canterbury Tale*, and S. Avella, *This Confident Church.*

CONGAR, Yves M.J. — Y. Congar, *Lay People in the Church.*

CONNELL, Francis J. — *Time*, 18 August 1952, and J. Deedy, *Literary Places.*

CONSALVI, Ercole — 1. *EB*; 2. John Jay Hughes in *Commonweal*, 3 November 1995.

COPLESTON, Frederick C. — 1. & 2. F. Copleston, *Memoirs of a Philosopher.*

COUGHLIN, Charles E. — 1. S. Marcus, *Father Coughlin;* 2. D. Warren, *Radio Priest.*

CUMMINGS, William T. — D. Rogers, *Since You Went Away.*

CURLEY, James M. — 1. W. Shannon, *The American Irish*; 2. J. Dinneen, *The Purple Shamrock*; 3. *New York Times*, 13 November 1958, and J. Curley, *I'd Do It Again!*

CURLEY, Michael J.

1. & 2. J. Ellis, *Catholic Bishops*.

CUSHING, Richard J.

1. J. Cutler, *Cardinal Cushing of Boston*; **2.** Joe Fitzgerald in the *Boston Herald,* 11 May 1995; **3.** James Carroll in the *Boston Globe,* 12 January 1992; **4.** P. Bailey to J. Deedy; **5.** *Commonweal,* 17 June 1983; **6.** R. Kaiser, *Pope ,Council and World,* and X. Rynne, *The Second Session*; **7.** W. Abbott, ed. *Twelve Council Fathers*; **8.** columnist Mike Barnicle in the *Boston Globe,* 17 March 1996, quoting Cushing's nephew, Father William C. Francis; **9.** George E. Ryan to J. Deedy; **10.** J. Lukas, *Common Ground*.

DAMIEN (Father)

See Veuster.

DAY, Dorothy

1. & 4. J. Forest, *Love Is the Measure*; **2.** D. Macdonald, "Revisiting Dorothy Day"; **3.** M. Traxler, "Weekends in Prison."

DE SMET, Pierre-Jean

Robert Folsom reviewing *Come Blackrobe* by John J. Killoren, S.J., in *NCR,* 29 July 1994.

DESMOND, Daniel F.

Herbert A. Kenny to J. Deedy.

DE VALERA, Eamon

1. & 2. H. Kenny, *Literary Dublin*; **3.** de Valera to J. Deedy.

DOZIER, Carroll T.

Dozier to J. Deedy.

DUCHESNE, Louis-Marie-Oliver

Marvin R. O'Connell in *The Catholic Historical Review,* July 1994.

EDGEWORTH, Henry Essex

1. *TCE*; **2.** *TCE* and *EB*.

ENGLAND, John

1. *TCE*; **2.** J. Ellis, *Documents of American Catholic History.*

FÉNELON, Francois

H. Daniel-Rops, *The Church in the Seventeenth Century,* vol 2.

FITZGERALD, F. Scott — 1. & 2. J. Allen, *Candles and Carnival Lights,* and Catholic News Service.

FOLEY, Thomas P.R. — Steven M. Avella in *The Catholic Historical Review,* April 1996.

FORGIONE, Francesco — 1. John McCaffery in *Saints Are Now,* ed. J. Delaney; 2. J. Deedy, *The Catholic Book of Days.*

FRANCIS, de Sales — 1. J. Adels, *The Wisdom of the Saints*; 2. T. Maynard, *Saints for Our Times.*

FRANCIS, of Assisi — 1. M. Bishop, *St. Francis of Assisi*; 2. *BLS*; 3. P. McGinley, *Saint-Watching.*

FRANCIS XAVIER — *See* Xavier.

GALILEO, Galilei — 1. G. de Santillana, *The Crime of Galileo,* and Larry N. Lorenzoni in *Religious Life Review,* November-December 1985; 2. & 3. *EB, TCE,* and M. Barthel, *The Jesuits;* 4. Desmond O'Grady in *Commonweal,* 21 October 1994.

GASPARRI, Pietro — A. Rhodes, *The Vatican in the Age of Dictators.*

GHIBERTI, Lorenzo — J. Burckhardt, *The Civilization of the Renaissance in Italy.*

GIBBONS, James — 1. J. Deedy, *Retrospect*; 2. M. Adelman to J. Deedy.

GILL, Eric — 1. M. Yorke, *Eric Gill*; 2. D. Attwater, *Eric Gill*; 3. *Overview,* September 1992; 4. M. Hoehn, *Catholic Authors,* and *The Tablet,* 11 February 1989.

GODFREY, William — F. Spellman, *Action This Day.*

GOGARTY, Oliver St. John — 1. M. Caulfield, *The Irish Mystique*; 2. O. Gogarty, *Start from Somewhere Else.*

GREENE, Graham	**1.** J. Deedy, *The Catholic Fact Book*; **2.** G. Greene, *A Sort of Life*; **3.** G. Phillips, *Graham Greene;* **4.** & **5.** G. Greene, *A Sort of Life,* and Leopoldo Duran in *The Tablet*, 17 September 1994; **6.** letter, *The Tablet*, 10 December 1988; **7.** "Notebook," *The Tablet*, 28 January 1995.
GREGORY, the Great	**1.** *BLS;* **2.** Paul Meyvaert in *The Tablet*, 25 June 1994; **3.** *Emmanuel College Magazine*, spring 1994; **4.** Walter J. Wilkins in *The Catholic Historical Review,* and B. Walker, *The Women's Encyclopedia of Myths and Secrets.*
GREGORY X	P. Granfield, *The Papacy in Transition.*
GUINEY, Louise Imogene	**1.** P. Kane, *Separatism and Subculture*; **2.** H. Fairbanks, *Louise Imogene Guiney.*
GUINNESS, Alec	**1.**, **2.**, & **3.** A. Guinness, *Blessings in Disguise.*
HADRIAN VI	J. Kelly, *The Oxford Dictionary of Popes,* and E. John, ed., *The Popes.*
HAYES, Helen	H. Hayes, *On Reflection.*
HEALY, James A.	**1.** & **2.** A. Foley, *Bishop Healy.*
HEALY, Timothy M.	Karl E. Meyer in the *New York Times*, 6 September 1994.
HEBBLETHWAITE, Peter	**1.** *The Tablet*, 24/31 December 1994, and Tom Fox in *NCR*, 6 January 1995; **2.** P. Hebblethwaite in *The Tablet*, 2 September 1992; **3.** Arthur Jones in *NCR*, 6 January 1995.
HERR, Daniel Joseph	**1.** D. Herr, *Stop Pushing!*; **2.** D. Herr, *Start Digging!*
HICKLEY, Dennis	*The Tablet*, 16 July 1994.
HILDEBRAND, Dietrich von	"Dietrich von Hildebrand: Human and Philosophical Profile" in *The Catholic Writer*, ed. R. McInerney.

HOPKINS, Gerard Manley — 1. H. Bloom, ed., *Gerard Manley Hopkins*; 2. H. Gardner, ed., *A Book of Religious Verse.*

HUME, George Basil — 1. Peter Hebblethwaite in *NCR*, 4 November 1994; 2. & 3. *NCR*, 15 November 1985.

HUNT, George W. — *America*, 24 September 1994.

HURLEY, Joseph P. — M. Adelman to J. Deedy.

IGNATIUS, of Loyola — 1. M. Barthel, *The Jesuits*; 2. J. Adels, *The Wisdom of the Saints.*

IRELAND, John — 1. J. Ellis, *Catholic Bishops*; 2. J. Cogley, *Catholic America*, and Rory T. Conley in *U.S. Catholic Historian*, summer 1994; 3. J. Ellis, *American Catholicism.*

JAMES II — O. Gogarty, *Start from Somewhere Else,* and M. Caulfield, *The Irish Mystique.*

JOAN, of Arc — T. Maynard, *Saints for Our Times.*

JOHANNES, Francis — M. Adelman to J. Deedy.

JOHN XXIII — 1. P. Hebblethwaite, *Pope John XXIII,* and D. Fraser, *Knight's Cross;* 2., 3., & 7. P. Hebblethwaite, *Pope John XXIII;* 4. G. Bull, *Inside the Vatican,* and P. Hebblethwaite, *Pope John XXIII;* 5. *Commonweal,* 17 May 1985; 6. G. Wills, *Certain Trumpets.*

JOHN PAUL I — 1. F. Murphy, *The Papacy Today,* and J. Deedy, *Matrix;* 2. J. Kelly, *The Oxford Dictionary of Popes.*

JOHN PAUL II — 1. & 3. T. Szulc, *Pope John Paul II;* 2. L. Longford, *Pope John Paul II;* 4. P. Johnson, *Pope John Paul II and the Catholic Restoration;* 5. *Boston Globe,* 30 April 1994; 6. Peter Hebblethwaite in *NCR*, 1 July 1994; 7. *Boston Globe,* 1 May 1995.

JOYCE, James	1., 2., & 3. R. Ellmann, *James Joyce.*
JULIAN, of Norwich	*TCE* and L. Cunningham, *The Catholic Heritage.*
JULIUS II	E. John, ed., *The Popes.*
KELLY, James Plunkett	*Boston Globe*, 7 August 1994.
KENNEDY, John F.	A. Menendez, *John F. Kennedy.*
KNOX, Ronald Arbuthknott	1., 2., & 4. E. Waugh, *Monsignor Ronald Knox*; 3. J. Deedy, *The Catholic Book of Days.*
KUNG, Hans	J. Deedy in *Thinkers of the 20th Century*, ed. R. Turner, and H. Kung, *Why I Am Still a Christian.*
LA FARGE, John	1. Edward S. Stanton in *Saints Are Now*, ed. J. Delaney; 2. J. La Farge, *The Manner Is Ordinary*; 3. J. La Farge, *An American Amen.*
LAW, Bernard F.	1. *The Pilot*, 15 April 1994; 2. *Quincy Patriot-Ledger*, 28 January 1995.
LENCLOS (l'Enclos), Ninon de	*EB* (1913 and 1986 editions) and *Context*, 1 December 1994.
LEO X	Morris L. West in *NCR*, 27 January 1995, and J. Kelly, *The Oxford Dictionary of Popes.*
LIPSCOMB, Oscar H.	*The Catholic Week,* 9 June 1995.
LUSTIGER, Jean-Marie	*The Tablet,* 8 April 1995.
MACAULAY, Thomas Babington	J. Deedy, *The Catholic Book of Days.*
McAULEY, Catherine Elizabeth	*The Irish Echo.*
McCARTHY, Eugene	J. Deedy recollection.
McNABB, Vincent	Paul Likoudis in *The Wanderer,* 25 April 1996.

McQUAID, John Charles — 1. H. Boylan, *A Dictionary of Irish Biography;* 2. Michael O'Toole in *The Tablet,* 14 October 1995.

MANNING, Henry Edward — 1. & 2. S. Leslie, *Henry Edward Manning.*

MARCINKUS, Paul C. — *The Tablet,* 21/28 December 1985 and 20 January 1986.

MARITAIN, Jacques — 1. Tim Unsworth in *NCR,* 2 December 1994; 2. Yves R. Simon in *Jacques Maritain,* ed. J. Evans.

MAXIMILIAN — *BLS.*

MERTON, Thomas — 1. E. Rice, *The Man in the Sycamore Tree*; 2. J. Baker, *Thomas Merton—Social Critic*; 3. M. Mott, *The Seven Mountains of Thomas Merton,* and T. Merton, *The Courage for Truth*; 4. F. Gray, *Divine Disobedience*; 5. R. Daggy, *Introductions East and West.*

METTERNICH, Klemens Wenzel Lothar von — 1. Janne Matlary in *The Tablet,* 28 October 1995; 2. & 3. *TCE.*

MEYER, Albert G. — Dr. Robert Kascht, *Catholic Herald,* 20 April 1995.

MINIHAN, Jeremiah F. — C. M. Buckley to J. Deedy.

MORE, Thomas — 1. & 3. D. Herr in *Saints for All Seasons,* ed. J. Delaney, and *The Saints,* ed. J. Coulson; 2. *Overview,* April 1983; D. Herr in *Saints for All Seasons,* ed. J. Delaney, and *The Saints,* ed. J. Coulson.

MOTHER TERESA — 1. Eileen Egan in *Saints Are Now,* ed. J. Delaney; 2. & 3. *The Patriot Ledger,* 17 June 1995.

MUNDELEIN, George W. — J. Ellis, *Catholic Bishops.*

MURRAY, John C. — 1. *America,* 30 November 1963; 2. D. Pelotte, *John Courtney Murray*; 3. J. C. Murray in *The Documents of Vatican II,* ed. W. Abbott; 4. Ben Birnbaum in *Boston College Magazine,* winter 1995.

MURRAY, Philip

1. P. McGeever, *Rev. Charles Owen Rice*, quoting from *100 Years of Labor in the USA* (London: Ink Links, 1979); **2.**, **3.**, & **4.** Charles Owen Rice to J. Deedy.

NERI, Philip

1. J. Deedy, *The Catholic Fact Book*; **2.** J. Deedy, *The Catholic Fact Book,* and P. McGinley, *Saint-Watching*; **3.** T. Maynard, *Saints for Our Times*; **4.** J. Adels, *The Wisdom of the Saints*; **5.** J. Coulson, ed., *The Saints*.

NEWMAN, John Henry

1. J. Deedy, *The Catholic Book of Days*; **2** & **4.** *The Tablet*, 21 July 1990; **3.** *The Tablet*, 4 June 1994; **5.** J. Newman, "On the Development of Ideas"; **6.** Garry Wills in *The New York Review of Books*, 22 December 1994.

NOVAK, Michael

The Tablet, 2/9 April 1994.

O'CONNELL, Daniel

1. & **2.** M. Glazier and M. Hellwig, eds., *The Modern Catholic Encyclopedia*.

O'CONNELL William H.

1. J. Deedy, *Seven American Catholics*; **2.** D. Wayman, *Cardinal O'Connell of Boston*; **3.** D. Wayman, *Cardinal O'Connell of Boston,* and M. Adelman to J. Deedy; **4.** M. Adelman to J. Deedy; **5.** J. Ellis, *Catholic Bishops.*

O'CONNOR, Flannery

1. S. Paulson, *Flannery O'Connor*; **2.** S. Fitzgerald, ed., *The Habit of Being*; **3.** Lawrence Janowski in *The Critic*, summer 1994.

ONASSIS, Jacqueline Kennedy

1. M. Adelman to J. Deedy; **2.** Dick Irish in *Georgetown Magazine*, fall 1994.

O'REILLY, John B.

1. & **2.** J. Roche, *Life of John Boyle O'Reilly*; **3.** J. Roche, *Life of John Boyle O'Reilly,* and J. Deedy in *The Encyclopedia of American Catholic History*, ed. M. Glazier and T. Shelley.

O'REILLY, Mary B.

1. & **2.** *Boston Globe*, 22 October 1939.

O'SULLIVAN — *See* Starkey.

OTTAVIANI, Alfredo — 1. R. Kaiser, *Pope, Council and World;* and T. Szulc, *Pope John Paul II;* 2. H. Fesquet, *The Drama of Vatican II.*

PADRE PIO — *See* Forgione.

PASCAL — B. Pascal, *Pensées.*

PAUL VI — 1. & 2. P. Hebblethwaite, *Pope Paul VI.*

PERCY, Walker — J. Tolson, *Pilgrim in the Ruins.*

PIUS IX — 1. R. Kaiser, *Pope, Council and World*; 2. F. Murphy, *The Papacy Today*; 3. A. Rhodes, *The Vatican in the Age of Dictators.*

PIUS X — 1. E. John, ed., *The Popes*; 2. J. La Farge, *The Manner Is Ordinary*; 3. P. McGinley, *Saint-Watching*; 4. *EB,* 1955 edition.

PIUS XII — *The Tablet,* 9 July 1994.

PLUNKETT, James — *See* Kelly.

POWERS, J.F. — *St. Anthony Messenger,* May 1990.

PREUSS, Edward — R. T. Conley in *U.S. Catholic Historian,* summer 1994.

QUELEN, Hyacinthe-Louis de — *TCE.*

RICE, Charles Owen — 1. P. McGeever, *Charles Owen Rice*; 2. J. Deedy in "Crusader for Social Justice," *Ave Maria,* 5 October 1963; 3. & 4. Rice to J. Deedy.

ROBERTS, Thomas d'Esterre — 1. P. Hebblethwaite, *Pope Paul VI*; 2. J. Horgan in a letter to J. Deedy, 16 November 1995; 3. H. Fesquet, *The Drama of Vatican II,* and *The Tablet,* 21/28 December 1985 and 20 January 1986.

ROLFE, Frederick — 1. & 2. D. Weeks, *Corvo.*

RUTH, George Herman	G. Ward and K. Burns, *Baseball.*
SARANDON, Susan	*Boston Globe,* 9 March 1995.
SCANLAN, Patrick F.	1. & 2. *The Tablet*, Brooklyn, 8 October 1994.
SHEED, Francis J.	1. & 2. W. Sheed, *Frank and Maisie.*
SHEEN, Fulton J.	1. & 2. B. Adler, ed., *The Wit and Wisdom of Bishop Fulton J. Sheen.*
SMITH, Alfred E.	1. Thomas E. Dewey in R. Moses, *A Tribute to Governor Smith*; 2. J. Deedy, *Seven American Catholics*; 3. *New York Times Magazine*, 13 March 1977.
SOUBIROUS, Bernadette	1. J. Coulson, ed., *The Saints*; 2. *Overview*, February 1981; 3. T. Maynard, *Saints for Our Times.*
SPELLMAN, Francis J.	1. & 2. R. Gannon, *The Cardinal Spellman Story;* 3. correspondence, Monsignor Thomas J. McCarthy to J. Deedy, 10 January 1977; 4. correspondence, Monsignor John Tracy Ellis to J. Deedy, 28 November 1976; 5. T. J. Shelley, "Francis Cardinal Spellman and His Seminary at Dunwoodie," *The Catholic Historical Review*, spring 1994; 6. G. Fogarty, *The Vatican and the American Hierarchy from 1870 to 1965.*
STARKEY, James Sullivan	H. Kenny, "Irish Wit and *Finnegans Wake.*"
STRITCH, Samuel A.	1. *DAB*, Supplement 6; 2. D. Herr to J. Deedy.
TEILHARD, de Chardin	1. M. and E. Lukas, *Teilhard;* 2. M. and E. Lukas, *Teilhard,* and R. Milner, *The Encyclopedia of Evolution*; 3. J. Deedy, *Literary Places*; 4. J. Deedy in *Saints Are Now*, ed. J. Delaney.
TERESA, of Avila	1. & 2. P. McGinley, *Saint-Watching*; 3. Mary Purcell in *Saints for All Seasons*, ed. J. Delaney.

THÉRÈSE, of Lisieux	**1.** Kenneth Meyers in the *Pittsburgh Catholic*, 18 November 1994; **2.** *BLS;* **3.** Naomi Burton Stone in *Saints for All Seasons*, ed. J. Delaney; **4.** J. Coulson, ed., *The Saints.*
THURSTON, Herbert	H. A. Kenny to J. Deedy.
TOBIN, Sister Mary Luke	**1.** & **2.** Sister Mary Luke to J. Deedy; **3.** Christine Dubois in *Catholic Northwest Progress,* 11 May 1995.
TOKLAS, Alice B.	L. Watts, "Can Women Have Wishes?" in *Journal of Feminist Studies in Religion,* fall 1994, and C. R. Stimpson in *Notable American Women,* ed. Sicherman et al.
TYRRELL, George	E. B. and G. W. Rutler in *Homeletic & Pastoral Review*, January 1991.
URBAN VIII	**1.** *TCE*; **2.** *EB.*
VEROT, Augustin	H. Jedin, *Ecumenical Councils of the Catholic Church.*
VEUSTER, Joseph D.	**1.** J. Deedy, *The Catholic Book of Days*; **2.** *The Tablet*, 17 September 1994.
VOLTAIRE, Francis-Marie Arouet	**1.** J. Orieux, *Voltaire*; **2.** & **3.** Anonymous; **4.** *Georgetown Magazine*, spring/summer 1994; **5.** K. Armstrong, *A History of God.*
VON LE FORT, Gertrud	J. Foster, *Contemporary Christian Writers.*
WALKER, James J.	**1.** G. Fowler, *Beau James*; **2.** G. Fowler, *Beau James,* and G. Walsh, *Gentleman Jimmy Walker*; **3.** *DAB*; **4.** "Biography," A&E television network, 19 November 1994.
WALSH, William Thomas	Jane Walsh Close to J. Deedy.
WARD, Mary J. ["Maisie"]	W. Sheed, *Frank and Maisie.*

WARD, William G.

1. *TCE*; 2. M. O'Connell, *The Oxford Conspirators*; 3. & 4. W. Irvine, *Apes, Angels, and Victorians*.

WAUGH, Evelyn

1. *Life*, 8 April 1946; 2. J. Deedy, *The Catholic Fact Book*; 3. M. Adelman to J. Deedy; 4. *The Tablet*, 3 September 1994; 5. Mark Feeney in reviewing *Evelyn Waugh: The Later Years 1939–1966* by Martin Stannard, *Boston Globe*, 20 September 1992.

WEIGEL, Gustave

1. P. Bussard, ed., *The New Catholic Treasury of Wit and Humor* (Juan Ochagavia in *Woodstock Letters*); 2. W. Abbott to J. Deedy.

WEST, Morris L.

America, 28 April 1990.

WHITFIELD, James

J. Ellis, *American Catholicism*.

WILLIAMS, Tennessee

1. *New York Times*, 26 February 1983; 2. R. Leavitt, ed., *The World of Tennessee Williams*.

WISEMAN, Nicholas

1. *The Tablet*, 24/31 December 1994; 2. *TCE*.

WOLSEY, Thomas

1. & 2. *EB* and *TCE*.

WOODRUFF, Mia

1. *The Tablet*, 16 April 1994; 2. P. Hebblethwaite, *Pope Paul VI*.

WRIGHT, John J.

1. R. Kaiser, *Pope, Council and World*; 2. G. MacEoin, *The Inner Elite*.

XAVIER, Francis

1. & 2. *BLS*.

YEO, Margaret

M. Hoehn, *Catholic Authors*.

Bibliography

Abbott, Walter M., S.J. *Twelve Council Fathers.* New York: Macmillan, 1963.

————, ed. *The Documents of Vatican II.* New York: Herder and Herder, 1966.

Adels, Jill Haak. *The Wisdom of the Saints: An Anthology.* New York: Oxford University Press, 1987.

Adler, Bill, ed. *The Wit and Wisdom of Bishop Fulton J. Sheen.* Englewood Cliffs, N.J.: Prentice-Hall, 1968.

Allen, Joan M. *Candles and Carnival Lights: The Catholic Sensibility of F. Scott Fitzgerald.* New York: New York University Press, 1978.

America, 106 West 56th Street, New York, NY 10019.

Armstrong, Karen. *A History of God: The 4000-Year Quest of Judaism, Christianity and Islam.* New York: Knopf, 1993.

Attwater, Donald. *Eric Gill: Workman.* London: Clarke, n.d.

Augustine, Saint. *Confessions.* Garden City, N.Y.: Image Books, 1960.

Avella, Steven M. *This Confident Church: Chicago Leadership and Life in Chicago, 1940–1965.* Notre Dame, Ind.: University of Notre Dame Press, 1992.

Baker, James Thomas. *Thomas Merton—Social Critic.* Lexington, Ky.: University Press of Kentucky, 1971.

Baring, Maurice. *C.* Oxford/New York: Oxford University Press, 1986.

Barthel, Manfred. *The Jesuits: History and Legend of the Society of Jesus.* New York: Morrow, 1984.

Bartlett's Familiar Quotations. 16th ed. Gen. ed., Justin Kaplan. Boston: Little, Brown, 1992.

Bishop, Morris. *St. Francis of Assisi.* Boston: Little, Brown, 1974.

Bloom, Harold, ed. *Gerard Manley Hopkins.* New York: Chelsea House, 1986.

Bossy, John. *Giordano Bruno and the Embassy Affair.* New Haven: Yale University Press, 1991.

Boylan, Henry, ed. *A Dictionary of Irish Biography.* New York: St. Martin's, 1988.

Boston College Magazine, 122 College Road, Chestnut Hill, MA 02167.

Bull, George. *Inside the Vatican.* New York: St. Martin's, 1982.

Burckhardt, Jacob. *The Civilization of the Renaissance in Italy.* London: Phaidon Press, 1944.

Bussard, Paul, ed. *The New Catholic Treasury of Wit and Humor.* New York: Meredith Press, 1968.

Butler's Lives of the Saints. Ed. Herbert Thurston, S.J., and Donald Attwater. New York: Kenedy, 1956.

Catholic Herald, 3501 Lake Drive, Milwaukee, WI 53207.

Catholic Historical Review, The, The Catholic University of America, Washington, DC 20064.

Catholic Northwest Progress, 910 Marion Street, Seattle, WA 98104.

Catholic Radical, The, 52 Mason Street, Worcester, MA 01610.

Catholic Week, The, P.O. Box 349, Mobile, AL 36601.

Caulfield, Max. *The Irish Mystique*. Englewood Cliffs, N.J.: Prentice-Hall, 1973.

Cogley, John. *Catholic America*. New York: The Dial Press, 1973.

———. *A Canterbury Tale: Experiences and Reflections 1916–1976*. New York: Seabury, 1976.

Commonweal, 475 Riverside Drive, Room 405, New York, NY 10115.

Congar, Yves M. J. *Lay People in the Church*. Westminster, Md: Newman Press, 1957.

Context, 205 West Monroe Street, Chicago, IL 60606.

Copleston, Frederick C., S.J. *Memoirs of a Philosopher*. Kansas City: Sheed & Ward, 1993.

Coulson, John, ed. *The Saints*. New York: Hawthorn Books, 1958.

Cowley, Malcolm, ed. *Writers at Work: The* Paris Review *Interviews*. New York: Viking, 1958.

Critic, The, 205 West Monroe Street, Chicago, IL 60606.

Cunningham, Lawrence S. *The Catholic Heritage: Martyrs, Ascetics, Pilgrims, Warriors, Mystics, Theologians, Artists, Humanists, Activists, Outsiders, and Saints*. New York: Crossroad, 1983.

Curley, James Michael. *I'd Do It Again!* Englewood Cliffs, N.J.: Prentice-Hall, 1957.

Cutler, John Henry. *Cardinal Cushing of Boston*. New York: Hawthorn, 1970.

Daggy, Robert E. *Introductions East and West: The Foreign Prefaces of Thomas Merton*. Greensboro, N.C.: Unicorn Press, 1981.

Daniel-Rops, Henri. *The Church in the Seventeenth Century*. 2 vols. Garden City, N.Y.: Image Books, 1965.

Deedy, John. *Literary Places: A Guided Pilgrimage, New York and New England*. Kansas City, Mo.: Sheed Andrews and McMeel, 1978

———. *Seven American Catholics*. Chicago: Thomas More Press, 1978.

———. 'Apologies Good Friends . . . ': An Interim Biography of Daniel Berrigan, S.J. Chicago: Fides/Claretian, 1981.

———. The Catholic Fact Book. Chicago: Thomas More Press, 1986.

———. The Catholic Book of Days. Chicago: Thomas More Press, 1989.

———. Retrospect: The Origins of Catholic Beliefs and Practices. Chicago: Thomas More Press, 1990.

———. Matrix: Exploring the Challenges of Contemporary Life. Chicago: Thomas More Press, 1992.

Delaney, John J. Dictionary of American Catholic Biography. Garden City, N.Y.: Doubleday, 1984.

———, ed. Saints for All Seasons. Garden City, N.Y.: Doubleday, 1978.

———. Saints Are Now: Eight Portraits of Modern Sanctity. Garden City, N.Y.: Doubleday, 1981.

Delaney, John J., and James Edward Tobin, eds. Dictionary of Catholic Biography. Garden City, N.Y.: Doubleday, 1961.

de Santillana, Giorgio. The Crime of Galileo. New York: Time Inc. Book Division, 1962.

Dictionary of American Biography. New York: Scribner's, Supplement 6, 1980.

Dinneen, Joseph F. The Purple Shamrock. New York: Norton, 1949.

Ellis, John Tracy. Documents of American Catholic History. Milwaukee: Bruce, 1962.

———. American Catholicism. Chicago: University of Chicago Press, 1969.

———. Catholic Bishops: A Memoir. Wilmington, Del.: Michael Glazier, 1984.

Ellmann, Richard. James Joyce. New York: Oxford University Press, 1959.

Emmanuel College Magazine, The Fenway, Boston, MA 02115.

Encyclopaedia Britannica. 11th ed. New York: Encyclopaedia Britannica Company, 1911.

Evans, Joseph W., ed. Jacques Maritain: The Man and His Achievement. New York: Sheed & Ward, 1963.

Fadiman, Clifton, gen. ed. The Little, Brown Book of Anecdotes. Boston: Little, Brown, 1985.

Fairbanks, Henry G. Louise Imogene Guiney: Laureate of the Lost. Albany, N.Y.: Magi Books, 1972.

Fesquet, Henri. The Drama of Vatican II. New York: Random House, 1967.

Fitzgerald, Sally, ed. The Habit of Being: Letters of Flannery O'Connor. New York: Random House, 1979.

Fogarty, Gerald P., S.J. The Vatican and the American Hierarchy from 1870 to 1965. Wilmington, Del.: Michael Glazier, 1985.

Foley, Albert S. *Bishop Healy: Beloved Outcaste*. New York: Farrar, Straus & Young, 1954.

Forest, Jim. *Love Is the Measure: A Biography of Dorothy Day*. New York: Paulist Press, 1986.

Foster, Joseph R. *Contemporary Christian Writers*. New York: Hawthorn, 1963.

Fowler, Gene. *Beau James: The Life and Times of Jimmy Walker*. New York: Viking, 1949.

Fraser, David. *Knight's Cross: A Life of Field Marshal Erwin Rommel*. New York: HarperCollins, 1994.

Gaines, James R. *Wit's End: Days and Nights of the Algonquin Round Table*. New York: Harcourt Brace Jovanovich, 1977.

Gannon, Robert I. *The Cardinal Spellman Story*. Garden City, N.Y.: Doubleday, 1962.

Gardner, Helen, ed. *A Book of Religious Verse*. New York: Oxford University Press, 1972.

Generation, Claretian Publications newsletter, 221 West Madison Street, Chicago, IL 60606.

Glazier, Michael, and Monika K. Hellwig, eds. *The Modern Catholic Encyclopedia*. Collegeville, Minn.: Liturgical Press, 1994.

Glazier, Michael, and Thomas Shelley, eds. *The Encyclopedia of American Catholic History*. Collegeville, Minn.: Liturgical Press, 1995.

Gogarty, Oliver St. John. *Start from Somewhere Else*. Garden City, N.Y.: Doubleday, 1955.

Granfield, Patrick. *The Papacy in Transition*. Garden City, N.Y.: Doubleday, 1980.

Gray, Francine du Plessix. *Divine Disobedience: Profiles in Catholic Radicalism*. New York: Knopf, 1970.

Greene, Graham. *A Sort of Life*. New York: Simon & Schuster, 1971.

Guinness, Alec. *Blessings in Disguise*. New York: Knopf, 1986.

Hayes, Helen. *On Reflection: An Autobiography*. New York: Evans, 1968.

Hebblethwaite, Peter. *Pope John XXIII: Shepherd of the Modern World*. Garden City, N.Y.: Doubleday, 1985.

———. *Pope Paul VI: The First Modern Pope*. New York/Mahwah, N.J.: Paulist Press, 1993.

Herr, Dan. *Stop Pushing!* Garden City, N.Y.: Hanover House, 1961.

———. *Start Digging!* Chicago: Thomas More Press, 1987.

Hoehn, Matthew, O.S.B. *Catholic Authors: Contemporary Biographical Sketches, 1930–1947*. Newark: St. Mary's Abbey, 1948.

Homiletic & Pastoral Review, 86 Riverside Drive, New York, NY 10024.

Irish Echo, 309 Fifth Avenue, New York, NY 10016.

Irvine, William. *Apes, Angels, and Victorians.* New York: Time Inc., 1963.

Jedin, Hubert. *Ecumenical Councils of the Catholic Church.* New York: Deus Books/Paulist Press, 1960.

John, Eric, ed. *The Popes: A Concise Biographical History.* New York: Hawthorn, 1964.

John Paul II, Pope. *Crossing the Threshold of Hope.* New York: Knopf, 1994.

Johnson, Paul. *Pope John Paul II and the Catholic Restoration.* New York: St. Martin's, 1981.

Journal of Feminist Studies in Religion, Scholars Press, P.O. Box 15399, Atlanta, GA 30333-0399.

Kaiser, Robert Blair. *Pope, Council and World: The Story of Vatican II.* New York: Macmillan, 1963.

Kane, Paula M. *Separatism and Subculture: Boston Catholicism, 1900–1920.* Chapel Hill: University of North Carolina Press, 1994.

Kelly, J. N. D. *The Oxford Dictionary of Popes.* Oxford/New York: Oxford University Press, 1988.

Kelly, Richard J., ed. *We Dream of Honour: John Berryman's Letters to His Mother.* New York: Norton, 1988.

Kenny, Herbert A. *Literary Dublin: A History.* New York: Taplinger, 1974.

———. "Irish Wit and *Finnegans Wake,*" offprint from *Proceedings,* Massachusetts Historical Society, vol. 95, 1983.

Kung, Hans. *Why I Am Still a Christian.* Nashville, Tenn.: Abingdon Press, 1987.

La Farge, John, S.J. *The Manner Is Ordinary.* New York: Harcourt, Brace and Company, 1954.

———. *An American Amen.* New York: Farrar, Straus & Cudahy, 1958.

Leavitt, Richard F., ed. *The World of Tennessee Williams.* New York: Putnam's, 1978.

Leslie, Shane. *Henry Edward Manning: His Life and Labours.* New York: Kenedy, 1921.

Longford, Lord. *Pope John Paul II: An Authorized Biography.* New York: Morrow, 1982.

Lukas, J. Anthony. *Common Ground.* New York: Knopf, 1985.

Lukas, Mary, and Ellen Lukas. *Teilhard.* New York: McGraw-Hill, 1981.

MacCarthy, Fiona. *Eric Gill: A Lover's Quest for Art and God.* New York: Dutton, 1989.

Macdonald, Dwight. "Revisiting Dorothy Day." *The New York Review of Books,* 28 January 1971.

MacEoin, Gary. *The Inner Elite: Dossiers of Papal Candidates.* Kansas City, Mo.: Sheed, Andrews and McMeel, 1978.

Marcus, Sheldon. *Father Coughlin: The Tumultuous Life of the Preist of the Little Flower*. Boston: Little, Brown, 1973.

Marek, George R. *Beethoven: Biography of a Genius*. New York: Funk & Wagnalls, 1972.

Markus, Gilbert, O.P., ed. *The Radical Tradition: Revolutionary Saints in the Battle for Justice and Human Rights*. Garden City, N.Y.: Doubleday, 1993.

Maynard, Theodore. *Saints for Our Times*. New York: Image Books, 1955.

McGeever, Patrick J., Rev. *Charles Owen Rice: Apostle of Contradiction*. Pittsburgh: Duquesne University Press, 1989.

McGinley, Phyllis. *Saint-Watching*. Chicago: Thomas More Press, 1982.

McInerney, Ralph, ed. *The Catholic Writer*. Papers Presented at a Conference Sponsored by the Wethersfield Institute, New York City, 29–30 September 1989. San Francisco: Ignatius Press, 1991.

McKenzie, John L. *The Civilization of Christianity*. Chicago: Thomas More Press, 1986.

McNabb, Vincent. *The Wanderer*

Menendez, Albert J. *John F. Kennedy: Catholic and Humanist*. Buffalo, N.Y.: Prometheus Books, 1978.

Merton, Thomas. *The Courage for Truth: The Letters of Thomas Merton to Writers*. Selected and edited by Christine M. Bochen. New York: Farrar Straus & Giroux, 1993.

Milner, Richard. *The Encyclopedia of Evolution*. New York: Facts On File, 1990.

Moses, Robert. *A Tribute to Governor Smith*. New York: Simon & Schuster, 1962.

Mott, Michael. *The Seven Mountains of Thomas Merton*. Boston: Houghton Mifflin, 1984.

Murphy, Francis X., C.S.S.R. *The Papacy Today*. New York: Macmillan, 1981.

National Catholic Reporter, 115 East Armour Blvd., Kansas City, MO 64111.

Newman, John Henry. "On the Development of Ideas," *Essay on the Development of Christian Doctrine*. *Great Ideas Today*. New York: Encyclopaedia Britannica, 1966.

Nobile, Philip. *Catholic Nonsense*. Garden City, N.Y.: Doubleday, 1970.

O'Connell, Marvin R. *The Oxford Conspirators: A History of the Oxford Movement 1833–1845*. New York: Macmillan, 1969.

O'Connor, Ulick. *Brendan*. Englewood Cliffs, N.J.: Prentice-Hall, 1970.

Orieux, Jean. *Voltaire: A Biography of the Man and His Century*. Garden City, N.Y.: Doubleday, 1979.

Overview, 205 West Monroe Street, Chicago, IL 60606.

Pascal, Blaise. *The Provincial Letters, Pensées, Scientific Treatises.* Vol. 23 of *Great Books of the Western World.* Chicago: Encyclopaedia Britannica, 1952.

Patriot Ledger, 400 Crown Colony Drive, Quincy, MA 02169.

Paulson, Suzanne Morrow. *Flannery O'Connor: A Study of the Short Fiction.* Boston: Twayne, 1988.

Pelotte, Donald E., S.S.S. *John Courtney Murray: Theologian in Conflict.* New York/Ramsey, N.J.: Paulist Press, 1976.

Phillips, Gene D., S.J. *Graham Greene: The Films of His Fiction.* New York: Teachers College Press, 1974.

Pilot, The, 49 Franklin Street, Boston, MA 02110.

Pittsburgh Catholic, 135 First Avenue, Suite 200, Pittsburgh, PA 15222.

Religious Life, 4200 North Austin Avenue, Chicago, IL 60634.

Rhodes, Anthony. *The Vatican in the Age of Dictators (1922–1945).* New York: Holt, Rinehart & Winston, 1973.

Rice, Edward. *The Man in the Sycamore Tree: The Good Times and Hard Life of Thomas Merton.* Garden City, N.Y.: Doubleday, 1970.

Roche, James Jeffrey. *Life of John Boyle O'Reilly.* New York: Cassell, 1891.

Rogers, Donald I. *Since You Went Away.* New Rochelle, N.Y.: Arlington House, 1973.

Ryan, Thomas R., C.PP.S. *The Sailor's Snug Harbor, Studies in Brownson's Thought.* Westminster, Md.: Newman Book Shop, 1952.

Rynne, Xavier. *Letters from Vatican II (First Session): Background and Debates.* New York: Farrar, Straus, 1963

————. *The Second Session: The Debates and Decrees of Vatican Council II, September 29 to December 4, 1963.* New York: Farrar, Straus, 1964.

Shannon, William V. *The American Irish.* New York: Macmillan, 1963.

Sheed, Wilfrid. *Frank and Maisie: A Memoir with Parents.* New York: Simon & Schuster, 1985.

Sicherman, Barbara, et al., eds. *Notable American Women: The Modern Period.* Cambridge, Mass.: Belknap Press, 1980.

Speaight, Robert. *The Life of Hilaire Belloc.* New York: Farrar, Straus & Cudahy, 1957.

————. *The Life of Eric Gill*. New York: Kenedy, 1966.

————. *Georges Bernanos: A Study of the Man and the Writer*. New York: Liveright, 1974.

Spellman, Francis J. *Action This Day: Letters from the Fighting Fronts*. New York: Scribner's, 1943.

Szulc, Tad. *Pope John·Paul II: The Biography*. New York: Scribner's, 1995.

Tablet, The, 1 King Street Cloisters, Clifton Walk, London W6 0QZ.

Tolson, Jay. *Pilgrim in the Ruins: A Life of Walker Percy*. New York: Simon & Schuster, 1992.

Traxler, Margaret Ellen. "Weekends in Prison." Chicago: Institute of Women Today, May 1977.

Turner, Roland, ed. *Thinkers of the 20th Century*. Chicago: St. James Press, 1987.

U.S. Catholic Historian, P.O. Box 16229, Baltimore, MD 21210.

Vaillancourt, Jean-Guy. *Papal Power: A Study of Vatican Control over Lay Catholic Elites*. Berkeley: University of California Press, 1980.

Walker, Barbara G. *The Woman's Encyclopedia of Myths and Secrets*. San Francisco: HarperCollins, 1983.

Walsh, George. *Gentleman Jimmy Walker: Mayor of the Jazz Age*. New York: Praeger, 1974.

Ward, Geoffrey C., and Ken Burns. *Baseball: An Illustrated History*. New York: Knopf, 1994.

Ward, Maisie. *Return to Chesterton*. New York: Sheed & Ward, 1952.

Warren, Donald. *Radio Priest: Charles Coughlin, the Father of Hate Radio*. New York: The Free Press, 1996.

Waugh, Evelyn, *Monsignor Ronald Knox*. Boston: Little, Brown, 1959.

Wayman, Dorothy G. *Cardinal O'Connell of Boston*. New York: Farrar, Straus & Young, 1955.

Weeks, Donald. *Corvo: Saint or Madman?* New York: McGraw-Hill, 1971.

West, Rebecca. *Saint Augustine*. Chicago: Thomas More Press, 1982.

Williams, Dakin, and Shepherd Mead. *Tennessee Williams: An Intimate Biography*. New York: Arbor House, 1983.

Wills, Garry. *Certain Trumpets: The Call of Leaders*. New York: Simon & Schuster, 1994.

Yorke, Malcolm. *Eric Gill: Man of Flesh and Spirit*. New York: Universe, 1982.